"Kashatus brings fresh insights into the interior life of Abraham Lincoln during the Civil War and shows that Quaker-established schools for free blacks were outstanding and necessary models for the work of Reconstruction that lay ahead."

Linda B. Selleck
Author of *Gentle Invaders: Quaker Women Educators and Racial Issues During the Civil War and Reconstruction*

"*Abraham Lincoln, the Quakers, and the Civil War* is a balanced treatment of Lincoln's relationship with the Society of Friends, showing his respect for and attention to the Quaker delegations that came to talk with him during the Civil War."

James McPherson
Emeritus Professor, Princeton University
Author of *Battle Cry of Freedom: The Civil War Era*

"I believe strongly in the message of this thorough study. In addition to their warm and practical interactions, Abraham Lincoln, the British, and the American Quakers experienced the same divine calling for the nation to become a people unified by the pain, doubts, and the depression of war."

Hugh Barbour
Author of *The Quakers in Puritan England*
Co-author of *The Quakers*

"This is a fascinating look at an intriguing, long-neglected subject—how Abraham Lincoln sought counsel and inspiration from the anti-war Quakers in the midst of the bloodiest war in world history."

Harold Holzer
Roger Hertog Fellow, New York Historical Society

"William Kashatus's *Lincoln, the Quakers, and the Civil War* is an excellent piece of historical writing by an author who has deep insight into American Quakers. He offers fascinating insights into Lincoln's presidency, his anguish, and his spirituality while also illuminating a little-known aspect of the Great Emancipator's own fascination with Quakers."

Max L. Carter
Professor of Religious Studies, Guilford College, Greensboro, NC

Abraham Lincoln, the Quakers, and the Civil War

"A Trial of Principle and Faith"

William C. Kashatus

AN IMPRINT OF ABC-CLIO, LLC
Santa Barbara, California • Denver, Colorado • Oxford, England

Copyright 2014 by William C. Kashatus

All rights reserved. No part of this publication may be reproduced, stored in a retrieval system, or transmitted, in any form or by any means, electronic, mechanical, photocopying, recording, or otherwise, except for the inclusion of brief quotations in a review, without prior permission in writing from the publisher.

Library of Congress Cataloging-in-Publication Data

Kashatus, William C., 1959–
 Abraham Lincoln, the Quakers, and the Civil War : "a trial of principle and faith" / William C. Kashatus.
   pages cm
 Includes bibliographical references and index.
   ISBN 978-1-4408-3319-9 (hardcopy : alk. paper) — ISBN 978-1-4408-3320-5 (ebook) 1. Lincoln, Abraham, 1809–1865—Relations with Quakers. 2. United States—History—Civil War, 1861–1865—Religious aspects—Quakers. 3. Quakers—United States—History—19th century. 4. Society of Friends—United States—History—19th century. I. Title.
 E457.2.K365   2014
 973.7092—dc23   2014015667

ISBN: 978-1-4408-3319-9
EISBN: 978-1-4408-3320-5

18 17 16 15 14   1 2 3 4 5

This book is also available on the World Wide Web as an eBook.
Visit www.abc-clio.com for details.

Praeger
An Imprint of ABC-CLIO, LLC

ABC-CLIO, LLC
130 Cremona Drive, P.O. Box 1911
Santa Barbara, California 93116-1911

This book is printed on acid-free paper ∞

Manufactured in the United States of America

*For Sarah and Charlie,
devoted friends and steadfast Quakers*

Contents

Acknowledgments	ix
Introduction	1
Chapter 1: Antislavery Kinship, 1861	9
Chapter 2: Justifying Emancipation, 1862	39
Chapter 3: Trials of War, 1863	71
Chapter 4: Redemption, 1864–1865	97
Conclusion	119
Notes	127
Selected Bibliography	165
Index	175

A photo essay follows page 96

Acknowledgments

Abraham Lincoln, the Quakers, and the Civil War: "A Trial of Principle and Faith" is a collaborative effort that began in 1977 when I entered Earlham College in Richmond, Indiana. At Earlham, I met Sarah Mullen and Charles Northrop, classmates and fellow Quakers who quickly became my best friends. Despite—or perhaps because of—my reclusive nature, Sarah and Charlie constantly pulled me away from Lily Library to visit local historical sites, participate in campus ministry, provoke others by dressing in Quaker garb, and, in our junior year, travel to England on a foreign study program and Quaker pilgrimage. They also challenged my intellect by reading my research papers, offering constructive criticism and engaging in thoughtful conversation. Most of all, they inspired me to become a better person by modeling Friends' values. It was most fitting that they married shortly after graduation in 1981. Sarah and Charlie remain my closest friends. This book is dedicated to them with eternal love, respect, and affection.

It was also at Earlham that I had the good fortune to study with several professors who inspired my interest in history and religion, including Hugh Barbour, Max Carter, Peter Cline, Lillie Johnson, Tom Mullen, Randall Shrock, and D. Elton Trueblood. Not only did they give selflessly of their intellect and time, but did so with gentle good humor and constant encouragement. In the process, they taught me that *what* I learned at Earlham was not as important as *how* I learned it. I am extremely grateful to all of these professors for making the learning process so enjoyable. I can only hope that my own teaching and scholarship does justice to their example.

A personal debt of gratitude is owed to Tom Haviland and Bill Vaselopulos, my closest friends on Earlham's varsity soccer team between 1978 and 1980. Tom, a Quaker, was a huge supporter at a time when I had doubts about my abilities, both on and off the soccer pitch. Bill, a native of Chicago, was another confidant and the person who took me on my first visit to Lincoln's home and burial site in Springfield, Illinois.

Special thanks are due to others who reviewed earlier drafts of the manuscript and provided constructive criticism including Hugh Barbour, emeritus professor of religion, Earlham College; Max Carter, campus minister at Guilford College; Christopher Densmore, curator of Friends Historical Library at Swarthmore College; Ruth Dobyns, curator of the Quaker Heritage Center at Wilmington College; Allen Guelzo, professor of history at Gettysburg College; Thomas Hamm, professor of history and curator of the Quaker Collection at Earlham College; Harold Holzer, senior vice president for external affairs at the Metropolitan Museum of Art and one of the nation's leading Lincoln scholars; and James McPherson, emeritus professor at Princeton University and a leading Civil War scholar. Of course, any errors or shortcomings that remain are mine alone, as are the views presented herein.

Another group of folks provided invaluable research assistance by granting access to special collections, historical photographs, and/or family memoirs: James M. Cornelius, curator of the Lincoln Collection in Springfield, Illinois; Gwen Gosney Erickson, librarian and archivist, Guilford College, Greensboro, North Carolina; Joan Kimball, Philadelphia, Pennsylvania; Patti Kinsinger, archivist at the Quaker Heritage Center, Wilmington College, Wilmington, Ohio; Susanna Morikawa of Friends Historical Library at Swarthmore College; John Anderies and Ann Upton of the Quaker Collection at Haverford College, Haverford, Pennsylvania; and Christine Hadley Snyder, Clarksville, Ohio.

Finally, special thanks is owed to my family. My parents, Balbina and Bill, gave me the gift of a Quaker education, as well as their unconditional support in my decision to become a writer. My sons, Tim, Peter, and Ben, have tolerated my twin passion for history and writing all their lives. Some day they will hopefully understand, like their mother, Jackie. Words cannot adequately describe the love and respect I have for her.

Introduction

On the rainy morning of Sunday, October 26, 1862, President Abraham Lincoln was visited at the Executive Mansion by a small delegation of the Religious Society of Friends. In the past, he had entertained many similar interviews from religious groups, who came to offer political advice under the guise of divine authority. Occasionally, a minister even had the presumption to request an appointment. Although Lincoln was compelled to endure such meetings, he detested them. On the other hand, he had infinite patience for those who called on a genuinely spiritual mission. Such was the case with four Quakers—Eliza P. Gurney, John M. Whitall, Hannah B. Mott, and James Carey—who were deeply affected by the trials of the Civil War and felt a special sympathy for the president in his position of overwhelming responsibility.

Gurney, a Quaker minister and the widow of a prominent English banker and philanthropist, assured Lincoln that it was "not from any motive of idle curiosity" that she and the others had requested the interview. Nor did the delegation seek any political favor, like other Friends who had earlier lobbied him and the War Department for leniency in dealing with Quaker conscientious objectors or the emancipation of the slaves. Instead, Gurney emphasized the delegation's "near sympathy" for the president in the "heavy weight of responsibility that rested upon him." Quoting from 1 Peter 4:12, the Quaker minister evoked the "fiery trail" experienced by the early Christians who were facing persecution for their faith. She compared Lincoln's circumstances to "God's chosen people," recognizing the "trials and persecutions" he would have to confront because of his recent decision to emancipate the slaves. Gurney urged him to "commit his way unto the Lord by prayer" whenever those trials emerged. If he did so, she believed that "the peace of God" would "keep the president in heart and mind."[1]

Lincoln, relieved that the delegation had not come to seek any favor, was charmed by the innocence and genuine sympathy of the Quakeress. Gurney knelt and offered a prayer "that light and wisdom might be shed down from on high, to guide our President," before the group settled into a silent meditative worship.[2] Whitall later noted that he would never forget the "deep solemnity, the almost awful silence [that] reigned within that room," or the "tears running down the cheeks of our honored President as E. P. Gurney solemnly addressed him." When the members of the delegation rose to go, Lincoln, profoundly affected by the meeting, encouraged the four Friends to stay longer than the 15 minutes scheduled for their visit. But Gurney declined, noting that the president had too many other responsibilities. Taking her hand, Lincoln, with unusual warmth, confided, "I am glad of this interview."[3]

Afterward, the president, who was usually guarded about his innermost thoughts, wrote a remarkably candid letter to Gurney. After thanking her for her "sympathy and prayer," Lincoln recalled Gurney's sermon and the invocation of Peter's letter to the early Christians. "We are indeed going through a great trial—a fiery trial," he wrote, wedding his own trial with that of the divided Union. It was a metaphor he would return to time and again for the remainder of his presidency. At the same time, the president was hopeful. Confessing his belief that he was an "instrument in the hands of the heavenly Father," Lincoln expressed a desire that his "words and actions may be in accordance with His will." But he did not succumb to the arrogance of most wartime leaders who believed that their cause was favored by the Almighty. Instead, the president reasoned that if his "efforts failed after endeavoring to do my best with the light which He affords me, then I must believe that, for some purpose unknown to me, He wills it otherwise." To underscore the point, Lincoln concluded with a statement that reflected his humility and a genuine desire to submit to the divine will. "If I had had my way, this war would never have been; but, nevertheless, it came," he wrote. "If I had had my way, the war would have ended before this; but, nevertheless, it still continues. We must conclude that He permits it for some wise purpose, though we may not be able to comprehend it; for we cannot but believe that He who made the world still governs it."[4]

After receiving the letter, Gurney must have been struck by the president's spirituality, which bore a striking resemblance to Quaker thought. His reference to a divine "light," for example, resonated with the Friends' fundamental belief that there is a presence of the Almighty in all people and that such an "inner light" provided ongoing revelation of His will. To be sure, Gurney was an *evangelical* Friend who emphasized the primary role of the Bible in the revelation of new truth. The sermon she delivered to Lincoln on 1 Peter and the "fiery trail" of those who are experiencing persecution reinforced that fact. But she did not totally discount the influence or necessity of the Holy Spirit. Instead, Gurney saw the two as separate influences: Scripture revealed God's will, and the Holy Spirit (Inner Light) acted as a guide for the correct reading of the Bible.[5] At the same time, Gurney, like most Quakers, shared Lincoln's perception that God's will was the ultimate factor in determining human affairs. The president, revealing a clear understanding of human fallibility, acknowledged the omnipotence of the Almighty by deferring to "His will" and His "wise purpose," though he himself "may not be able to comprehend it." This strong sense of spirituality determined his course of action. That Gurney understood and appreciated such a decision-making process would endear her to the president, who encouraged a correspondence.[6] "Many times, since I was privileged to have an interview with thee, nearly a year ago, my mind has turned towards thee with feelings of sincere and Christian interest," she wrote to Lincoln on August 8, 1863, assuring him of her "continued hearty sympathy in all thy heavy burdens and responsibilities." She also confirmed the president's belief that "the Almighty did design to make thee instrumental in accomplishing His will when he appointed thee thy present post of vast responsibility, as the Chief Magistrate" and concluded with a prayer that "the Almighty ... may strengthen thee to accomplish all the blessed purposes" that He intended.[7]

Lincoln, burdened with the prosecution of the war as well as a reelection campaign, did not respond until September 4, 1864. But his reassurance that he had "not forgotten" her visit to the White House and the rare personal tone of the letter suggests that the president was genuinely moved by Gurney and her sincere effort to serve him in a time of terrible personal anguish:

> I have not forgotten—probably never shall forget—the very impressive occasion when yourself and friends visited me on a Sabbath forenoon two years ago. Nor has your kind letter,

written nearly a year later, ever been forgotten. In all, it has been your purpose to strengthen my reliance on God. I am much indebted to the good Christian people of the country for their constant prayers and consolations; and to no one of them, more than to yourself. The purposes of the Almighty are perfect, and must prevail, though we erring mortals may fail to accurately perceive them in advance. Your people—the Friends—have had and are having a very great trial. On principle, and faith, opposed to both war and oppression, they can only practically oppose oppression by war. In this hard dilemma some have chosen one horn and some the other. For those appealing to me on conscientious grounds, I have done, and shall do, the best I could and can, in my own conscience, under my oath to the law. That you believe this, I doubt not; and, believing it, I shall still receive, for our country and myself, your earnest prayers to our Father in Heaven.

Your sincere friend,
Abraham Lincoln[8]

What's most revealing about Lincoln's letter, however, is his depth of understanding of and compassion for the Quaker dilemma created by the Civil War. Indeed, the conflict presented the Society of Friends with a "trial of principle and faith."

While most Quakers were not active in the abolitionist movement, they were opposed to chattel slavery on moral principle. Their opposition stemmed from the Society of Friends' social testimony on the spiritual equality of all human beings, regardless of race. Most Quakers considered slavery an evil that denigrated all, as well as the cause of the war, which was God's punishment.[9] Accordingly, individual Friends sought to abolish slavery in a variety of ways. Some appealed to the moral conscience of those who held slaves and refused to purchase goods procured by slave labor. Others established antislavery organizations, like the Pennsylvania Anti-Slavery Society, which raised funds for the cause and elevated public awareness through the publication of newspapers and pamphlets. Still others lobbied the state and federal governments to adopt antislavery legislation. At the same time, Quakers did not always agree on the best approach to abolitionism. There were those who advocated gradual emancipation followed by the relocation, or colonization, of former slaves in Africa. There were others who demanded immediate emancipation and the amalgamation, or complete integration, of former slaves into white mainstream society. Naturally, there were also those who held positions that ran the gamut between these two extremes.[10] Among the more controversial Friends were those who violated federal law by participating in the Underground Railroad, a clandestine network of abolitionists who channeled runaway slaves from the border states to freedom in Canada. These Quakers firmly believed that God's law superseded civil law, which required every citizen to aid in the recapture of runaway slaves or face a fine and/or imprisonment.[11] Thus, Quakers formed a significant part of the abolitionist minority that elected Lincoln to the presidency in 1860, expecting that he would further the antislavery cause. When Lincoln, in 1863, wedded the cause of emancipation to preserving the Union as an inextricable objective of the war, Quakers struggled mightily with the combative means to achieve such highly desired objectives.

If human equality was a highly valued moral principle with strong theological implications, pacifism was a fundamental article of the Quaker faith. Friends had opposed the violent resolution of conflict since their founding in the mid-seventeenth century. Any violation of the historic Peace Testimony, whether through the individual's involvement in the military or by paying taxes levied purely for the purpose of war, was cause for disownment from the Society of Friends throughout the eighteenth and early nineteenth centuries.[12] But Quaker meetings became more willing to labor with those members who deviated from the Peace Testimony during the Civil War because of the very dilemma Lincoln had articulated, namely, that to abolish slavery meant going to war. Many young Quakers enlisted in the Union army. After Congress passed the first Conscription Act in 1863, Lincoln, as promised, pardoned those young Friends who appealed for a religious exemption, but many were still arrested and imprisoned for refusing to serve. A second draft act, passed at the urging of Friends in 1864, exempted religious objectors from military service, provided they did medical work, assisted with recently freed slaves, or paid $300 to be used for the welfare of the freedmen. But many yearly meetings along the East Coast did not approve of alternative service or paying an exemption for military duty, insisting that the commitment to the Peace Testimony be absolute.[13]

Confronted with such a trial of principle and faith, mid-nineteenth-century Quakers wrestled to find an approach that would further the cause of emancipation without deviating from their historic Peace Testimony. Many directed their attention to nursing and aiding the recently freed slaves who congregated behind Union lines. Working with freedmen's aid associations, Quakers were among the most active groups in freedmen's relief. Some Friends raised money for their food and shelter, collected clothing, and sent generous contributions to give the former slaves a start in free society. Others traveled south to establish schools for the religious and educational instruction of the freedmen and their children.[14] Promoting the cause of emancipation first as active abolitionists and later by working for the relief of freedmen, individual Quakers sought to resolve the peculiar trial presented by the war. Together with the Society of Friends' ongoing appeal for military exemption and expressions of sympathy for Lincoln's own spiritual welfare, these efforts allowed Quakers to exercise a profound effect on the manner in which the president prosecuted the Civil War.

To be sure, Lincoln, as president, was influenced by many groups, and it is impossible to determine the precise nature of the Quaker impact on his wartime policies. However, the president was no stranger to the Society of Friends and had great sympathy for as well as a genuine interest in their faith and practice. He was acutely aware of his own Quaker ancestry, noting in his 1860 campaign biography that his "family were originally Quakers, though in later times they have fallen away from the peculiar habits of that people."[15] This knowledge may have inspired him to adopt some of their peculiar practices. Lincoln exhibited many Quaker traits in his own lifestyle such as refusing to swear oaths, pretend affection, or remove his hat in deference to people in positions of authority. He also demonstrated a preference for simplicity—another quality associated with early Quakers—by dressing in plain black-and-white clothing; writing speeches, addresses, and letters noted for their austerity and brevity; and shunning the use of titles for people, including himself. "Call me Lincoln," he requested, "not Mr. President."[16] Just as appealing to him was the nondoctrinal character of the Quaker faith.

Lincoln did not embrace formal religion. Although he often attended religious services, he rejected his parents' Baptist faith and never claimed membership in a religious denomination. Nor did he accept any definite creed.[17] As a result, there are those like William Herndon, Lincoln's law partner and early biographer, who considered him an "infidel."[18] Other, more recent historians, like Richard Carwardine and Eric Foner, view Lincoln as a "Christian without a creed," a man of deep faith but one who relied on intellect, "applying the same sort of reasoning to the problems of theology that he applied to the problems of the law."[19] Still other scholars, such as Allen Guelzo, Harold Holzer, and Stephen Mansfield, see Lincoln as a "skeptic" with a "darkly Calvinist twist." According to this argument, Lincoln tended to rely on reason and personal intellect rather than religious doctrine in his decision-making process until faced with a crisis, when he yielded to the same "backdrop of necessity, providence and predestination" of a Calvinist worldview. Though he was not a Christian in a technical sense, Lincoln evolved during his presidency from a skeptic who used biblical language as rhetoric to curry favor with the voters to a spiritually devout leader who relied on a sustained personal encounter with God to help him overcome the death of a son and to make the difficult decisions on prosecuting the war and Emancipation.[20]

While Lincoln did not necessarily accept the lessons of Calvinism or the Bible, there is at least one that he valued—the "doctrine of necessity," or the belief that the actions of any individual were predetermined and shaped by the unknowable wishes of a higher power.[21] During the course of his presidency, Lincoln became more firmly convinced that behind all of his own struggles and the Union defeats there was a divine purpose at work. This is what he meant when he wrote to Gurney that he believed that he was an "instrument in the hands of the heavenly Father" and hoped that his "words and actions [as president] may be in accordance with His will." It was almost always through this lens of providential necessity that Lincoln assessed the meaning of the Civil War. The doctrine of necessity, as well as Lincoln's rejection of creeds, reflected a distinctively Quaker tone in his spirituality, factors that led to the publication of two works on Lincoln and the Quakers. In his 1973 book *Abraham Lincoln: Theologian of American Anguish*, D. Elton Trueblood identified the similarities between Quaker thought and Lincoln's religious beliefs and suggested an ongoing relationship between the Society of Friends and the president during the Civil War.[22] Daniel E. Bassuk followed Trueblood's work with the publication, in 1987, of a pamphlet titled *Abraham Lincoln and the Quakers*. It is a brief collection of primary and secondary source excerpts of Lincoln's relationship with the Society of Friends offering compelling evidence of a reciprocal influence between the two.[23] The works of Trueblood and Bassuk inspired me to do my own study of Lincoln's Quaker connection.

Abraham Lincoln, the Quakers, and the Civil War: "A Trial of Principle and Faith" explores Lincoln's relationship with the Religious Society of Friends during the years of his presidency, 1861 to 1865. It argues that Lincoln and the Quakers faced a similar dilemma during the Civil War—how to achieve the desired goal of emancipation without extending the bloodshed and physical and emotional hardship of war—and that they supported each other throughout the conflict in seeking a resolution to the dilemma. The argument focuses on Lincoln's evolution in thinking about and his treatment of the institution of slavery during his four years as president. What began as a matter of political expedience (i.e., honoring his constitutional obligation as president to preserve and protect slavery in those areas of the nation where it already existed in order to secure the loyalty of the border states) ended as a moral and spiritual imperative to abolish the peculiar institution altogether. Throughout Lincoln's presidency, the Society of Friends, individually and collectively, encouraged the process by lobbying the president and the federal government for emancipation and amnesty for conscientious objectors among their members and by offering their spiritual support and guidance to him. In the process, Lincoln and the Quakers gained mutual respect for each other and, with Emancipation and the end of the war, a resolution of their common dilemma.

Although the true Lincoln can never be known, just as the precise influence of any group on his thinking can never be determined, there is a small but compelling body of primary source documents that suggests a strong kindred bond between the president and Friends. To be sure, Lincoln kept no diary and wrote few personal letters. Most of his papers consist of speeches and wartime directives. Of the 18,350 papers that compose the eight volumes of his collected works, however, there are 12 papers sent to Lincoln by English and American Quakers and another half dozen papers sent to Quakers by the president. These include personal correspondence and appeals from monthly and yearly meetings on both sides of the Atlantic.[24] In addition, there are another dozen or so journal entries, reminiscences, and memorials by Friends who had dealings with the president.[25] These papers underscore the basis of the book's thesis and present a never-before-told story about our nation's greatest president and his relationship with one of its most respected humanitarian and religious groups.

CHAPTER 1
Antislavery Kinship, 1861

On the evening of February 21, 1861, Abraham Lincoln, en route from Springfield, Illinois, to Washington, D.C., arrived in Philadelphia. It was just his second visit to the City of Brotherly Love, and Lincoln, a great admirer of the founding fathers, wanted to see Independence Hall, where the Declaration of Independence was adopted and signed. His personal political credo had been formulated on the principles of the Declaration, and now, as the country moved hopelessly toward civil war, the president-elect was seeking inspiration for the difficult circumstances that confronted him.[1]

Two months earlier, on December 20, 1860, South Carolina seceded from the Union. The legality of secession, the doctrine of state's rights, and the institution of black slavery were issues of debate in the United States for decades. Slavery had been the backbone of the South's economy for nearly two centuries, and the states felt that the Northern plan to abolish their peculiar institution infringed on their rights to govern themselves, as it was not a power explicitly awarded to the federal government in the Constitution. Time after time the South had forced political compromises by threatening to dissolve the Union, but by 1860 many Northern politicians had come to view the threat as a bluff and had grown tired of compromising over slavery. The election of Lincoln, who ran on an antislavery platform, proved to be the final straw. In January, Mississippi, Florida, Alabama, Georgia, and Louisiana also seceded, followed by Texas on February 1.[2]

On Capitol Hill, many felt that Lincoln, a prairie lawyer chosen by a minority of the popular vote, was ill-equipped to hold the nation together. His detractors believed that he had stolen the election through cunning and luck. Only by shrewd manipulation of the slavery issue was Lincoln able to secure the Republican nomination. Instead of alienating the competing factions within the party, Lincoln united radicals, moderates, and conservatives by conceding that the South had a constitutional right to preserve slavery where it already existed while also demanding that Congress prohibit the extension of the peculiar institution.[3] The same reasoning allowed Lincoln to win a clear majority of electoral votes in the general election, while the Democrats, divided over the slavery issue, split their vote between Northern and Southern candidates. Now there were concerns that he lacked the will and purpose to lead the nation in the face of a mounting crisis.[4]

Lincoln's reverence for the nation's founding was intimately bound to his vision for its future, a point he made clear on February 22, when he delivered a brief address at Independence Hall. Arriving at 7:00 a.m., the president-elect was ushered into the east wing chamber where the Declaration had been signed 85 years earlier. In reply to welcoming remarks by Theodore L. Cuyler, president of the Select Council of Philadelphia, Lincoln made an extemporaneous speech, admitting that he was "filled with deep emotion" as he stood on the same site as the founders. Speaking of his strong reverence for the Declaration, he admitted that he had "never had a feeling politically that did not spring from the sentiments embodied in the [document], which gave liberty, not alone to the people of this great country, but hope to the world for all future time." Then, addressing the impending crisis, Lincoln added, "If this country cannot be saved without giving up that principle—I would rather be assassinated on this spot than to surrender to it." "It is the only principle," he resolved, "that I am willing to live by, and, in the pleasure of Almighty God die by."[5]

Lincoln's fierce determination to sacrifice his life in order to preserve the Union might have been intended to put the South on notice that he refused to buckle under the threat of assassination. The night before, Allan Pinkerton, the head of the Pinkerton National Detective Agency, informed the president-elect of an assassination plot to be carried out at Baltimore, a strongly pro-Southern city with an infamous reputation for street violence. Pinkerton urged Lincoln to leave Philadelphia immediately, passing through Baltimore on a midnight train before the conspirators learned of the change of plans. Lincoln refused to alter his schedule, however, insisting on making the visit to Independence Hall and traveling to Harrisburg later in the day to address the Pennsylvania legislature.[6] What is certain is that the president-elect's unshakable commitment to "liberty, not alone to the people of this great country, but hope to the world for all future time" underscored his reverence for the Declaration as well as his determination to preserve its principles regardless of the costs.

Lincoln rejected the popular notion that the rights of liberty and the pursuit of happiness were confined to the white race. While he understood that the founding fathers employed the rhetoric of universal liberty to justify American independence from Great Britain and that they did not advocate either equality of condition or equal opportunity for the back race, Lincoln, throughout his political career, routinely invoked the Declaration to defend his antislavery beliefs.[7] He had always been morally opposed to slavery. His first encounter with the peculiar institution came in 1828, when at age 19 he sailed a cargo of produce down the Mississippi River to New Orleans, where he witnessed the physical brutality of slave markets, a scene that remained a "continual torment" to him.[8] A decade later, he was one of only two representatives in the Illinois state legislature to take a stand against slavery, calling it a "monstrous injustice."[9] During his single term in the U.S. House of Representative in 1847–1849, Lincoln supported such antislavery measures as the Wilmot Proviso, which excluded slavery from the territory acquired through the Mexican War. Having been exposed to the horrors of Washington's slave auctions, he also introduced an unsuccessful bill that would forever outlaw slavery in the nation's capital.[10] Of the 175 speeches Lincoln delivered between 1854 and 1860, virtually all addressed his antislavery sentiments.[11] But his most articulate moral objection to the institution came on October 16, 1854, at Peoria, Illinois, when he addressed the Kansas–Nebraska Act. Ignoring the economic issues that had previously defined his career as a Whig politician devoted to internal improvements, Lincoln focused on slavery as a political and moral evil. Politically, he argued that the Kansas–Nebraska Act violated the founding fathers' intent to restrict the spread of slavery, leading to its eventual demise. Then, he moved seamlessly to a strong moral condemnation to the institution itself. "I cannot but hate the spread of slavery . . . . because of the monstrous injustice of slavery," he declared. "I hate [slavery] because it deprives our republican example of its just influence in the world and enables the enemies of free institutions—with plausibility—to taunt us as hypocrites because it forces so many really good men amongst ourselves into an open war with the very fundamental principles of the *Declaration of Independence*, insisting that there is no right principle of action but *self-interest*."[12]

Essentially, Lincoln's position on slavery as a moral wrong and his desire to prevent its extension were well known by 1861, when he assumed the presidency. What was not clear was his solution to the problem. He had often given serious consideration to gradual emancipation accompanied by colonization, or relocating the freedmen to Liberia on the coast of West Africa. Such a policy was consistent with his beliefs on the social and political inferiority of the black race, but it represented a middle ground in the spectrum of Northern antislavery opinion. At one extreme were radical abolitionists, who demanded immediate emancipation and equal citizenship for black slaves. Some were Radical Republicans, largely located in New England, upstate New York, and the upper Midwest. Among them were Senators Salmon Chase of Ohio and William Seward of New York, both of whom had challenged Lincoln for the Republican nomination and would soon be appointed to the executive cabinet. Others worked outside the political system, violating federal law by participating as agents of the Underground Railroad, the clandestine network of safe houses where fugitive slaves sought refuge en route to freedom. Underground Railroad agents resided throughout the North, but were concentrated in the Mid-Atlantic states of Pennsylvania, New Jersey, and New York; the border states of Maryland and Delaware; and the Midwestern states of Ohio and Indiana, all of which served as destination points for runaway slaves. At the other end of the antislavery spectrum were the conservatives, mostly former Whigs who opposed the expansion of slavery because it would retard the nation's economic development. But they refused to act on their antislavery convictions, fearing that to do so would endanger the Union.[13] Quakers, among the most active abolitionists, could be found on every conceivable level of the antislavery spectrum.

II

The Religious Society of Friends was a pioneer in the antislavery movement. Inspired by a theological belief of the presence of a divine spark, Quakers reasoned that if God made His presence available to each person, then, in His eyes, all human beings were of equal value regardless of race, sex, or creed. This so-called "Inner Light" doctrine and a concomitant testimony on human equality placed Friends well ahead of other American churches in acknowledging the evils of slavery. As early as 1688, a small group of Quakers in Germantown, near Philadelphia, challenged the institution by urging slaveholders in their church to "stand against" the practice of "bring[ing] men [to this country], or to rob and sell them against their will."[14] The Society of Friends, however, could not bring itself to a complete realization of the testimony, especially when many prominent Philadelphia Quakers themselves owned slaves or participated in the slave trade. Consequently, individual members served to plant the seed for abolitionism within the Society of Friends.

There was Benjamin Lay, an eccentric hunched-back dwarf, whose sensationalist behavior confronted Friends with the inconsistency between slaveholding and the Society's testimony on equality. In one of his most shocking demonstrations, Lay, in 1738, went before Philadelphia Yearly Meeting, the body that set the policy for the Quaker meetings of Pennsylvania, New Jersey, and Delaware, and plunged a sword into a hollowed-out Bible containing a bladder of red pokeberry juice. Splattering those seated nearby with "blood," Lay accused the slaveholding Quakers of hypocrisy.[15] Lay represented the most radical impulse of Quaker abolitionism, one that placed a single-minded commitment to eradicating slavery at any cost above the practical necessity of achieving that cause through society's established institutions. Such a radical impulse could also be found among those nineteenth-century Friends who participated in the Underground Railroad. A less impassioned but every bit as passionate Quaker abolitionist was John Woolman, whose work, *Some Considerations on the Keeping of Negroes* (1754), aroused the moral conscience of Philadelphia Yearly Meeting. Appealing to the Christian sympathies of his readers, Woolman reminded them that slavery was a "contradiction to true religion itself," but that one should "exercise lovingkindness towards all men," including the slaveholder, in order to enjoy the "blessing of God."[16] By focusing on the temporal as well as spiritual welfare of the slaveholder, rather than the demoralization of the slave, Woolman made abolitionism the catalyst of a spiritual reformation among Friends. That reformation emphasized the need of Philadelphia Yearly Meeting to distance itself from worldly practices and to purify the church by requiring all members to return to a primitive simplicity in behavior and lifestyle.

Thus, Friends became more insistent that their children not mix with non-Quakers at school, preferring a more guarded education. Marriage outside the Society of Friends was discouraged and often resulted in disownment. Members were strenuously urged to rid themselves of "vain customs of the world" such as wearing ostentatious clothing and participating in music, theater, and art. Quakers also placed a greater emphasis on their historic Peace Testimony.

Unable to reconcile their pacifist convictions with their public responsibility to defend the frontier during the French–Indian War, Friends resigned en mass from the Pennsylvania government. Swift and sometimes severe disciplinary action was taken against wayward members who deviated from Quaker practice.[17] Abolitionism was a fundamental objective of this spiritual reformation, but one that was not easily achieved.

In 1754, Philadelphia Yearly Meeting declared its "uneasiness and disunity with the importation and purchasing of Negro and other slaves," stating that these practices were "not consistent with both Christianity and common justice." Rather than disown those Friends who engaged in the slave trade, the yearly meeting urged them to "make the case of the Africans [their] own, and consider what [they] should think . . . . and feel, were [they] in their circumstances."[18] Four years later, the yearly meeting directed its constituent monthly meetings to "eliminate from membership all those who continued to buy or sell slaves and, through visiting committees, to persuade owners to free the black slaves they already owned."[19] However, enforcement of the 1758 discipline varied widely among the Quaker monthly meetings of southeastern Pennsylvania, ranging the spectrum from disownment to lenient treatment for those who claimed ignorance of the change in discipline and promised to treat their slaves well in the future.[20]

The antislavery example pioneered in Philadelphia Yearly Meeting quickly spread to other yearly meetings in colonial America. But the final step of disowning from membership those Friends who refused to free their slaves did not come to fruition until the American Revolution. That decision was closely tied to the Quaker refusal to support a war-born government and the persecution Friends suffered at the hands of American patriots. Suspected of loyalty to the British government, Friends who refused to fight, swear oaths of allegiance, or pay war taxes experienced the confiscation or destruction of their property by patriot neighbors and the forcible requisition of supplies from their households by the Continental army.[21] To prove their allegiance to and influence events in the fledgling United States, Quakers expanded their involvement in humanitarian reform, and no reform held more importance than abolitionism.[22] Between 1776 and 1784, every Quaker yearly meeting in North America adopted the discipline of disownment for slaveholding among members.[23] What had begun a century earlier as a moral protest by a small group of Quakers within Philadelphia Yearly Meeting had become a matter of spiritual integrity for the Society of Friends itself. Once this decisive step was taken, however, abolitionism was not as pressing a concern for the Society of Friends as it had been earlier. It was clear that the American yearly meetings viewed slavery as a moral and spiritual evil that had now been purged from the church. Having achieved that goal, the Society of Friends, as a religious body, did not feel compelled to accept blacks into church membership or to involve themselves in a larger campaign to abolish slavery. In fact, a strong fear of miscegenation resulted in subtle forms of discrimination within the Society of Friends well into the mid-nineteenth century. Quakers on the East Coast, for example, welcomed African Americans to attend worship services, but they were required to sit in special sections reserved for them, and only a tiny number were received into formal membership.[24] Instead, individual Friends assumed the responsibility of shifting the antislavery campaign to the larger, non-Quaker society. Even after the Society of Friends experienced a series of theological schisms in the first half of the nineteenth century, individual Quakers, regardless of dogma, continued to participate in the antislavery crusade.

The first and arguably the most serious schism in American Quakerism occurred during 1827–1828 when Friends came under the growing influence of the Methodists and other evangelical groups. Younger and more progressive-thinking Friends, often living in large cities, were affected by the new and vibrant evangelical movement. They accused the elder members of the Society of undervaluing Jesus Christ and the Bible, which was, for them, the authoritative source of knowledge about Jesus. These evangelically oriented Friends argued that no one could be saved without the blood of Christ, who was equal with God, a person in the Trinity, born of the Virgin Mary and without sin. While they did not stress an emotional conversion experience like other evangelical groups, the young Friends did emphasize the virgin birth, scriptural inerrancy, the Trinity, a physical resurrection, and a strong belief in heaven and hell.[25] As these Friends gained influence in their yearly meetings, they pressed for changes in religious discipline that complemented evangelical thought. For example, in 1806, Philadelphia Yearly Meeting revised its discipline and introduced for the first time an article making it a cause for disownment to "deny the divinity of our Lord and Savior Jesus Christ, the immediate revelation of the Holy Spirit, or the authenticity of the Scriptures."[26] This shift in discipline led some Quakers to leave the Society of Friends and join other, more evangelical denominations, and others to resist the new ideas.

During the next two decades, their frustrations coalesced around the ministry of Elias Hicks, a traveling Quaker minister from Long Island, New York, who championed a more spiritualistic and less dogmatic approach. Although Hicks accepted the truth of scripture, the divinity of Christ, and the resurrection, he emphasized the Inner Light, or indwelling Christ, was the unerring source of divine revelation. Tensions between urban and rural Friends, issues of control, and personality conflicts compounded the difficulties. Matters came to a head in 1827 when Philadelphia Yearly Meeting split into two yearly meetings. One group, the "Hicksites," followed the beliefs of Elias Hicks and retained the majority of members in Philadelphia Quakerdom. The other yearly meeting was established by the "Orthodox," the minority who embraced evangelical thought. Each faction consolidated its control of meeting houses, schools, graveyards, and trust funds. The following year, New York and Baltimore yearly meetings split with the Hicksites enjoying the numerical majority in both meetings. In the Midwest, Ohio Yearly Meeting split roughly in half between the opposing factions, and Indiana Yearly Meeting became Orthodox after a small number of Hicksites separated from it.[27]

Between 1830 and 1860, the evangelical movement became stronger in the United States, and Orthodox Friends felt pressured to conform to its principles. Joseph John Gurney, an evangelical from a prominent family of British Quakers, came to the United States in the 1840s to strengthen evangelical thought among Orthodox Friends. Gurney's theology appealed to the authority of the Bible and to the human need for atonement. But he did not deny the importance of such Hicksite beliefs as silent worship, plain speech and dress, and pacifism. Nor did he deny the significance of the Inner Light, only that the Bible was the primary source of revelation. He also favored working closely with other Christian groups in such humanitarian reforms as abolitionism.[28] However, Gurney's ministry served to divide Orthodox Friends. The conflict, known as the "Wilburite–Gurneyite controversy," pitted the followers of John Wilbur, a New England Friend who defended the authority of the Holy Spirit as primary and worked to prevent what he saw as the dilution of the Friends' tradition of Spirit-led ministry, against those of Gurney. To that end, Wilbur traveled across the Midwest and East Coast, going from meeting to meeting to oppose Gurney's views.

The Wilburite-Gurneyite controversy had the most damaging effect on Indiana Yearly Meeting, resulting in a schism among

Orthodox Quakers in the early 1840s. Levi Coffin, the state's most prominent Underground Railroad agent, and two other leading abolitionists, Walter Edgerton and Charles Osborn, led a group of radicals who advocated immediate emancipation against the more conservative Indiana Yearly Meeting, which advocated gradualism and discouraged members from joining with non-Quakers in their antislavery activities. The yearly meeting responded to the growing controversy by closing its meetinghouses in 1841 to antislavery lecturers, while the radicals continued to hold joint abolitionist meetings with non-Quakers. Matters came to a head in October 1842 when Senator Henry Clay of Kentucky appeared before Indiana Yearly Meeting at Richmond. Clay, a slaveholder who advocated gradual emancipation followed by colonization, was campaigning for the Whig Party in the congressional elections. While he was received warmly by the conservative Friends, the radicals presented him with a petition urging that he could at least free his own slaves. Clay, noticeably angered, was whisked away by Elijah Coffin, Levi's cousin and the clerk of the yearly meeting. When the dust settled, the Coffins, Osborn, Edgerton, and some 2,000 radicals had established their own Indiana Yearly Meeting of Anti-Slavery Friends and separated from the main conservative body, which retained a membership of 25,000.[29]

Quaker historian Thomas Hamm argues that the rhetoric of Indiana Yearly Meeting was an "amalgam of the arguments of both Wilburites and Gurneyites." The yearly meeting's leadership believed that the activities of abolitionists like the Coffins, Osborn, and Edgerton "endangered the purity of the Society of Friends by associating with non-Friends who did not wait for the leadings of the Holy Spirit and who were, in some cases, of doubtful religious and moral standing." The Anti-Slavery Friends "embraced an equally confusing set of ideas." Like the Gurneyites, they considered it their duty as Quakers to work with *anyone* who sought to advance the antislavery cause, regardless of their denominational affiliation. At the same time, there were those Anti-Slavery Friends, like Osborn and Edgerton, who embraced Wilburite beliefs accusing the larger body of Indiana Friends of being "corrupted by the wealth and worldliness" condoned by Gurney. They believed it was the responsibility of the Anti-Slavery Friends to "raise a higher standard of discipline, reaffirming the historic Quaker position on slavery and disciplinary issues." Thus, Hamm argues that the Anti-Slavery Friends were in a "doubly isolated position ... as abolitionists they repulsed the Wilburites, and as separatists they were anathema to the Gurneyites."[30]

The schism between Anti-Slavery Friends and the main body of Indiana Yearly Meeting did not last very long. Many of the yearly meeting's members sympathized with the abolitionists but were not driven to the necessity of separating from the main body.[31] Still their antislavery sympathies as well as a growing animosity within the yearly meeting toward John Wilbur and the desire to avoid further conflict in their religious body led to a reconciliation of the two sides in 1857.[32] While the Wilburite–Gurneyite controversy still divided Orthodox Friends in Ohio and Philadelphia yearly meetings, Orthodox Friends in New York, Baltimore, and North Carolina yearly meetings embraced Gurneyite beliefs. Essentially, Orthodox Quakerism was slowly moving toward mainstream evangelical religion in the United States, being driven by common ties in politics and humanitarian reform, especially the abolition of slavery.[33] Despite their theological differences, Quakers shared a basic antipathy to slavery, believing that human bondage was a disgrace to the nation and must be abolished. That shared belief transcended theological differences between the Orthodox and Hicksite, Wilburite and Gurneyite, Conservative and Progressive, and even those who were Congregational Friends.[34] Thus, *doctrine* was much less important than the *approach* used to eradicate human slavery.

Quaker historians Hugh Barbour and Jerry Frost contend that there is a "lack of statistics on numbers of Friends from each branch of Quakerism in each form of program to determine which Friends embraced a particular approach."[35] However, there *were* significant differences in approach. Some Quaker abolitionists appealed to the moral conscience of slaveholders, and refused to purchase goods procured by slave labor. Many of these were Southern Friends who had been ridiculed for their antislavery beliefs and migrated to the free states of Ohio, Indiana, Illinois, and Iowa. There were those Friends who refused to work with non-Quaker abolitionists in eradicating slavery. Others joined non-Friends in establishing antislavery organizations, such as the Pennsylvania Anti-Slavery Society, which raised funds for the cause and elevated public awareness through the publication of newspapers and pamphlets. Still others lobbied state and federal governments to adopt antislavery legislation. And there were even those Friends who violated federal law by assisting fugitive slaves to escape to freedom on the Underground Railroad.[36] There were also differences in the timetable for emancipation advocated by various Quaker abolitionists. There were those who advocated a gradual approach followed by the relocation, or colonization, of former slaves in Africa. There were others who demanded immediate emancipation and the amalgamation, or complete integration, of former slaves into white mainstream society. Naturally, there were also those who held positions that ran the gamut between these two extremes.[37] The point is that by the time Lincoln became president in 1861, not every Quaker was active in the antislavery cause, and those who were abolitionists were divided on how to achieve emancipation, not over matters of theology.

Lincoln understood the Friends' fierce devotion to human equality and pacifism, and he was careful not to alienate his Quaker supporters. On February 22, 1861, when he traveled to Harrisburg to address the Pennsylvania legislature, the president-elect was greeted at the train station by Governor Andrew Curtin and a large crowd. Anticipating their concern about the possibility of civil war, Lincoln acknowledged the "peaceful principles upon which this great Commonwealth was originally settled" and underscored his "praise for those peaceful principles." "I hope no one of the Friends who originally settled here, or who lived here since that time, or who live here now, has been or is a more devoted lover of peace, harmony and concord than my humble self," he added. Noting the impressive presence of the Pennsylvania militia in dress uniform, Lincoln complimented the governor on the "finest military array, I think, that I have ever seen." But he quickly expressed his hope that "their services may never be needed, especially in the shedding of fraternal blood." "It shall be my endeavor," he concluded, "to preserve the peace of this country so far as it can possibly be done."[38] He expressed a similar wish to avoid the "shedding of fraternal blood" when he addressed the Pennsylvania General Assembly later that day, assuring them that if war came, it "shall be through no fault of mine."[39] To be sure, Lincoln, by nature, was a peaceful man who shared the Quakers' desire to prevent war. But he was also a shrewd politician who sought to affirm Pennsylvania's faith in his leadership. Lincoln was acutely aware of the fact that the Keystone State and its influential Quaker vote had been critical to his success in the 1860 election. Republican leaders were convinced that Pennsylvania would decide the presidential contest and that if the Quakers turned out to vote, "Honest Abe" would win. When large numbers of Friends voted in the state election, which occurred several weeks before the general election, Lincoln's victory became a certainty. Elated by the outcome, John G. Whittier, a Quaker poet and journalist, penned a spirited campaign song predicting that "Lincoln goes [into the presidency] when the Quakers are out [to vote]."[40] Whittier's words were prophetic.

Quakers joined the Republican Party in droves in 1856.[41] Prior to that date, most Friends had been staunch supporters of the Whig Party with its emphasis on free labor and free soil. That political ideology motivated Quakers to migrate from the South to the free states of Ohio and Indiana during the first part of the nineteenth century. Federal land grants made migration an attractive option for Quaker families who hoped to secure enough farmland to pass on to their sons. Property in the west could be purchased for as little as 50 cents to $5.00 an acre. What's more, Friends from Virginia and the Carolinas had grown frustrated with Southern laws, which forbade the manumission and education of slaves, and were encouraged to relocate "west of the Ohio River where there was no slavery" by traveling Quaker ministers from London, Philadelphia, and New England.[42] As a result, Southern Quakerism suffered a dramatic decline between 1800 and 1850. During that span, North Carolina laid down 83 of the 136 meetings that had been established in the state. North Carolina Yearly Meeting issued certificates of removal for 16 families who relocated to Pennsylvania, 294 to Ohio, and 784 to Indiana. In 1804–1805, Wrightsborough Monthly Meeting in Georgia was laid down because 50 families removed to Ohio, and by 1844, Virginia Yearly Meeting had so few members that it merged with Baltimore Yearly Meeting.[43] A secondary migration of Quakers from Indiana to Iowa, also motivated by the free soil ideology, occurred in 1835 after the Black Hawk War. Indiana Quakers resettled at Salem in southeastern Iowa and later moved to Oskaloosa in central Iowa and Indianola and Bear Creek in the western part of the state. The growth of Iowa Quakerism was so dramatic that by 1863 a new Iowa Yearly Meeting was established from Indiana Yearly Meeting, just five years after that body had created Western Yearly Meeting for all the monthly meetings south of Indianapolis.[44]

As the Whig Party yielded to a new Republican Party in the mid-1850s, so too did Quakers shift their partisan allegiance. Friends were at the forefront of Northern ideas of human rights that constituted the core beliefs of the Republican platform, especially a man's right to work where and how he wanted and to accumulate property in his own name. The extension of slavery was the primary obstacle to the Republican Party's principles of "free soil, free labor, free men." By 1860, the Republican vision had become synonymous with the Northern vision of the nation's future. At issue was whether that vision (based on a modern, more industrial economy and free labor) or the Southern vision (based on a traditional agricultural economy and slavery labor) would take root in the West, whose development would determine the nation's destiny.[45] Since most Quakers were either Northern merchant-entrepreneurs or Western farmers, the Society of Friends had a major stake in the fortunes of the Republican Party and its free soil ideology. By that time, Quaker involvement in abolitionism had intensified with the establishment of Underground Railroad networks emanating from one of three major nerve centers: Philadelphia, Cincinnati, and Newport, Indiana.[46] Although Lincoln opposed such illegal methods, he certainly viewed the Society of Friends as an important constituency because of their abolitionist and free soil sentiments.

Lincoln had initially used the rights of Northern free labor as an attack against slavery in his 1858 senatorial campaign against Stephen Douglas, but he later placed a greater emphasis on the free labor ideology to appeal to a broader spectrum of Northerners. Pitting the industrial growth of the North against the economic stagnation of the South, Lincoln attributed the difference to the superiority of free to slave labor. He scoffed at the Democrats' assumption that "the slave is in a better condition than the hired laborer because he remains a hired laborer." "There is no such thing as a man who is a hired laborer always remaining in his early condition," Lincoln declared while stumping in Ohio for Republican candidates in 1859. "Improvement in condition is the great principle for which this government was formed." But the slaveholders, according to Lincoln, had "taken labor, the common burden of [the human] race, and placed it on the shoulders of [black slaves]." In so doing, they "degraded" their own society, "destroy[ing] hope for self-improvement, which is a more powerful incentive than the rod." Predictably, Lincoln couched his rhetoric in the context of the Declaration of Independence. He viewed the dual concerns of *free labor* and *abolitionism* as inextricably tied to the founders' emphasis on inalienable rights, specifically the right of every man to pursue his own happiness. "In the exercise of this right," he declared, "you must have room to grow. Where shall we go to? To those new territories which belong to us, which are God-given for that purpose? Can they make that national advance in their condition if they find the institution of slavery planted there?"[47] It was a shrewd argument. By wedding his own antislavery views to the free labor ideology, Lincoln redefined slavery from a moral wrong to a threat to the economic self-interest of white Northerners as well as a threat to the entire nation itself.[48] The logic resonated with a broad cross-section of Friends, from the Philadelphia merchant who was concerned about his profits and social advancement, to the New England abolitionist who cared deeply about the immorality of slavery, to the Western farmer who feared the expansion of slavery. Now Lincoln would have to prove to Friends that he possessed the ability, leadership, and resolve to implement their shared vision.

III

Lincoln rose at 5:00 a.m. on March 4, 1861, the morning of the inauguration. The clouds over Washington were heavy with rain, threatening to dampen the enthusiasm of the occasion with showers. A few drops fell occasionally before 8 a.m., but eventually the cloudy skies yielded to bright sunshine. By mid-morning, the weather was cool and bracing but, on the whole, favorable to the momentous event.

Despite his excellent accommodations at Willard's Hotel on 14th Street, the president-elect was restless and eager to begin the day's events. After an early breakfast, Lincoln listened attentively while his son, Robert, read aloud his inaugural address. Some final touches were added, and the former prairie lawyer retired to his closet, where he prepared for the ceremonies.[49]

Orville Browning, a personal and political friend, paid a brief visit and asked Lincoln if he preferred to accompany President James Buchanan to the Capitol Building or make the trip alone. Proper etiquette required the president-elect to share a carriage with the incumbent, but it was also Lincoln's privilege to show his contempt for Buchanan, a lame duck who reverted to a policy of inactivity as seven slave states seceded from the Union.

"That puts me in mind of a story," Lincoln replied with a wry smile. "Once there was a man dressed like a Quaker, who, coming into court as a witness, was asked if he would swear or affirm. 'I don't give a damn which', was the reply."[50]

Of course, Lincoln did *give a damn* and achieved both objectives by accompanying Buchanan in an open carriage down Pennsylvania Avenue to the Capitol but making little effort at conversation. The outgoing president appeared pale, sad, and nervous. In his discomfort, he made a feeble attempt at levity, which only intensified Lincoln's resentment of him. "If you are as happy entering the presidency as I am leaving it," said Buchanan, "then you are a very happy man."[51] Lincoln acknowledged the remark with a slight smile, breaking the tension that existed on a historic but ominous day.

Southern sentiment in the city was strong. There were rumors of assassination plots, and Lincoln could sense the hostility of Confederate sympathizers among the crowds lining the streets as the carriage made its way to the Capitol Building. Of those things, he had little control. The burden of Lincoln's safety fell on the aged shoulders of Lieutenant General Winfield Scott, head of the U.S. army, who had also received death threats if he "dared to protect the ceremony by military force." Undeterred, Scott made sure to surround the president-elect's carriage on all sides by marshals and cavalry, almost hiding it from view. Green-coated riflemen with orders to "shoot anyone crowding toward the President's carriage" were stationed on the rooftops of the buildings lining the parade route, and cannon stood on the Capitol grounds ready to be fired if there should be trouble.[52]

The procession arrived at the unfinished Capitol Building without incident, and Lincoln took his place on the platform erected over the steps of the eastern portico. After Chief Justice Roger B. Taney administered the oath of office, Lincoln delivered a stirring inaugural address that was both firm and conciliatory. While he denied the right of any single state to secede from the Union and vowed to "hold, occupy and possess" federal installations in the rebellious states, the new president also declared that he had no intention, or inclination, to abolish slavery in those states. "Apprehension seems to exist among the people of the Southern States, that by the accession of a Republican administration, their property, and their peace, and personal security, are to be endangered," he stated. "There has never been any reasonable cause for such apprehension." To reassure those who doubted him, Lincoln identified his duty under the federal constitution to respect the property of all U.S. citizens. "I have no purpose, directly or indirectly, to interfere with the institution of slavery in the States where it exists," he declared. "I believe I have no lawful right to do so, and I have no inclination to do so." This was not an empty or politically expedient promise. Lincoln acknowledged the fact that "those who nominated and elected [him] did so with full knowledge that [he] had made this, and many similar declarations, and had never recanted them." Furthermore, the Republican Party had "placed in the platform, for [his] acceptance, and as a law to themselves, the clear and emphatic resolution" not to interfere with slavery in those states where it already existed.[53] As a gesture of reconciliation, Lincoln ended his address with an appeal to the people of the South: "We are not enemies, but friends. We must not be enemies. ... The mystic chords of memory, stretching from every battlefield, and patriot grave, to every living heart and hearthstone, all over this broad land, will yet swell the chorus of the Union, when again touched, as surely they will be, by the better angels of our nature."[54]

To be sure, Lincoln's inaugural, though directed at the South, was a strong forceful appeal to all the American people to hold the Union together and to trust that he would abide by his constitutional duties to do the same. As much as he hated slavery, he would not interfere with the institution where it already existed, but hold firm in preventing its extension into the new territories. While much of the Northern press praised or at least accepted Lincoln's speech, initial impressions among Philadelphia's Quakers were mixed. Elizabeth Newport, a member of Green Street Monthly Meeting, was moved by Lincoln's earnest desire for divine guidance and wrote a letter encouraging him to "hold fast the profession of thy faith." She also assured the new president that "there are many in the Society of Friends whose hearts beat in unison with his desire to preserve the Union" and that his "nomination and election to the presidency has been hailed with an intensity of interest among [Quakers] never before equalled."[55] Similarly, Martha Schofield, a Hicksite Quaker of Darby, Pennsylvania, was also enthusiastic, viewing Lincoln's election as "evidence that the people have been roused from their lethargy." Although he "may not be an abolitionist," she added, the new president is "far better than a Democrat who would submit to Southerners' laws."[56] Other Quakers were more cautious. The *Friend*, for example, editorialized that Lincoln's inaugural "was mild and peaceful, and evidenced that he appreciated the serious difficulties of his position."[57] Still other Friends, like Lucretia Mott, a radical abolitionist and a leading Hicksite minister, was put off by the address. Mott, after reading the inaugural speech in the newspaper, told relatives that it was "infernal and diabolical." She accused Lincoln of appeasing the South by promising not to interfere with slavery where it already existed and condemned his "willingness to strengthen the pro-slavery parts of the [Federal] Constitution."[58] Mott probably would have welcomed secession, believing that disunion would eventually lead to the disintegration of slavery itself.[59] Outside of Philadelphia, the inaugural was received by Friends with silence, probably a reflection of a "wait-and-see" attitude.

In the South, Lincoln's address was met with contempt. Margaretta Walton, a traveling Quaker minister from Ercildoun in Chester County, Pennsylvania, was visiting friends in Montgomery, Alabama, when she heard the inaugural address read aloud in public. "The men in the audience were feeling sore and extremely cross," she noted in her journal. "They could see nothing but war in it and feel that nothing Lincoln does is right. Their feelings are so bitter that reason has no place among them."[60] Southern contempt for the new president reached fever pitch on April 12, with the Confederate bombardment of Fort Sumter in Charleston Harbor, South Carolina. The president responded to the assault with a virtual declaration of war, calling for 75,000 state militia volunteers to crush the southern "insurrection." To prevent Washington from being encircled by prosecessionist state governments in Maryland and Delaware and to ensure the transportation of loyal troops to the isolated Union capitol, Lincoln ordered federal soldiers to arrest secessionists in those states and suspend the writ of habeas corpus. He also called up the state militias, expanded the navy, ordered a naval blockade of the South, and approved the expenditure of military funds—all without congressional approval. In peacetime, such actions would have been unconstitutional. But Lincoln defended their legitimacy—and necessity—by pointing to the Constitution's war emergency clauses, which, he claimed, existed to give the nation a reasonable capacity for self-defense. Still, these unprecedented actions provoked the wrath of antiwar Democrats who chastised the president as "King Linkum I, a race-mixing dictator who aimed to centralize, militarize and mongrelize the Union of states."[61] The Society of Friends was more measured in its response to the outbreak of war.

Philadelphia Meeting for Sufferings (Orthodox), which served as a de facto executive committee in carrying out the wishes and policies of Philadelphia Yearly Meeting (Orthodox), immediately expressed its "concern" over the "serious commotions now agitating the community" and the "threat of civil war." Urging members to maintain the peace testimony, the Meeting for Sufferings issued an epistle "to conform to the doctrines in which Friends have always believed and to stand firm during these trials."[62] While New England Yearly Meeting (Orthodox) affirmed their loyalty to the federal government and the antislavery cause, it urged its members to avoid taking up arms for the defense of either.[63] Western Yearly Meeting, held at Plainfield, Indiana, encouraged members to "follow after the things that make for peace" instead of giving into "[human] temptations and shortsightedness ... when the strife of civil war is around us."[64] Indiana Yearly Meeting for Sufferings condemned the Confederacy for the "disloyalty and the civil strife ... [it] has brought upon our beloved country." It also entreated members to "maintain our peace testimony and against the taking of human life" in case the "trials of war should come upon us individually."[65] Indiana Yearly Meeting (Orthodox) continued to uphold their allegiance to the Union while discouraging members from fighting throughout the war with similar advices. "We love our country and highly appreciate the excellent government under which we have enjoyed so large a share of liberty and security to person and property, and look with heartfelt sorrow upon the efforts to destroy it," according to another epistle written shortly after the First Battle of Bull Run in July. "But we have been made especially to feel the great evil of war, the horrors of the battlefields, the terrible suffering connected therewith ... and cannot believe that any cause is sufficient to justify such scenes or warrant us in violating what we believe to be the law of our Lord."[66]

Despite the appeals, there were those Quakers who eagerly responded to Lincoln's call for troops. Students from Friends colleges and at least one boarding school were especially vulnerable to the patriotic impulse. Isaac J. Wistar and Norwood Penrose Hallowell, students at Haverford College, an Orthodox institution near Philadelphia, enlisted shortly after the Confederate assault on Sumter. Wistar, a lieutenant colonel in the California volunteers, served with distinction during the Peninsula campaign and achieved the rank of brigadier general by war's end. Hallowell, a white lieutenant colonel, served in the 54th Massachusetts, the first African American regiment in the U.S. Army.[67] At Westtown, an Orthodox Friends' boarding school in Chester County, Pennsylvania, some of the older boys also felt the need to enlist.[68] In November 1861, Joseph Pratt, an 18-year-old student, ran away from the school with two classmates to join the Brandywine Guards, 30th Pennsylvania Regiment.[69] The following month, two other students—Thomas Bundy and Alfred Whitaker—"ran off to the war," taking a train to Washington, D.C., where they enlisted in the Union army.[70] Male students continued to run away from school as they reached age 18. Edward Wood, for example, "made a faithful promise to his father that he would not [sic] go to war." But in June 1863 he broke that promise and joined the Union army.[71] With so many of their male schoolmates leaving for the battlefront, Westtown's female students were eager to learn anything they could about the war and feared that their older brothers and even fathers might also enlist. Margaret Gummere wrote that she was "nearly crazy to hear the war news," but her teachers "are all very much troubled and try to hide [the news] to keep the girls from being excited." Not knowing only proved to be more nerve-wracking. Margaret constantly worried about her older brother, Morris, and her father joining the Union ranks and begged her mother to prevent them from enlisting.[72]

The temptation to serve in the military was particularly strong at Earlham College, a Gurneyite institution in Richmond, Indiana. Excitement over the war reached fever pitch early on. "A good deal of excitement here," John Harvey wrote home to his sister, Hannah, in Clinton County, Ohio. "We have daily newspapers, one boy reads and the others gang around. One-hundred-and-eighty soldiers left here a few days ago, hundreds of them passing from the west. I went to the depot yesterday to see 3,000 pass in detachments. Some of the boys talk of going home. They say they can't study."[73] Despite counsel by teachers and meeting elders to adhere to the Peace Testimony, several Earlham students dropped out to enlist in the Union army.[74] Among those students who enlisted in the Union ranks was Daniel Wooten, who insisted that the Confederate rebellion "against the laws of our country" took precedent over the biblical commandment "thou shalt not kill" "so long as God gives us the power to quell them by any means."[75] Another student, Levinus King, was motivated to fight for the Union by his fierce abolitionist beliefs. Even the pleas of his father, who wrote to the college superintendent to discourage his son from "joining the bloody strife," could not dissuade him.[76] Unfortunately, the young Quaker died for his antislavery convictions just four weeks after enlisting.[77] Nor were Northern and Midwestern Friends the only ones to deviate from the Peace Testimony. Several Quakers in Loudoun County, Virginia, enlisted in the Union army and even a few in the Confederate army, depending on their antislavery convictions or their belief in the inviolability of states' rights.[78]

Perhaps as many as 300 Quakers enlisted in the Union army. While those who went to war received a good deal of public attention, there was no mass enlistment among Friends. Those who enlisted did so as individuals—not as a group—breaking with the majority of American Friends who remained loyal to the Society's pacifist principles. In fact, there is no accurate record of those Quakers who participated in the Civil War either by enlisting or by allowing themselves to be drafted. Thus, the numbers are subject to the speculation of historians. Rufus Jones, for example, estimated that by the end of 1863, monthly meetings in the North "averaged just 2 or 3 enlistees, with the exception of Indiana Yearly Meeting, which had nearly 300 men serving in the Union army."[79] Peter Brock agrees with Jones that the number of Quakers serving in the Union army was small. He also points out that there are no accurate records of those who paid a commutation fee.[80] But Jacquelyn Nelson calculated that there were considerably more Friends who served in the federal army, at least from Indiana. Nelson, using local church records, the minutes of Indiana and Western yearly meetings, and monthly meeting records, identified that 1,212 Indiana Quakers served in the Union army between 1861 and 1865, roughly 21 percent of the male Quaker population in the Hoosier state at the time. Nelson also noted that many of the records she examined were incomplete. As a result, she believed that perhaps as many as 45 percent of Indiana's Quaker males might have joined the military.[81] Thomas Hamm refutes Nelson's findings. Although he does not dispute that many Indian Friends served in the Union army, he argues that Nelson's figures are inflated because she counted some men "who had been disowned decades earlier and who, in some cases, had joined other churches." He also believes that Nelson included in her estimate many non-Quakers with surnames that are common to many Quaker families.[82]

Regardless of the numbers, no Friend who went to war suffered disownment automatically because of his decision. Instead, monthly meetings tended to labor with those who deviated from the Society's Peace Testimony, understanding the difficulty of compromising one Quaker principle in order to fight for another.[83] Not all Quakers were as patient. Lucretia Mott, Philadelphia Quakerdom's most outspoken abolitionist, had no sympathy for any Friend who took up arms in violation of the Peace Testimony. When her son-in-law, Edward M. Davis, was disowned by the Cherry Street Meeting for joining the Union army, Mott scoffed, "Who would have thought when Edward was exerting himself to make converts to peace principles that he would be among the active officers in this war? He flatters himself that the abolition of slavery-end justifies the means."[84] Davis, a captain posted to General John C. Fremont's Union forces in the West, told his mother-in-law that there was a "good understanding on emancipation" between him and his commanding officer.[85] But the 68-year-old Quaker matron remained unconvinced. Nothing—not even the emancipation of the South's 4 million slaves—could compromise Mott's belief in pacifism. She viewed the Civil War as "divine punishment for the nation's wrongdoings and atrocious cruelties" to the black race, and believed that the "moral protest and demand of the people [were] likely to do more than any army can accomplish."[86] Even when Fremont, in August 1861, declared martial law in Missouri and ordered the emancipation of slaves employed for Confederate military purposes—a decision that cost the general his command—Mott refused to soften her position.[87] Instead, she vented her wrath on the machinations of the Lincoln administration. "Old Abe," Mott complained to her sister, Martha, in a November 6, 1861, letter, "seemed a miserable compromiser, sacrificing young lives and then firing Fremont for personal and partisan effect."[88] She was not alone in this opinion.

Henry H. G. Sharpless, a Philadelphia Quaker and dry goods merchant, was deeply disturbed by Lincoln's decision to relieve Fremont of his command and to rescind the general's emancipation order. Sharpless, a devout abolitionist, viewed the action as a "deficiency in firmness." His disappointment probably came from the dashed hope of a speedy end to the war since four of his sons had enlisted in the Union army. However, when one of those sons wrote home to express his "disgust with the president," the Quaker merchant insisted that Lincoln was "under great pressure from his cabinet" and had been "imposed upon in the Fremont matter." Asking that his son reconsider his opinion, Sharpless insisted that "if there is honesty and integrity in America, it can be found in the heart of Abraham Lincoln."[89]

To be sure, Lincoln's decision met with widespread disapproval. According to the *New York Times*, Fremont's actions were "in harmony with public sentiment throughout the North," which saw his proclamation as a justified punishment of the rebels and a legitimate means of weakening the Confederate war effort. "Lincoln," declared the editorial, "miscalculated by revoking the order."[90] Radical Republicans, both in Congress and in the executive cabinet, also criticized the president for not prosecuting the war more vigorously, as Fremont's proclamation proposed.[91] But the president was in a precarious position that few could appreciate. He had a responsibility to reject extreme courses of action on the slavery issue as he had sworn to be faithful to the entire nation, both North and South. Thus, Lincoln's rejection of Fremont's emancipation order was consistent with his inaugural pledge not to interfere with slavery where it already existed. However, it also challenged the Confiscation Act passed by Congress earlier that summer. According to the act, Confederate property, including slaves utilized for Southern military purposes, would be confiscated, and the owner forfeited his claim to any slave so employed. Both Lincoln and Congress understood the measure as applicable to *individual* slaves who were bound to labor for the Confederate war effort; it did not apply the *law* of slavery.[92] Still, the president, pressured by the unanimity of every Republican member of Congress, signed the bill "with great reluctance."[93] Lincoln feared that the Confiscation Act would alienate the border states of Delaware, Maryland, Kentucky, and Missouri. Those four states, which remained loyal to the Union, had a white population of 2.6 million, just less than half that of the Confederacy, and about 400,000 slaves.[94] The president knew if he made emancipation a war aim or declared emancipation in any of the border states, he risked losing the support of all of them. That he simply could not afford if he hoped to win the war.

At the same time, the Confiscation Act allowed Lincoln to pursue the issue of emancipation more aggressively because it marked a turning point in the federal government's interpretation of slavery. The measure treated slaves as "human beings held to labor," not as "chattel property," as previously recognized by federal law. In addition, the act applied to both the seceded as well as the border states, affording the possibility of taking a broader action against slavery.[95] Armed with such a law, Lincoln enjoyed a legal foundation to pursue his ultimate goal of complete and unconditional emancipation. The first step in that process began in November 1861, when he formulated a plan for gradual compensated emancipation in the border states. Instead of launching the plan in Missouri, where it had little chance for success, Lincoln saw Delaware as the ideal border state for the experiment. Delaware offered the advantages of a small slaveholding population, few slaves, and one of the largest free black communities south of the Mason–Dixon Line. Of the 90,500 white residents, just 587 owned a total of 1,800 slaves. If manumitted, those slaves would be able to assimilate into a free black population of 19,800 persons, who could help them make the transition to freedom. In addition, Delaware had barred the sale of slaves outside its borders, thereby decreasing the total value of human chattel. Finally, the state was home to a considerable Quaker population with a strong antislavery tradition and an active Underground Railroad network that witnessed an increasing stream of fugitive slaves after the passage of the federal Confiscation Act. All of these factors placed Delaware on the course of abolitionism beginning in 1847 when a bill for gradual emancipation just missed passage in the state legislature by a single vote.[96]

With the support of George P. Fisher, Delaware's lone member of the House of Representatives and a strong Unionist, Lincoln drafted two bills for gradual compensated emancipation. One bill abolished slavery in five yearly stages, culminating in 1867 with slave children to serve an apprenticeship to adulthood. The other bill immediately freed slaves above the age of 35 but extended the process of emancipation to 1893. Both bills required the federal government to compensate owners with $400 per slave and barred the sale of slaves outside the state. Lincoln soon extended the plan to the three remaining border states, expressing his belief that "colonization should be connected with it." Gradual compensated emancipation went far beyond the Confiscation Act of 1861, which aimed at freeing *individual* slaves as part of the Union war effort. Instead, Lincoln's plan sought to abolish the *institution* of slavery and did so within the well-established framework of the federal constitution since its initiation and success would depend on the action of state authorities, not the federal government. The president believed that if Delaware adopted one of these two bills, the other border states would follow its example. As a result, Confederate leaders would recognize the futility of their cause, putting an end to war and eventually paving the way for emancipation in the South.[97]

IV

As the first year of the war was drawing to a close, Quakers on both sides of the Atlantic became concerned over the possibility of a British alliance with the Confederacy. There was nothing new about such a concern. Ever since the United States won its independence from Great Britain in the late eighteenth century, there were occasional attempts by disgruntled groups to secede from the Union and seek economic and military assistance from England to further their cause. Britain always appeared willing to entertain the possibility, hoping to reclaim its political and economic control over its former North American colonies. The American Civil War presented the most formidable opportunity to realize that goal.

At the beginning of the war the British government acknowledged the belligerent rights of the Confederacy. The strong dependence of the British textile industry on Southern cotton already inclined many members of Parliament to favor the Confederacy and some to the point of intervening on their behalf. In fact, the Confederate government believed that it could force the British into an alliance by withholding their most valuable cash crop from the market. Such a policy of "cotton diplomacy" would also cripple Northern industry and, along with the threat of a war against Great Britain, force the Union into a settlement.[98] On May 13, 1861, however, the British government, probably recognizing the hastiness of its earlier position, issued a proclamation of neutrality. While the proclamation recognized the South's right to contract loans and purchase supplies from neutral nations, it did not grant diplomatic recognition to the Confederacy.[99]

Still hoping to secure formal recognition from the British government, Confederate leaders, in November, dispatched two emissaries, James Mason and John Slidell, to England. The Confederate ship carrying the two agents reached Cuba, where they boarded the *Trent*, a British mail ship. On November 8, the Union sloop *San Jacinto* intercepted the *Trent*, and Captain Charles Wilkes ordered Mason and Slidell to be taken into custody. Parliament considered the action "an affront to her national honor," demanding that the two prisoners be returned to "British protection."[100] Their demand was fueled by the conservative British press, which viewed the Confederate cause as "gallant" and "heroic." Accordingly, most of England's newspapers portrayed the *Trent* affair as a deliberate attempt by the Lincoln administration to instigate a European conflict that might reunite his divided country. "President Lincoln has proved himself a feeble, confused and little-minded mediocrity," wrote London's *Morning Chronicle*, echoing the sentiments of many newspaper editors. "Mr. Seward, the firebrand at his elbow, is exerting himself to provoke a quarrel with all Europe."[101] Pro-war sentiment prevailed in Great Britain, promoted by the press as well as the prime minister, Henry John Temple, the third Viscount Palmerston.

When Lord Palmerston learned of the *Trent* affair, he called an emergency meeting of his cabinet. "I don't know whether you are going to stand this," he fumed, "but I'll be damned if I do!"[102] Palmerston believed in a cold, rational foreign policy that would above all promote national interests. While he recognized that it would be in Britain's best interests to stay out of the American Civil War, he also saw the *Trent* affair as a challenge to his country's prestige. What's more, Palmerston was convinced that U.S. Secretary of State William Seward had planned the seizure of the *Trent* to provoke a war with Britain in order to reunite the North and the South.[103] Accordingly, the British prime minister prepared for war.[104] Fortunately, Lincoln had an important ally in Parliament in the liberal statesman John Bright.

Bright, a wealthy Quaker merchant and ardent abolitionist, initially approved of the neutrality proclamation. In a May 28 speech to the House of Commons, he addressed the concerns of fellow free traders who favored the Confederacy because it advocated freedom of trade in contrast to the protectionist economic policies of the North. Rejecting this simplistic argument, Bright contended that "freedom of choice in the economic marketplace ... must be subordinated to the freedom of the individual and to peace between nations."

Eliminating the "degradation of human beings in the form of slavery, followed by [eliminating] the degradation of countries in war, take precedence over free trade," he explained, because "democratic choice for the individual and for nations" are "expressions of the highest ideals of man" and a "properly united America reflects those ideals." He concluded his speech with a request that his fellow legislators "refrain from discussion on the American conflict" in order to maintain the country's formal position of neutrality.[105] Later, on December 4, when the *Trent* affair threatened war between the two nations, Bright took to the floor again to ease tensions. Repeating his argument for supporting the Union cause, the Quaker statesman reminded his fellow legislators that within a short time span the Northern states would have a population "equal to or exceeding that of our kingdom."

> When that time arrives, I pray that it may not be said amongst [the Northerners], that in the darkest hour of their country's trials, England, the land of their fathers, looked on with icy coldness and saw unmoved the perils and calamities of their children. If all other tongues are silent, mine shall speak for that policy which gives hope to the bondsmen of the South, and which tends to generous thoughts, generous words, and generous deeds, between the two great nations who speak the English language.[106]

While Bright's speech did little to change the pro-war sentiment in Parliament, it was received with tremendous gratitude by Lincoln and his cabinet. Unknown to Bright, the president's admiration for him dated to the early 1850s when the British parliamentarian began to voice his unconditional support for free trade, democracy, and reforms such as the abolition of slavery. These were the very same issues that dominated Lincoln's political career and inspired his run for the presidency. Thus, he followed Bright's political career so closely that his admiration bordered on hero worship. In fact, Lincoln, when he became president, went so far as to place a full-length portrait of the English statesman on the mantle of his fireplace in the executive office.[107] Bright's interest in his administration must have been flattering to Lincoln, who paid special attention to his counsel.

As the *Trent* affair lingered on, Bright worked behind the scenes to prevent war between England and the United States. He considered Palmerston, an old antagonist, a "hoary imposter," and he relished the idea of taking him on in the matter.[108] Bright, a Quaker pacifist, repeatedly took the floor of the House of Commons to argue that commercial ties bound Britain firmly to the United States and discouraged war. Palmerston, however, was itching for a fight. He lectured the Quaker parliamentarian for his "unrealistic" approach to the problem. "If your utopia could be realized and if the nations of the earth would think of nothing but peace and commerce," declared Palmerston, "the world would give up fighting altogether. But unfortunately, man is a fighting and quarreling animal." "Conflict," he concluded, "is part of human nature."[109]

Bright also worked behind the scenes, writing to allies in Parliament as well as to friends in the U.S. Congress urging peace and offering timely advice.[110] Understanding the British government's distrust of U.S. Secretary of State Seward, the liberal statesman communicated primarily with Senator Charles Sumner, chairman of the Senate Foreign Relations Committee, who, he believed, exercised tremendous influence with both Seward and Lincoln.[111] "At all hazards," he wrote to Sumner on December 5, "you must not let this matter grow into a war with England, even if you are right and we are wrong." Bright also suggested that Lincoln ask for arbitration by a European tribunal regarding international law. He reasoned that such a "moderate course" would "meet with great support" by the British government and lessen support for the Confederacy in his country.[112] Sumner shared the letter with Lincoln, who immediately began drafting such a proposal. But subsequent letters from Bright to Sumner revealed that there was no time for arbitration.

The British government was already taking steps toward war, sending 8,000 soldiers to protect Canada, and planning an embargo on the shipment of war materials to the United States.[113] On December 23, Parliament presented formal demands for the release of Mason and Slidell and for an apology from the U.S. government, giving the Lincoln administration just seven days to respond with a satisfactory answer.[114] With the deadline in mind, the president called for a cabinet meeting on Christmas Day, and Sumner was invited in order to read the most recent letters he had received from Bright. In one letter, the Quaker parliamentarian stated his belief that Palmerston's reputation depended on the public belief that "he is plucky and instant in the defense of English honor" and that a war against the United States would not only keep him in power but also enhance his reputation for conflict.[115] In a second communication, Bright urged Lincoln to "make every concession that can be made" rather than risk "the breaking up of your country," which meant releasing Mason and Slidell.[116] Everyone agreed that it was essential to avoid war with

Great Britain and the president said that it was imperative that he avoid the folly of having "two wars on his hands at a time." To preserve the peace, Lincoln released the two Confederate diplomats, thereby removing the threat that the Civil War would erupt into an international conflict.[117]

Bright, like Lincoln, found the *Trent* affair a bitter and trying experience. The British Quaker confided to Richard Cobden, his closest liberal ally in the House of Commons, that if war broke out with the United States, he would "retire from Parliament."[118] To that end, Bright maintained a stream of correspondence with key American diplomats and Lincoln's inner circle throughout the Civil War offering insightful counsel on how to insure peace between the two nations. His steadfast support for Lincoln emerged time and again in his speeches to the English people and in Parliament, often in the face of significant opposition by such prominent statesmen as William Gladstone.[119] As a result, Lincoln considered Bright a "noble and good friend," and sent him a portrait of himself to reinforce their friendship.[120]

For Quakers on both sides of the Atlantic, the *Trent* affair evoked great fear of a potential alliance between the Confederacy and Britain. London Yearly Meeting was the first body to recognize the danger. Appealing for "peace with America," the leaders of the yearly meeting urged the British government to "maintain a perfectly temperate and conciliatory attitude [toward the United States] at a time when they are engaged in a struggle for their national identity, if not for their national existence." They emphasized the "nearly two-centuries-old relationship" English Quakers had with their American brethren and the "special religious as well as national interest they had in this issue." The memorial also suggested that it would be "deeply humiliating [for England] to be involved in active cooperation with the South and slavery against the North and freedom" considering the "vast sacrifices which England had made for the abolition of the slave trade and slavery in our own [colonial] possessions." A copy of the memorial was also sent to Baltimore Yearly Meeting, which distributed copies among the other yearly meetings across a divided United States.[121] At least one copy of the memorial found its way into the hands of Lincoln, who assured the sender that "any fears of serious derangement of our amicable relations with Great Britain is without foundation" and that he appreciated the Quakers' "prompt and generous suggestions in the interest of peace and humanity."[122] Similarly, Lincoln was visited by a delegation of British Friends in early December, who reminded him that in spite of the enthusiasm for war among the public, there were those in Parliament, like John Bright, who were extremely sympathetic to the Union cause. Thanking them for their visit, Lincoln stated that theirs were the "first words of cheer and encouragement we have had across the water."[123]

American Friends also wrote to Lincoln expressing their strong concern that the United States resolve immediately the conflict with England. "For two hundred years the Society of Friends has been an integral portion of this government as well as that of Great Britain and has maintained an unbroken correspondence in Christian Fellowship," stated Western Yearly Meeting of Friends in western Indiana and eastern Illinois. "When the friendly relations of these governments have been disturbed we have made an appeal to both governments that Christian nations should adopt pacific measures for the adjustment of national disputes." Emphasizing the "many fraternal ties" between the United States and Great Britain, the elders express the desire that "no false standard of national honor may induce the men in power [of the two countries] to take any other than pacific ground in resolving their differences." This, they explain is the "rightful approach that inspires all men of faith" and one consistent with the "Divine Law." "While our government is struggling for national existence and for the support of its national integrity against the rebellion of its own citizens," they conclude, "we feel a deep solicitude that the rulers of nations . . . not be forgetful of the King of Kings and the Lord of Lords, and that peace and order may be established to secure the natural rights of all men and guarantee the blessing of Heaven by recognizing and incorporating the Divine principles in our national policy."[124] In a similar letter to Lincoln, Samuel Boyd Tobey, clerk of New England Yearly Meeting, expressed the Quaker belief that "war is inconsistent with the teachings of the Savior" and that Friends have "steadfastly maintained this doctrine, enduring much suffering in its defense." At the same time, he "sympathizes" with the president's "very responsible position" and "prays that [he] might be engaged to seek wisdom from on high." The letter closed with the reminder: "Blessed are the peacemakers, for they shall be called the children of God."[125]

Lincoln was optimistic that peace would be preserved between the United States and Great Britain and conveyed those feelings in his reply to Tobey. "Engaged as I am in a great war, I fear it will be difficult for the world to understand how fully I appreciate the principles of peace inculcated by the Society of Friends," he wrote in a March 19,

1862, letter. "Grateful to the good people you represent for their prayers in behalf of our common country," the president concluded the letter with a hope for "an early end of war, and return of peace."[126] Whether Lincoln's optimism was based on personal confidence or a diplomatic assurance that England would not interfere in American affairs is uncertain. But he had already taken precautions to prevent any military or financial assistance to the Confederacy. From the outset of the war, Union strategists used their naval superiority to prevent the Confederacy from selling its cotton abroad. By the closing months of 1861, the Union navy controlled vast stretches of the Atlantic and Gulf coasts with an effective blockade.

On February 15, 1862, British Foreign Secretary Lord John Russell officially recognized the fact that under international law the effectiveness of the blockade made it legally binding on neutral powers, and he had no intention of challenging it. His decision was influenced in part by Britain's strong economic ties to the North. Just as important, Quaker parliamentarian John Bright had successfully discouraged other members of Parliament with constituencies involved in Confederate contracts from lobbying for war against the United States.[127] Clearly, the South had underestimated those ties and overestimated England's dependence on American cotton.[128] Ultimately cotton diplomacy failed and, to the relief of Lincoln as well as Quakers on both sides of the Atlantic, the British government refused to grant diplomatic recognition to the Confederacy.

CHAPTER 2

Justifying Emancipation, 1862

Lincoln was overwhelmed with the responsibilities of the presidency in the early winter of 1862. Confederate troops were positioned just 25 miles to the south, threatening to strike Washington, while General George B. McClellan, the arrogant but talented 37-year-old officer Lincoln recently appointed as general in chief of the Union armies, remained in the capitol training federal troops. As a result, Lincoln was compelled to give more attention to his duties as commander in chief than to any other function of the presidency. He devoured books on military history and strategy and spent considerable time in the War Department telegraph office reading reports from his generals in the West and sending instructions to them. With public pressure for Union action growing, Lincoln, on January 27, 1862, ordered McClellan to launch an offensive action "against the insurgent forces" on February 22.[1] It was a desperate effort to force his reluctant commanding general into action.

Considered the most promising general in the Union ranks at the beginning of the Civil War, McClellan proved highly capable of reorganizing the Army of the Potomac and restoring its pride after the devastating defeat at the Battle of Bull Run the previous July. As a result, the dashing young officer had won the hearts of both soldiers and citizens. The press was so enamored of the five-foot-eight-inch general that it awarded him the romantic title "Young Napoleon" after France's Napoleon Bonaparte, the military genius of the nineteenth century. Some enthusiasts even promoted McClellan as the next president. But McClellan was far from the ideal combat leader, lacking the stamina and courage for bold action. Instead, he sought to avoid unnecessary loss of life and property, intending to win the war "by maneuvering his troops rather than fighting." Surrounded by a grateful public and an adoring press, McClellan began to regard himself not as Lincoln's subordinate but rather his master. Once he secured command of the Union forces, his erratic military conduct, inflated ego, and unchecked political ambitions resulted in a stalemate with the president, who demanded a decisive offensive action.[2] The relationship grew even more strained over the next several months. McClellan was not the only problem, either.

Lincoln's political family, the executive cabinet, was a constant source of tension during the early years of the war. Comprised of men who were better known, better educated, and more politically experienced than the president, the original cabinet also included some of the most fractious members of the Republican Party. In fact, four campaigned against Lincoln for the presidency: Senator William H. Seward of New York, Senator Salmon P. Chase of Ohio, Senator Simon Cameron of Pennsylvania, and Judge Edward Bates of Missouri. Each of these men considered the president a well-meaning but incompetent administrator. Yet Lincoln possessed the self-confidence and political acumen to take the unprecedented step of incorporating these rivals into his cabinet because he believed that their collective talent and patriotism would allow the Union to prevail. Seward became secretary of state, Chase secretary of the treasury, Cameron secretary of war, and Bates attorney general. The remaining posts were awarded to former Democrats as a gesture of political reconciliation. Gideon Welles was made secretary of the navy and Montgomery Blair postmaster general, and Edwin Stanton eventually replaced Cameron as secretary of war. They, too, had a low opinion of Lincoln's abilities. Thus, cabinet meetings were often contentious. Time and again, thoughtful deliberation was impeded by petty grievances and personal resentments. Some members, most notably Seward and Chase, sought to relegate the president to a figurehead role by circumventing his authority. Through it all, Lincoln delegated administrative authority to cabinet members to run their respective departments and carefully listened to their advice, while making the most important decisions himself.[3] Together with McClellan's open hostility, the raucous cabinet added to the appalling pressures Lincoln faced day after day, testing his patience and personal resolve.

During times of stress, Lincoln found a welcome diversion in his younger sons, Willie and Tad. His eldest child, Robert, age 18, was emotionally distant from his father. A student at Harvard College, he was self-disciplined, sensitive to criticism, and concerned about outward appearances. More like his mother's family, who were Southern aristocrats, Robert carried himself with an air of superiority. The death of a younger brother, Eddie, as a toddler, denied him a childhood playmate and left him with a reserved personality. Lincoln spent most of Robert's childhood away from home, riding the circuit and building his political career. The president recognized that fact and made a greater effort to befriend his eldest son, writing frequent letters, sending money, and taking Robert into his confidence whenever he visited the Executive Mansion.[4] Lincoln's relationship with his younger sons was much closer. Willie, age 11, was the "idolized child." Intelligent, polite, and thoughtful, he was mature for his age and was very much like his father in interest and personal disposition. They were both sensitive to those in need, deeply religious, and loved to read, write poetry, and tell humorous stories. According to one childhood friend, Willie was "everybody's favorite, a most lovable boy ... bright, sensible, sweet-tempered and gentle-mannered."[5] What's more, Willie seemed to be the only person who could cheer up his father when he was sad.[6] Thomas, age 9, had a quick, fiery temper. Nicknamed "Tad" because of a large head that resembled a tadpole, the youngster was slow, suffered from a speech impediment, and was unable to read. Being the youngest of the three sons, Tad was so indulged that outsiders considered him "the family pet." When he teamed up with Willie, the two boys did as they pleased often at the expense of others.[7] Lincoln himself was partly to blame.

The president doted on his two younger sons, giving them free reign of the White House. Pet animals—including dogs, rabbits, goats, and ponies—poured into the Executive Mansion. No room was off limits, not even Lincoln's office. Cabinet members were outraged when Willie and Tad burst into meetings and "clambered over their father's legs, pulled his nose and poked their fingers in his eyes without even causing reprimand."[8] The two boys could pull down all the books from the shelves, overturn inkstands, and scatter documents over the floor, and Lincoln could care less. Often absorbed in thought, the president was oblivious to their antics. When he did witness the mischief, he was amused by it and rarely disciplined them. Lincoln believed that "love is the chain that locked a child to his parent" and encouraged his sons to be "free, happy, and unrestrained by parental tyranny."[9] Such a liberal philosophy of parenting allowed Lincoln to establish a loving relationship with his younger sons and distinguished him from most fathers of the time period.[10] What's more, playing with Willie and Tad became an important physical and emotional release for the president during this stressful period.[11] Then suddenly, in early February 1862, Lincoln was deprived of this precious relief when Willie and Tad took sick.[12]

Illness had been prevalent in the capital that winter. Snow and sleet left the streets with a foul-smelling mud. The unsanitary conditions were made worse by the refuse of army camp latrines and broken sewage mains that drained into the Potomac.[13] The two boys probably contracted typhoid fever from the White House water supply, which was drawn directly from the polluted river. For weeks the brothers lay in unremitting pain and fever. The doctors assured the president and the First Lady that their sons would recover and treated the illness as they would an ordinary fever. But the boys' conditions did not improve.[14] By mid-February, Willie's illness became life threatening. Lincoln could transact little business, appearing to stumble through the many demands on him. Instead, he spent hours at Willie's bedside, stroking his son's hair, checking his brow, and trying to comfort him as the youngster slipped in and out of consciousness. Try as he might to deny the painful truth that he was losing his favorite son, Lincoln's worst fear was realized at 5:00 p.m. on Thursday, February 20, when Willie passed away. Mary Keckley, Mary Lincoln's seamstress, was washing the boy's body when the president entered the room and saw his dead son for the first time. Slowly lifting the cover from Willie's pale face, he stared at it for a long time. "My poor boy," he murmured, choking back his tears. "He was too good for this earth. I know that he is much better off in heaven, but then we loved him so. It is hard, hard to have him die." Unable to control his emotions, Lincoln buried his head in his hands and began to sob, his tall body convulsed with emotion.[15] After a few minutes, he left the room and made his way unsteadily down the hall to the office of John Nicolay, his personal secretary. "Well, Nicolay, my boy is gone, he is actually gone," said the grief-stricken father, trying to grasp the painful reality that he would never see his beloved son again.[16] Bursting into tears, Lincoln left to give comfort to Tad, who was slowly recovering from his illness.

Mary Lincoln's grief was even more devastating. For three weeks she took to her bed, unable to attend Willie's funeral or care for Tad. Even after she resumed her duties as First Lady, Mary continued to dress in black mourning attire, and for months the mere mention of Willie's name sent her into convulsive fits of weeping. Nor could she bear to enter the bedroom where he died nor the Green Room where his body had been embalmed.[17] Mary's behavior had always been unpredictable, probably due to the mental instability that was evident in several other members of the Todd family. But after Willie's death, her mental health became increasingly fragile. She began to consort with spiritualists who she believed put her in communication with her deceased son's spirit. So desperate was Mary to conjure his spirit that she took part in as many as eight séances. Lincoln indulged her by attending one but remained unconvinced.[18] He feared that his wife was going insane. During one fit of weeping, the president took his wife by the arm, led her to a window, and pointed across the Anacostia River to the Government Hospital for the Insane. "Mother," he said to her, "do you see that large white building on the hill yonder? Try to control your grief, or it will drive you mad, and we may have to send you there."[19] Concerned for his wife's mental health, he hired a nurse to look after her and tried to resume his duties as president.[20]

Still, Lincoln was deeply despondent. He had no close friends, no one in whom he could confide. Orville Browning, his closest companion, had recently lost his bid for reelection to the Senate and returned to Illinois. Instead, the president was surrounded by ambitious bureaucrats, incompetent generals, and civilian job seekers who seemed to pull at him from all directions. Accordingly, the winter and spring of 1862 was a very dark and lonely time when he struggled with profound grief and despair. Some scholars claim that Lincoln suffered from chronic depression and that the period after his son's death was among the most trying of his life.[21] Even Lincoln admitted repeatedly in the months following Willie's death that the loss of his son was "the hardest trial of my life."[22]

But Lincoln's pervasive sadness was not due so much to chronic depression as to a melancholy temperament. Unlike depression, melancholy is a personality characteristic, *not* a mental illness, and does not immobilize those who possess it.[23] As a result, the president was able to retain his ability to function at a very high level during times of great stress, proving to be more even tempered than the contentious members of his cabinet. Lincoln possessed a great self-awareness that triggered a reflexive impulse to escape these periods of profound sadness by telling a humorous anecdote. It was his way of remaining productive amid all the tragedy, tensions, and seemingly insurmountable challenges that would destroy lesser men. This peculiar blend of sadness and humor was perhaps the most prominent characteristic of the president's personality. "Mirthfulness and melancholy, hilarity and sadness were strangely combined in him," observed

Congressman Isaac Arnold, who became one of Lincoln's early biographers. "His mirth was sometimes exuberant. It sparked in jest, story and anecdote, while at the next moment, his peculiarly sad pathetic melancholy eyes would seem to wander far away, and one realized that he was a man familiar with sorrow and acquainted with grief."[24]

Lincoln's story-telling became more frequent in times of crisis. Most often, his audience was the members of his cabinet, who did not always appreciate—or understand—the levity. One of his favorite stories involved two Quaker women who were trying to determine who would win the war—Lincoln or Jefferson Davis, the president of the Confederacy.

"I think Jefferson Davis will succeed," said the first woman.

"Why does thee think so?" asked the other.

"Because he is a praying man," she replied.

Surprised by the response, the second woman insisted that, "Abraham Lincoln is a praying man, too."

"Yes," agreed the first woman, "but the Lord will think Abraham is only joking."[25]

What Lincoln liked so much about this particular story was that it involved Quakers, who had such a straitlaced reputation, and that the humor was made at his own expense. He often related the story to cabinet members to bring them into his orbit and diffuse contentiousness when the discussions became especially heated. But Edwin Stanton, his secretary of war, was much less amused, believing that the telling of humorous stories was inappropriate during the deliberations of the cabinet. Once, Stanton, noticeably irritated by Lincoln's story-telling, stood up and announced: "Mr. President, I did not come here this morning to hear stories. It is too serious a time!"

"Please, Mr. Stanton, sit down," Lincoln said regretfully. "I understand that these are serious times. So serious, I'm afraid that if I didn't laugh, I should cry."[26]

Lincoln made his struggle with melancholy a virtue in others ways, too. Like depression, melancholy has been recognized for centuries by writers and artists as a source of creativity, inspiration, and empathy. Such profound sadness tends to intensify the emotional experience of those who possess it, making them highly sensitive to the suffering of others, strengthening their sense of moral purpose, and deepening their spirituality. Lincoln experienced all of these behaviors. They not only made him a more compassionate leader but also catapulted him to greatness.[27] At the same time, Lincoln already possessed most of these behaviors before he assumed executive office. The most profound change he experienced during his presidency was a spiritual one. Together with the absence of a close friend and the inability to rely on his wife for emotional support, Lincoln's melancholy inspired him to turn to a higher power to save himself in the winter and spring of 1862.

To be sure, Lincoln's religious beliefs are a matter of controversy. While he often referenced God and quoted the Bible in his public speeches and private conversations, he never formally joined any church. According to William Wolf, author of *The Almost Chosen People: A Study of the Religion of Abraham Lincoln*, the 16th president not only rejected formal creeds and dogmas but was private about his religious convictions and respected those of others.[28] There is no better articulation of these beliefs than Lincoln's own statement on formal religion:

> Religion is a private affair between a man and his God. I doubt the possibility, or propriety, of settling the religion of Jesus Christ in the models of man-made creeds and dogmas ... I cannot without mental reservations assent to long and complicated catechisms. And when any church will inscribe over its altar as its sole qualification for membership the Savior's condensed statement of the substance of both the law and Gospel, "Thou shalt love the Lord thy God with all thy heart, and with all thy soul and with all thy mind, and thy neighbor as thyself"—that church will I join with all my heart and soul.[29]

In addition, two of Lincoln's contemporaries noted that there was no change whatsoever in the president's views on religion during the Civil War.[30] In other words, he remained a skeptic in matters of religion. But there is evidence of a growing spirituality in the president's conduct and outlook.

Although Lincoln certainly did not experience the kind of religious conversion common among nineteenth-century evangelicals, he later admitted that he underwent what he called a "process of crystallization" in his religious beliefs during this period.[31] It began at Willie's funeral when the Reverend Phineas Gurley, pastor of the New York Avenue Presbyterian Church, delivered the eulogy.[32] "In the hour of trial one must look to Him who sees the end from the beginning and doeth all things well," preached Gurley on that sad occasion. "With confidence in God," he continued, "our sorrows will be sanctified and made a blessing to our souls, and by and by we shall have occasion to say with blended gratitude and rejoicing, 'It is good for us that we have been afflicted.' "[33] After the service ended, Lincoln asked Gurley for a copy of the eulogy. The president continued to meet with the minister over the next several weeks to gain greater clarity on the meaning of the sermon.

While Lincoln scholars are divided on the exact nature of his spiritual transformation, most seem to agree that it was triggered by the idea that his son's death held a deeper meaning, one beyond his control, and that one day he would understand that higher meaning.[34] Under these tragic circumstances, the president came to realize that he could not influence events by his own will. Instead, he began to think of himself as an "instrument of God's will." Quaker theologian D. Elton Trueblood argues that Lincoln's eventual realization of "a Guiding Hand, which makes possible a genuine calling for both individuals and nations" allowed him to "grow immeasurably" and to navigate the "unjust criticism he constantly faced as well as the Union's military defeats." More important, Lincoln, according to Trueblood, "had come really to believe that God molds history and that He employs erring mortals to effect His purpose."[35] Lincoln's belief in the doctrine of necessity—the conviction that the actions of any individual are predetermined and shaped by the unknowable wishes of a higher power—enabled him to discern a pattern beneath the seeming irrationality of events he faced and gave him a new sense of moral strength.[36]

He spoke more frequently about God than ever before—about how the Almighty had taken Willie and how He controlled the fates of everyone. "I have all my life been a fatalist," he said to a congressman one day, admitting that "there is a divinity that shapes our ends."[37]

Lincoln's recognition of his own inadequacy in the face of the war's daunting challenges freed him from the personal anguish that had once overwhelmed him. Instead, he placed his confidence in the Almighty. Central to the president's new spiritual development was a fundamentally mystical experience—an immediate, intuitive, experiential knowledge of God—and the acceptance of achieving His will on Earth.[38] Less and less did Lincoln think that he was acting merely in his own will or depending on his own meager resources. According to Carl Sandburg, the president "grew immeasurably as he came to think of himself as an 'instrument of God's will.' "[39] By the summer of 1862, Lincoln was beginning to reflect a newfound confidence, emboldening him to confront the pressing issue of emancipation.

II

On Friday, June 20, 1862, Thomas Garrett, Oliver Johnson, William Barnard, Eliza Agnew, Dinah Mendenhall, and Alice Hambleton called on the president at the White House. The delegation had been sent by the Longwood Progressive Friends Meeting in Chester County, Pennsylvania, to present a *Memorial* urging the "immediate and universal emancipation" of the slaves.

The *Memorial*, drafted two weeks earlier, expressed the view that the Civil War was caused by the sins of slavery, an "un-Christian and barbarous system," and had resulted in a "frightful effusion of blood" in the North as well as in the South. Citing Lincoln's "House Divided" speech, delivered at Springfield, Illinois, before his election to the presidency, the *Memorial* quoted the president's belief that the "government cannot endure permanently half slave and half free" and that it will "cease to be divided ... becoming all one thing, or all the other."

Asserting the Progressive Friends' preference for a free country, the *Memorial* concluded by urging the president to "decree the entire abolition of slavery throughout the land" or risk "the fiery judgments to be poured out, until the work of national destruction is consummated beyond hope of recovery."[40]

After the presentation, Lincoln, with a wry smile, expressed his relief that the delegation had not come to seek any office, for those were his most troublesome visitors. Truth be told, there was at least one Quaker visitor who also tried his patience. A week earlier, the president greeted a Quaker woman who also asked that he emancipate the slaves. Assuming the role of a prophetess, she told Lincoln that the Almighty had come to her and informed her that "He had appointed [the president] to do the work of emancipation and establish freedom throughout the land." The Quakeress, with an air of self-righteousness, went on for several minutes quoting from scripture and imploring the president to answer his divine mission.

"Has the Friend finished?" Lincoln asked, having heard enough.

Recognizing his impatience, the Quaker woman ended her sermon.

"Friend," Lincoln replied, "I have neither the time nor the disposition to enter into discussion with you on this matter. Let me end this occasion, however, by asking the Friend to consider that if the Lord has appointed me to do the work you have indicated, is it not probable He would have communicated that knowledge to me as well?"[41]

It is important to note that Lincoln had a low tolerance for clergy and religious delegations pretending to have a more direct pipeline to God than he did. Whenever such self-righteous attitudes surfaced in a conversation, he quickly ended the interview, regardless of the religious denomination.[42] But he was more tolerant of the Progressive Friends, sensing the genuine sympathy of the small delegation. While the president agreed with their belief that slavery was a moral wrong, he admitted his difficulty with any practical method of eliminating the institution. To this end, Lincoln pointed out that the memorialists had omitted a critical sentence from his "House Divided" speech. That sentence articulated his belief that "either the opponents of slavery will arrest the farther spread of it, placing slavery on the course of ultimate extinction; or its advocates will push the institution forward till it becomes lawful in all the states, North as well as South." In other words, Lincoln believed that whatever was done about slavery would be accomplished by the American people themselves, and not him.

After all, said the president, "if a decree of emancipation could abolish slavery, John Brown [the radical abolitionist who unsuccessfully attempted to lead a slave insurrection] would have done the work most effectually." Even with his executive powers, Lincoln doubted whether such a decree could be any more binding on the South than on the federal constitution itself. It would be impossible to enforce. He also doubted that a "proclamation of freedom" would be "any more effective."

Oliver Johnson, having listened attentively to the president's reasoning, privately mused, that "if John Brown had been Commander-in-Chief of the army and navy, with the slaveholders in open revolt, he would not only have made a proclamation of freedom for the slaves, but executed it as well."

The Progressive Friends had, by 1862, rejected their earlier pronouncements in favor of passive nonresistance and welcomed any means—even war—by which to eliminate slavery.[43] Choosing to be more respectful of Lincoln, however, Johnson said, "True, Mr. President, the Constitution cannot now be enforced in the South; but you do not on that account intermit the effort to enforce it, and we are convinced that the abolition of slavery is indispensable to your success."

Unknown to the delegation, Lincoln had been privately wrestling with this very point for some time but could not bring himself to say anything more than that he "felt the magnitude of the task before him" and that he "hoped to be rightly directed in these very trying circumstances."

William Barnard, impressed by the president's humility, expressed sympathy for him and an earnest desire that he "might, under Divine guidance, be led to free the slaves, and thus save the nation." By doing so, Barnard added, "nations yet unborn would rise up to call [the president] blessed, and better still, he would secure the blessings of God."

Lincoln was deeply moved. He confided that he had "sometimes thought that he might be an instrument in God's hands of accomplishing a great work" and that he "welcomed the role." Perhaps God's way of accomplishing emancipation was "different from theirs," he proposed, but regardless, he would "seek light from above, to do his duty in the place to which he had been called."[44] Thanking the delegation for their visit, the president shook hands with each member and ushered them to the door, ending the interview.

To be sure, it is impossible to determine the degree of influence Pennsylvania's Progressive Friends had on Lincoln, just as it is impossible to determine the influences of *any* religious denomination on his thinking or actions. Historian Richard Carwardine contends that Lincoln's conversations with ministers and religious delegations were "constant" and "extended across the full gamut of denominational affiliation." Lincoln "worked hard to keep open two-way channels with the leaders of this influential constituency, and to deal sensitively and respectfully with them, aware not only of their power but also that those contacts provided him with a way of both reading and reaching potent opinion-formers." At the same time, Carwardine emphasizes that it is "not clear how far Lincoln's cultivation of the company of religious leaders influenced his own spiritual quest."[45] Ward Lamon, the president's bodyguard, confirms this point. "The President was visited almost daily by reverend gentlemen, sometimes as single visitors," he observed, "but more frequently in delegations, and especially during the early years of the war. Generally, these interviews involved a speedy proclamation of emancipation and were entertaining and agreeable on both sides."[46] An examination of Earl Shenk Miers's *Lincoln Day by Day: A Chronology, 1809–1865* and the website *The Lincoln Log: A Daily Chronology of the Life of Abraham Lincoln* proved inconclusive in determining the numbers of contacts the president had with each of the various denominations compared to those interviews and correspondence he maintained with Quakers.[47] Predictably, James M. Cornelius, curator of the Lincoln Collection in Springfield, Illinois, believes that the number of contacts Lincoln had with each of the major religious denominations is "anyone's guess." "Eleven denominations have claimed Lincoln as a member in some fashion," said Cornelius. "To the extent that he knew he had a Quaker ancestor or two or was impressed by their faith, he may've given those visitors more time during the presidency."[48] Thus, while it is difficult to determine the degree of influence Pennsylvania's Progressive Friends had on Lincoln's decision to emancipate the slaves, the June 1862 interview probably had a stronger impact on the president's thinking about emancipation than those of other church delegations earlier in the war. The Progressives' influence was due not only to a shared view of God's role in human affairs but also to the timing of the interview, which corresponded with Lincoln's increasing faith in the doctrine of necessity and the fundamental mystical impulse that inspired it. At the same time, the Longwood Friends did *not* speak for the larger Religious Society of Friends, which tended to have a stronger commitment to the Peace Testimony and maintained many different perspectives on the issue of emancipation.

Pennsylvania's Progressive Friends were unique among antebellum Quakers. While they can trace their origins to Philadelphia Yearly Meeting, they took the Quakers' humanitarian impulse to an extreme. Founded at Longwood, Chester County, in 1853, the Pennsylvania Yearly Meeting of Progressive Friends was one of 16 co-operating but independent activist "comeouter" groups from the Middle Atlantic and Midwest states.[49] Alternatively known as Congregational Friends, the Progressives had revolted from their rural monthly meetings, which were more conservative on matters of religious doctrine, humanitarian reform, and especially becoming involved with non-Quakers in benevolent activities. Theirs was a religion of reform that sought to include all those who shared their belief in the moral improvement of society, regardless of religious denomination. Defining their fellowship by a quest for the world's moral improvement, Progressives believed that Christian faith and good works were "interchangeable, a marked departure from the conventional belief that faith must exist in a Christian antecedent to works."[50] By advancing such "ecumenical spirituality," Progressive Friends opened their fellowship to the supporters of many causes, including temperance, women's rights, common schooling, prison reform, and especially the abolition of slavery. Thus, the 57 Chester County Quakers who separated from Kennett Monthly Meeting (Hicksite) in 1852 did so over the issues of religious doctrine and involvement in inter-denominational reform. They also represented a radical minority of antislavery Friends, most of whom freely violated the federal Fugitive Slave Law by serving as agents on the Underground Railroad.[51]

According to their "Exposition of Sentiments," or "mission statement," Longwood's Progressive Friends operated on three inextricable beliefs, all of which were reflected in their antislavery activities. The first was a conviction that the "universe was governed by a divinely-ordained Higher Law."[52] Believing that God's law superseded civil law, many members rejected the federal Fugitive Slave Law of 1850 requiring every citizen to aid in the recapture of runaway slaves or face a fine or imprisonment or both. Instead, they established a network of safe houses for fugitive slaves and channeled runaways to conductors along the Underground Railroad's Eastern Line, which ran from Maryland and Delaware through southeastern Pennsylvania and ultimately to Canada. Many of the fugitives were sent into Chester County by Thomas Garrett of Wilmington, Delaware. Garrett often sent the escapees to his relatives, Isaac and Dinah Mendenhall in Kennett, just over the Mason–Dixon Line. One of the most outspoken Progressive Friends, Garrett is known to have assisted more than 2,300 runaways—including Harriet Tubman—in his three decades as an Underground Railroad agent.[53]

The second operating tenet of Longwood's Progressive Friends was that the individual can become "more free and responsible by learning about the natural and moral law through study, reflection and discussion." To that end, the meeting held regular conventions to discuss their reform activities. Members came armed with facts and figures, as well as with proposals to submit for discussion and to achieve a better understanding of moral and natural law. The truth these Progressive Friends were seeking was not based so much on historical fact but was the result of "continuous revelation" that would inspire action for a "virtuous purpose."[54] Oliver Johnson was perhaps the most gifted of the Progressive Friends' leaders in this respect. Likened to a biblical prophet, Johnson knew how to articulate the sense of the meeting and help guide the proceedings without imposing his will. He also authored many of the antislavery testimonies drafted by the Longwood Meeting. Not surprisingly, Johnson was appointed to lead the delegation that met with President Lincoln in June 1862.[55]

The third and final operating principle of the Progressive Friends was that they, like all Americans, had a mission to make democracy work in this country, allowing it to serve as an example for the rest of the world. In this sense, Progressive Quakerism was not simply an attempt to reconstitute the Quaker faith on a purer, more ecumenical footing, but a "moral revolution" based on "concrete political demands" that would ultimately achieve such radically unpopular causes as the abolition of slavery.[56] All people were invited to join the Progressive Friends in this moral revolution, without regard to gender, race, or religious denomination. While most were well-educated members of the middle class, they were a socially diverse bunch. At any given convention, you could find earnest-faced Quakers clad in plain brown coats and broad-brimmed hats seated alongside free-thinkers with long hair and beards. In fact, the West Chester *American Republican* described Longwood as a place where "long-haired men and short-haired women met to threaten the stability of society."[57] The only test of membership was the ability to demonstrate faith in God by leading a life that combined personal purity with increased practical benevolence. It was a radical policy for the time period, even among Quakers. But the Progressive Friends genuinely believed that they could achieve their democratic mission only if the obstacles of human prejudice, superstition, and greed could be eliminated.[58] They also realized it was a never-ending mission that demanded outreach, including spreading the word through publications and camp-style meetings. So committed were the Progressive Friends that between their annual sessions of 1857 and 1858, they conducted 26 missionary meetings in 12 different locations across the eastern seaboard in the Midwest, and in 1858, their yearly meeting appointed a 64-member committee to proselytize for reform in Ohio, Delaware, New Jersey, New York, Indiana, and Iowa through personal visits and an ongoing correspondence.[59]

To be sure, Longwood's Progressive Friends had elevated "reform" to a "religion" of itself, and no reform was more important to them than the abolition of slavery. Each year from their beginnings in 1853, the group issued forceful testimonies against the peculiar institution and listened to impassioned denunciations of slavery by such prominent reformers as William Lloyd Garrison, Lucretia Mott, Charles Burleigh, and Sojourner Truth. In fact, most if not all of the Progressive Friends subscribed to Garrison's call for the immediate emancipation of slaves. "In dealing with such a sin as slavery," they stated in a testimony encouraged by Garrison himself, "we can adopt no half-way measures. The whole truth must be proclaimed, without concealment, without compromise. No church, no government, no constitution, no union which requires us to support or sanction such a crime, can have any binding force upon our consciences. We seek not alone to prevent the extension of slavery, but to exterminate it from every part of the land."[60] This was the very same position the six memorialists—Thomas Garrett, Oliver Johnson, William Barnard, Eliza Agnew, Dinah Mendenhall, and Alice Hambleton—had presented to Lincoln when they met with him on June 20, 1862.

Unknown to the Quaker delegation, the president was evolving toward the same position himself. Despite his best intentions, his plan for compensated, gradual abolition in the border states met with growing resistance, first by Delaware's state legislature and later by the governors of the other border states. Both bodies would eventually reject the plan altogether.[61] At the same time, Lincoln's initiative to achieve border emancipation was being undermined by yet another Union officer. In May, Major General David Hunter, commander of the Department of the South, declared the 900,000 slaves in the South Carolina Sea Islands "forever free," and instructed his officers to accept black volunteers. Like Fremont's earlier declaration, Hunter acted without the permission of Lincoln or the War Department. Although Secretary of the Treasury Salmon Chase urged the president to accept Hunter's declaration, Lincoln immediately revoked the order, stating that "no commanding officer shall do such a thing upon *my* responsibility without consulting me."[62] The impending failure of border emancipation was made worse by the fact that the Union war effort was not going well at all. Although General George McClellan, commander of the Army of the Potomac, finally launched his offensive in mid-March, it was a feeble effort at best. Cautiously advancing his troops up the Virginia Peninsula en route to the Confederate capitol at Richmond, the Union commander still refused to attack, chronically overestimating the strength of enemy units and demanding that Lincoln send reinforcements. In fact, McClellan's troops outnumbered those of Confederate General Joseph E. Johnston's forces and the Union delay allowed the rebels to slip away unnoticed fooling McClellan with logs painted black to appear as cannons. The so-called Quaker Gun affair was an embarrassment to the administration and one that presaged the ultimate failure of the Peninsula campaign in late June. It was clear to Lincoln that McClellan lacked both the courage and the resolve to launch a decisive engagement, a stark contrast to the success of General Ulysses Grant, commander of the Union troops in the West, who scored a string of resounding victories, but often at the expense of appallingly high casualty rates.[63] With the Union death toll rising and the impending failure of border emancipation, Lincoln resolved that those soldiers who gave their lives for the Union would not die in vain.

His search for a deeper meaning to the war was given further direction by the Progressive Friends, who urged him to pursue a policy of universal emancipation.

Although Lincoln had entertained dozens of similar interviews by the delegations of other religious groups, his visit with the Progressive Friends is significant in two respects.[64] First, Lincoln revealed his belief that he *might* be "an instrument in God's hands of accomplishing a great work," something he had yet to admit to any other group, including his cabinet. The revelation suggests that the president's belief in the doctrine of necessity was coming to fruition and that he felt comfortable enough to share his feelings with a delegation of Friends because of their deep and abiding conviction in mysticism, or the ability of human beings to communicate directly with God himself. Second, the *timing* of the Progressive Friends' interview had a profound impact on Lincoln because, as he put it, "things had gone from bad to worse and I felt that we had reached the end of the rope."[65] Considering the dismal fortunes of the Union army to that point and the impending failure of his plan for gradual, compensated emancipation in the border states, the president was acutely aware of his need for divine guidance and eager to receive it. It was at this critical juncture that the Progressive Friends validated Lincoln's growing belief that emancipation was the divinely ordained purpose of the war, and it was God's will for him to achieve that objective.[66] For Lincoln, moral purpose and political expedience were beginning to merge, strengthening his resolve to emancipate the slaves.

III

On Sunday morning, July 13, President Lincoln shared a carriage with his Secretary of State William Seward and his Secretary of the Navy Gideon Welles en route to the funeral of Edwin Stanton's infant son at Oak Hill Cemetery. Three days earlier the baby died from complications of a vaccination, leaving the secretary of war to hide his personal pain behind a stoic façade, while his grief-stricken wife tried to cope with the sudden loss of her newborn son. The war had forced the nation to deal with death on a daily basis, but nothing could prepare a parent for the loss of a child. For Lincoln, the occasion must have been an especially painful reminder of his own son's death earlier in the year. Once again, he was returning to the cemetery where Willie's body was entombed in a private vault awaiting final interment at Springfield. The mood was somber, very little being said as the carriage bounced over the rutted streets of Georgetown Heights.[67]

The events of the past week also weighed heavily on Lincoln. Having lost patience with McClellan and his refusal to go on the attack, the president, on July 11, replaced him with Henry W. Halleck as general-in-chief of the Union armies. While McClellan would remain in command of the Army of the Potomac, Halleck's appointment effectively ended Lincoln's four-month experiment of serving as his own general, allowing him to concentrate more on the slavery issue.[68] It came not a moment too soon, either. On July 12, the border states rejected the president's idea of compensated emancipation, insisting that such an action should be initiated by the slave states themselves.[69] Lincoln now realized that he would have to explore other alternatives for freeing the slaves, including a second confiscation act recently approved by Congress. The measure strengthened an earlier 1861 confiscation act in regard to fines, imprisonment, and loss of property for anyone assisting the Confederate cause. "Property" included the chattel of any slave owner in Union-occupied territory who had supported the rebellion. This was a distinct departure from the first confiscation act that freed only those slaves who were directly involved in the Confederate war effort and considered "contraband." Lincoln was also granted the authority to declare as "forever free" those rebel-owned slaves who escaped to the Union lines or who lived in Confederate territory later occupied by Union troops. Since the new measure prohibited the federal army from returning fugitives to their owners, the president could now employ these former slaves in any way he deemed "necessary and proper for the suppression of this rebellion" as well as to provide for their future colonization "in some tropical country." Nearly every Republican in Congress had voted for the Second Confiscation Act, and now turned to their president to sign the bill into law. Lincoln was being forced by his generals and Congress to act.

The president had *always* reserved the authority to make all decisions regarding slavery, emancipation, and race on his own, jealously guarding the constitutional powers vested in the executive branch. He did not appreciate military or congressional interference on these matters. He was especially disturbed by the Second Confiscation Act's provision granting him the power to declare rebel-owned slaves "forever free." It directly contradicted the Republican platform on which he and most of the congressman of his party had been elected. He was also troubled by the absence of a provision in the bill for determining whether fugitive slaves belonged to Confederate or Union owners.[70] At the same time, the president must have been secretly pleased that the measure reinforced his own thinking on emancipation and colonization. In fact, Lincoln, just a week earlier, met with James Mitchell, recently appointed as commissioner of emigration in the Department of the Interior, to schedule a meeting with a delegation of local African American leaders to discuss his plans for colonization.[71] For Lincoln, personal conviction and political expedience were converging in a providential manner.

Breaking the silence, the president informed Seward and Welles that he was considering "emancipating the slaves by proclamation in case the Rebels did not cease to persist in their war." Having "dwelt earnestly on the gravity, importance, and delicacy" of the subject, Lincoln said that he had "come to the conclusion that it was a military necessity absolutely essential for the salvation of the Union, that we must free the slaves or be ourselves subdued."[72] It was a shrewd way of overriding the constitutional protection of slavery by evoking the constitutionally sanctioned war powers of the president. Lincoln had ample justification for such a military declaration, too. For some time he had been receiving daily reports of slaves being put to work for the Confederate cause. Some served as teamsters carting the dead off battlefields. Others built military fortifications. Still others labored on farms so that their masters were free to fight. If the South were divested of their slaves, the North would achieve a significant advantage. Viewed in this context, emancipation was a "military necessity," and one that was validated by the president's constitutional war powers.[73]

Astonished by Lincoln's revelation, Welles noted that it was "a new departure for the president, for until this time ... he had been prompt and emphatic in denouncing any interference by the General Government on the subject" of slavery. But clearly, circumstances had changed. Congressional sentiment had caught up to the opinion of Northern abolitionists whose efforts had been focused on emancipation from the start. Still, Lincoln was not convinced that the North as a whole was ready to accept such a radical departure in the federal government's policy toward slavery. Seward also recognized this fact. Although he had always been more firmly rooted in the abolitionist camp than the president, the secretary of state confessed that he needed time for "mature reflection before giving a decisive answer" because the subject "involved consequences so vast and momentous."[74]

While Seward mulled over the issue, Lincoln began to take action. Despite his reservations, the president, on July 17, signed the Second Confiscation Act into law. He also completed a first draft of the

Emancipation Proclamation that he planned to introduce to his cabinet later that month.[75] Such calculated actions and thoughtful consideration reflect Lincoln's deliberate intention to wed emancipation to his original war aim of preserving the Union. They also contradict the assertion of some scholars who insist that Lincoln was "forced into glory" by African Americans intent on freeing themselves, most notably fugitive slaves who swarmed into Union camps from both border and rebel states and colluded with Fremont and Hunter to be sheltered and employed by the federal army.[76] "Emancipation" was *not* against Lincoln's "white supremacist instincts," as the argument maintains. In his mind, the beliefs were complementary. In fact, Lincoln's early and consistent hatred of slavery as a violation of human rights was intertwined with a deep-seated ambivalence over the social and intellectual status of blacks compared to whites. During his youth and well into his presidency, Lincoln had a penchant for blackface minstrels and "darky" jokes. He also doubted the capacity of black men to serve with courage in the Union army or to live in white mainstream society. As a result, he held off on allowing blacks to serve in the military, even if he realized that it could benefit the Union war effort. Similarly, Lincoln, for the first two years of his presidency, pushed for the voluntary colonization of freed slaves either in the Caribbean or back in Africa.[77] The critics, by imposing modern notions of civil rights on Lincoln, a figure who operated in a dramatically different culture, fail to understand that the president was a product of the early-to-mid nineteenth century. As such, he entertained many of the moral and social conventions of that time period. Thus, to impose contemporary standards and values on Lincoln is historically irresponsible. What made Lincoln such a complex and fascinating figure was his ability to redefine the moral and political conventions of the nineteenth century, which had validated slavery, in a way that made emancipation acceptable, even desirous, among the American people. His remarkable achievement was rooted in a deeply held spiritual belief that came to fruition through careful timing, political expedience, and military necessity.

On July 21, the president met with the cabinet to discuss the implementation of the Second Confiscation Act. Members agreed unanimously that three provisions of the new measure be executed: that field commanders would be given the authority to appropriate civilian property in hostile territory, that blacks were to be used as military laborers, and that the Union army would be instructed to keep records of all confiscated property, including slaves, so loyal owners could receive compensation. But Lincoln's proposal that the freed slaves would be "colonized in some tropical territory" received little support and was left unsettled.[78]

When the discussion resumed the next day, the president introduced a new draft order that he had been preparing for weeks. The proclamation cited the new Confiscation Act's warning to rebel loyalists to cease the rebellion within 60 days or face confiscation of their property, including slaves. Cabinet members nodded their heads in assent as they listened attentively. There was nothing surprising as the provision was firmly rooted in congressional actions. Next Lincoln affirmed his support for compensated gradual emancipation. While Postmaster General Montgomery Blair and Treasury Secretary Salmon Chase were not pleased with the idea, they, like the other members, appreciated the president's commitment to the plan and remained silent.[79] Lincoln proceeded to the next point almost as an afterthought, though its implications were earth-shattering.

Invoking his constitutional authority as commander in chief, the president declared that on January 1, 1863, "all persons held as slaves within any state or states" still under Confederate control "shall then, thenceforward, and forever, be free."[80] The declaration went far beyond the Second Confiscation Act, which applied only to states under Union control. Lincoln, asserting his executive authority in bold and unprecedented terms, was proposing to extend wartime emancipation in most places where the institution existed. What's more, on January 1, 1863, and thereafter, emancipation would be *immediate* and *without compensation*. The silence in the room was deafening. Cabinet members were stunned. With the exceptions of Seward and Welles, who had learned of Lincoln's plan a week earlier, no one was prepared for the bombshell that had just been dropped.

Attorney General Edward Bates was the first to break the silence. Expressing his "very decided approval for immediate promulgation," Bates's endorsement came with one condition—that "deportation," or colonization, immediately follow emancipation. His remarks came as a surprise since he had always opposed wholesale emancipation. Salmon Chase, initially shocked by the revelation, found his voice. Fearing that the state courts would not recognize such a proclamation, Chase worried that immediate emancipation would lead to "depredation and massacre." He preferred a more incremental process that would be implemented by local commanders in Union-occupied Southern territory. Montgomery Blair echoed the treasury secretary's concern. Blair, ever politically minded and lukewarm on the idea of emancipation, stated his belief that the proclamation would drive the border states into the Confederacy and be used by Lincoln's enemies on Capitol Hill as a weapon against the administration. Blair's greatest fear, however, was that the proclamation would cost Lincoln votes in the next election. Only Stanton gave his immediate and unconditional support to the measure. Interestingly, Welles said nothing. But in a diary entry he later recorded, the secretary of the navy recognized that the proclamation was "fraught with consequences, immediate and remote, such as human foresight could not penetrate." He also predicted that immediate emancipation would result in "a revolution of the social, civil and industrial habits and condition of society in all the slave states."

That left Seward, who long believed that slavery was the cause of the Civil War and welcomed immediate emancipation. Yet when asked for his opinion, the secretary of state confessed that he questioned the expediency of the proclamation "at this juncture." Seward was rightfully concerned that the Union army's lack of a decisive victory in the East had diminished public morale for the war effort and that an *Emancipation Proclamation* issued at this time might be viewed "as a last measure of an exhausted government [and] a cry for help." Therefore, the secretary of state suggested that the matter be postponed "until you can give it to the country supported by military success, attended by fife and drum and public spirit."[81]

After acknowledging the "differences in the cabinet on the slavery question," Lincoln informed members that he had already "resolved" to free the slaves. In other words, he "had not called them together to ask for their advice," but simply to inform them of his decision. At the same time, the president was "struck by the wisdom" of Seward's suggestion to postpone emancipation until a military victory could be achieved. Accordingly, Lincoln put the idea aside, stating that he would wait for "some sign from the Divine" to publicly issue the proclamation.[82] Still, he proceeded with his own plans to prepare the American people for emancipation by leaking his views through the press.

On August 14, for example, Lincoln met with a delegation of five black leaders, most of them local ministers, at the White House hoping to achieve consensus on the issue of colonization. While the president condemned slavery, he acknowledged the painful reality that the racism of white society would not allow the black race to prosper in the United States. "You and we are different races," he told them. "Even when you cease to be slaves you are yet far removed from being placed on equality with the white race. It is better for us both, therefore, to be separated." Lincoln offered colonization in Central America as the solution with the understanding that its success depended on "a hundred tolerably intelligent [black] men with their wives and children" to lead the emigration. He also assured the delegation that he would not impose colonization on the African American race but rather leave the final decision to blacks themselves.[83] There was virtually no dialogue; Lincoln dominated the meeting. At the outset, E. M. Thomas, the chairman of the delegation, stated his understanding that the group was there by invitation to hear what the president had to say. After Lincoln completed his remarks, Thomas briefly replied that the delegation would "hold a consultation and in a short time give an answer."[84] It is also important to note that the delegation did not consist of any nationally recognized black leader like Frederick Douglass, Samuel Ringgold Ward, Henry H. Garnet, Martin R. Delany, or William Wells Brown. All of these men were articulate—and outspoken—leaders of their race and would have immediately challenged the president on his view of race relations. Instead, the delegation was hand-picked by Lincoln's own commissioner of emigration, the Reverend James Mitchell. A reporter assigned by the president was also present taking meticulous notes of his remarks to ensure that they would appear verbatim in the national press the very next day. This was not a meeting, but rather a scripted performance choreographed by Lincoln to make emancipation more palatable to the white race.[85]

Indeed, the president's remarks on colonization appeared in newspapers across the nation the following day just as he intended. The *New York Times* added that Lincoln's remarks "committed him more strongly than ever to the colonization policy as the surest solution of Negro complications."[86] Even the black delegation's initial response was favorable. "We were entirely hostile to the [colonization] movement," wrote Chairman Thomas to Lincoln a few days later, "until all the advantages were so ably brought to our attention by you."[87] Not all blacks were pleased with the proposal, though. Frederick Douglass, the antislavery radical and the most famous African American in the nation at the time, was the most indignant of all. Colonization was the polar opposite of his vision of an integrated society that transcended white racism. When he read of the president's remarks, Douglass fumed that they exposed Lincoln's "pride of race and blood, his contempt for Negroes and his canting hypocrisy." "Worse," the black orator charged, the "widespread publication" of Lincoln's remarks gave "license to all the ignorant and base" racists "to commit all kinds of violence and outrage upon the colored people of the country." Douglass advised the president not to patronize blacks by deciding "what was best" for them, but simply to "allow [them] [their] freedom."[88] Douglass's anger was understandable. For him, colonization "presupposed racism, the spirit of slavery." For Lincoln, on the other hand, colonization "presupposed emancipation."[89]

Despite Lincoln's ultimate failure to convince black leaders of the benefits of colonization, he had achieved his intended goal of preparing white Americans for a society without slavery. In the process, he enlisted the support of an unwitting accomplice. Horace Greeley, the radical abolitionist editor of the *New York Tribune*, had grown impatient with the president's reluctance. It appeared to Greeley that everyone—Congress, military leaders, abolitionists, clergy, even the North itself—was ready to accept the abolition of slavery. Yet Lincoln still hesitated.

Unaware of the impending proclamation, Greeley, on August 19, tried to force Lincoln's hand on emancipation by publishing a public letter to the president. Titled "The Prayer of Twenty Millions," as if it was stating the feelings of the entire North, the letter expressed only the wishes of antislavery Republicans who were "sorely disappointed by the policy [Lincoln] seems to be pursuing with regard to the slaves of Rebels." Greely went on to state that he and his fellow abolitionists expected the president to "EXECUTE THE LAWS . . . with regard to the emancipating provisions of the new Confiscation Act" and stop listening to "certain fossil politicians hailing from the Border Slave States."[90] Lincoln responded a few days later on August 22 with his own letter. Insisting that the "preservation of the Union" was the primary aim of his war policy, the president suggested that emancipation was a much lesser consideration. "My paramount object in this struggle is to save the Union, and is not either to save or to destroy slavery," he declared. "If I could save the Union without freeing any slave I would do it, and if I could save it by freeing all the slaves I would do it; and if I could save it by freeing some slaves and leaving others alone I would also do that. What I do about slavery and the colored race, I do because it helps to save the Union."[91] Most contemporary readers understood Lincoln to mean that the abolition of slavery was a moot point; preserving the union was his only real objective. But the letter actually provided the indirect revelation that Lincoln was open to the possibility of a broad emancipation by cloaking it in his constitutional obligation to preserve the union. *That*, after all, was his stated goal from the very beginning of the war. Viewed in this light, Lincoln was preparing the American people to interpret the forthcoming *Emancipation Proclamation* as a conservative gesture, simply the latest action of a consistent policy to restore the Union.

While Lincoln, the politician, prepared the country for emancipation, Lincoln, the spiritual seeker, continued to rely on divine guidance to validate his actions. The fullest expression of his belief in the doctrine of necessity can be found in an undated writing known today as "Meditation on the Divine Will." This personal reflection is believed to have been written sometime in early September 1862 and was never meant for publication. In it, Lincoln reveals his belief that the "will of God prevails" and describes a God whom neither the Union nor the Confederacy could claim as their own. "I am almost ready to say this is probably true—that God wills this contest, and wills that it shall not end yet," Lincoln wrote. "He could give the final victory to either side any day. Yet the contest proceeds."[92] The "Meditation" not only reflects Lincoln's theological depth but also illuminates how far he had traveled "on his journey from fatalism to providence."[93] No longer did he see God as a distant being, but one who "made Himself accessible to those who seek Him out." Lincoln now understood that "God was at once the ultimate and personal reality," the primary actor in a war over which the Union and the Confederacy had little control.[94]

Quakers played a significant role in Lincoln's spiritual transformation constantly assuring him that Emancipation was the natural end of God's providence. Individually and collectively, Friends appealed to Lincoln's view of a divine role in human affairs, drawing an important distinction between human agency and God's will. Progressive Friends reminded him that the "immediate and universal emancipation" of the slaves was a manifestation of "Divine guidance," and the war's "frightful effusion of blood" a direct consequence of man's "sins for [practicing] the un-Christian and barbarous system of slavery."[95] Similarly, individual Friends implored the president to transcend the human fallibility that gave rise to the war in favor of God's will in emancipating the slaves. "Everyone has an influence if rightly exerted for the good of society, however, small," Lydia Longstreth, a member of Germantown Meeting in Philadelphia, wrote to Lincoln in September 1862. "Whence comes war? Is it not a relic of barbarism?" She asks that he "follow [God's] leading to emancipate the slaves" through "moral suasion" as it "is better than the power of the sword, which commands but cannot convince."[96] Similarly, Mary Schofield, a Quaker from Bucks County, Pennsylvania, wrote to Lincoln insisting that "the war and all the bloodshed is the result of our own disobedience to His divine laws." "Our nation, both North and South, have sinned against the Most High," she contends, and the only way for the nation to "recover [its] former greatness is to repent" by "removing the heavy burden of slavery and letting the oppressed go free." Schofield concludes the letter by asking Lincoln to submit to the "mercies of God" and "free the slaves," reminding him of Willie's death and the painful suffering it caused him. "Will thee not sympathize with the widows and orphans who mourn those who have fallen on the battlefield owing to the dreadful curse of slavery?"[97] These pleas reached Lincoln during a prolonged period of melancholy, triggered by his son's death in February 1862. It was a critical time in Lincoln's decision-making on emancipation according to D. Elton Trueblood because the president was "driven to deep soul-searching at times of sorrow and strain." Such "intensely painful experiences" made him especially receptive to a "sign from the Divine" for emancipation.[98] The "sign" arrived on September 17 with the Battle of Antietam at Sharpsburg, Maryland.

Antietam was the bloodiest day of fighting in the Civil War. The Union sustained casualties amounting to 2,108 killed and 9,549 wounded, and the Confederacy, 2,700 killed and 9,029 wounded. Although inconclusive from a military standpoint, the battle represented a strategic setback for the South since Confederate commander Robert E. Lee felt compelled to abandon his invasion of the North and retire across the Potomac River. Lincoln seized upon Antietam as the victory he had been waiting for to issue the *Emancipation Proclamation*, though McClellan's reluctance to pursue Lee's army exasperated him and led to the arrogant general's removal from command two months later.[99] On September 22, Lincoln met with his cabinet and announced his decision to issue a preliminary proclamation, confessing that he had promised God he would free the slaves if Lee's army was driven out of Maryland.[100]

Divine guidance had prevailed.

IV

The *Preliminary Emancipation Proclamation* appeared on the front page of every major urban Northern newspaper on September 23 and word of it spread into the South shortly after. Initial responses were predictable. In the South, reaction among whites was uniformly negative. Confederate President Jefferson Davis denounced it as an attempt to "stir up servile insurrection" and one that reinforced the South's decision to fight for its independence. Even Tennessee's Thomas A. R. Nelson, one of the most vigorous opponents of secession, denounced the "atrocity and barbarism of Mr. Lincoln's proclamation." It was more difficult to gauge the response of slaves. Most were illiterate, and if they heard about the proclamation through the grapevine, they dared not admit it, lest they raise their masters' suspicion of attempts to escape to freedom.[101]

Conversely, the North's initial response was overwhelmingly positive. Abolitionists were euphoric. "God bless Abraham Lincoln," exclaimed Horace Greeley's *New York Tribune*, while Joseph Medill's *Chicago Tribune* considered it the "grandest proclamation ever issued by man."[102] Every major city celebrated with huge rallies marked by bonfires, parades, and oratory. Radical Republicans gloried in the triumph. Even those like Thaddeus Stevens and Benjamin F. Wade, who once attacked Lincoln for his incompetence and reluctance to move against slavery, were forced into silence, at least for the moment.[103] In England, the *Emancipation Proclamation* was celebrated by the majority of people, thanks to Quaker parliamentarian John Bright's assiduous efforts. Bright's championing of the cause in the House of Commons and the force of his moral arguments against slavery won over a nation that had abolished slavery in 1833. What's more, Lincoln's explicit declaration that Emancipation was a major war aim for the Union forced British statesmen like Lord Palmerston, Earl Russell, and future prime minister William Gladstone, who supported the Confederacy, to change their position or face censure.[104]

American Quakers also praised the president's proclamation feeling as if their prayers had been answered. Rachel Moore, a Philadelphia Quaker minister, wrote in her journal that "Friends rejoice and give glory to Him who proclaimed freedom throughout the nation through our noble-souled president, Abraham Lincoln." Moore believed that the *Emancipation Proclamation* "brought the four million slaves out of their graves to such a resurrection as the world never saw; not all the annals of history can furnish a parallel with it." At the same time, Moore made sure to credit several Friends for "bringing the subject of emancipation into our legislative halls at an early day of the abolitionist movement." Among those Quakers she cites as "Saviors of the [black] race" are Maria Child, who "wrote an able and full truth of slavery"; Elias Hicks, who "refused to partake of the unrequited labor of slaves for many years"; and the "intrepid Lucretia Mott," who "conducted abolitionist meetings despite the threat of mobs."[105] Caleb Russell and Sallie Fenton of Prairie Grove Monthly Meeting (Hicksite) in Iowa wrote to Lincoln to "express [their] united approval" of the proclamation and urged the president to seek the "counsel of Him who holds the destinies of nations in His Hand" so that he could "bring about a permanent peace in our beloved country."[106] Encouraged by the letter, Lincoln replied that he was "upheld and sustained by the good wishes and prayers of God's people" and assured them that "no one is more deeply than myself aware" of the need for "His favor."[107] What meant even more were the visits of Quaker ministers who traveled to Washington to offer their prayers in person.

The most significant visit was that of Eliza Gurney and three other Friends on Sunday morning, October 26, 1862. Born and raised in Philadelphia, Eliza Kirkbride met Joseph John Gurney, a wealthy banker and Quaker reformer 13 years her elder, on a visit to England in 1836 and married him five years later. She became a recorded Quaker minister in 1841 and traveled throughout Europe with her husband urging the monarchs of Denmark, Holland, and France to free slaves in their West Indian colonies. After Joseph died in 1847, Eliza returned to the United States and settled at Burlington, New Jersey, where she continued her abolitionist activities.[108] In October 1862, Gurney "felt constrained to make a religious visit" to the president and express her gratitude for the *Preliminary Emancipation Proclamation*.[109] Gurney was also deeply troubled by the trials of the Civil War. It is not clear if she and her companions—John M. Whitall, Hannah B. Mott, and James Carey—traveled to Washington as a delegation appointed by a specific monthly or yearly meeting or if they had initiated the interview themselves.[110] What is known is that they did not seek any political favor, which greatly pleased Lincoln. Instead, Gurney emphasized the delegation's "near sympathy" for the president in the "heavy weight of responsibility that rested upon him." Although she expressed her gratitude for Lincoln's recent decision to emancipate the slaves, Gurney recognized the "trials and persecutions" the president would have to confront because of that decision and hoped that he would "commit his way unto the Lord by prayer" whenever those trials emerged. If he did so, she believed that "the peace of God" would "keep the president in heart and mind."[111]

Lincoln was charmed by the innocence and genuine sympathy of the Quakeress. Gurney knelt and offered a prayer "that light and wisdom might be shed down from on high, to guide our President," before the group settled into a silent meditative worship.[112] Whitall later noted that he would never forget the "deep solemnity, the almost awful silence [that] reigned within that room," or the "tears running down the cheeks of our honored President as E. P. Gurney solemnly addressed him." When the members of the delegation rose to go, Lincoln, profoundly affected by the meeting, encouraged the four Friends to stay longer than the 15 minutes scheduled for their visit. But Gurney declined, noting that the president had too many other responsibilities. Taking her hand, Lincoln, with unusual warmth, confided, "I am glad of this interview."[113]

Conversely, John G. Nicolay, one of the president's secretaries, was much less impressed by the visit. Later that evening, Nicolay wrote a letter to his fiancée, Therena Bates, complaining about a "small Quaker delegation" that came to "hold a prayer meeting" with Lincoln. He stated his sympathy for the president, who was "compelled to bear the infliction until the 'spirit' moved them to stop." "Isn't it strange," Nicolay concluded, "that so many and such intelligent people often have so little common sense?"[114] Although Nicolay prided himself in being privy to most, if not all, of Lincoln's interviews, his negative impression of this one was off the mark. The secretary was, in demeanor and temperament, a brooding, pessimistic figure. He tended to scrutinize others for ulterior motives.[115] Thus, Nicolay probably likened the Quaker delegation to those of other religious groups who came to seek favors or to convert the president to Emancipation through unwelcome preaching. In fact, Lincoln was so moved by the interview with Gurney that he wrote a remarkably candid letter to her confessing his belief:

> We are indeed going through a great trial—a fiery trial. In the very responsible position in which I happen to be placed, being a humble instrument in the hands of our Heavenly Father, as I am, and as we all are, to work out His great purposes, I have desired that all my works and acts may be according to His will, and that it might be so, I have sought His aid—but if after endeavoring to do my best in the light which He affords me, I find my efforts fail, I must believe that for some purpose unknown to me, He wills it otherwise. If I had had my way, this war would never have been commenced; if I had been allowed my way this war would have been ended before this, but we find it still continues; and we must believe that He permits it for some wise purpose of His own, mysterious and unknown to us; and though with our limited understandings we may not be able to

comprehend it, yet we cannot but believe, that He who made the world still governs it.[116]

It is a revealing letter in two respects. First, Lincoln, who was usually guarded about his innermost thoughts, trusted Gurney so completely that he shared his belief in being an "instrument in the hands of our Heavenly father," something he had previously confided only to his cabinet. Such a high degree of trust reflects the spiritual kinship that existed between the president and the Quaker minister. That point is reinforced by Lincoln's own sympathy for her, as he acknowledges the "fiery trial" she and her fellow Quakers are experiencing. What's more, historian Ronald C. White credits Gurney with inspiring his use of the term "fiery trial" in his *Annual Message to Congress* later that year. White believes that Lincoln "carried the image of a fiery trial with him" from the letter to Gurney, making it synonymous to the circumstances of the nation in his December 1 address. On that occasion, Lincoln appealed to a divided legislature to unite behind him and his efforts at Emancipation.[117] Using the plural pronouns "we" and "us," the president, in his concluding paragraph, asked that Congress hold themselves accountable to the ideals of the founding fathers and the experiment in democracy that they began:

> Fellow-citizens, *we* cannot escape history. We of this Congress and this administration, will be remembered in spite of ourselves. No personal significance, or insignificance, can spare one or another of us. The fiery trial through which we pass, will light us down, in honor or dishonor, to the latest generation. We *say* we are for the Union. The world will not forget that we say this. We know how to save the Union. The world knows we do know how to save it. We—even *we here*—hold the power, and bear the responsibility. In *giving* freedom to the *slave*, we *assure* freedom to the *free*—honorable alike in what we give, and what we preserve. We shall nobly save, or meanly lose, the last best hope of earth. Other means may succeed; this could not fail. The way is plain, peaceful, generous, just—a way which, if followed, the world will forever applaud, and God must forever bless.[118]

Second, Lincoln's letter to Gurney represents the most complete expression of his belief in the doctrine of necessity to that point in time, a theme that began with the "Meditation on the Divine Will" a month earlier and reached its fullest expression in his second inaugural address of March 4, 1865, when he declared:

> If we shall suppose that American slavery is one of those offenses which, in the providence of God, must needs come, but which, having continued through His appointed time, He now wills to remove, and that He gives to both North and South this terrible war as the woe due to those by whom the offense came, shall we discern therein any departure from those divine attributes which the believers in a living God always ascribe to Him? Fondly do we hope, fervently do we pray, that this mighty scourge of war may speedily pass away. Yet, if God wills that it continue until all the wealth piled by the bondsman's two hundred and fifty years of unrequited toil shall be sunk, and until every drop of blood drawn with the lash shall be paid by another drawn with the sword, as was said three thousand years ago, so still it must be said "the judgments of the Lord are true and righteous altogether."[119]

Placed in this context, the influence of Eliza Gurney on Lincoln's spiritual development was profound. He recognized her earnest desire for his welfare later writing that he had "not forgotten" and "probably never shall forget the very impressive occasion when you and your friends visited me."[120] Lincoln was so moved by the interview that he urged Gurney to write him, transmitting his request through Isaac Newton, a Quaker who also served as the U.S. commissioner of agriculture. She agreed, becoming an important source of spiritual support for the president.[121]

The importance Lincoln attached to prayer and spiritual fellowship cannot be exaggerated, particularly in times of national crisis and personal distress. Although he often prayed alone, he welcomed spiritual fellowship with others, especially Quakers, who shared his belief in the ability of the individual to communicate directly with the Almighty. One of these occasions took place in mid-December 1862 after Lincoln learned of the high Union casualties sustained at the Battle of Fredericksburg. Frustrated with McClellan's replacement, General Ambrose E. Burnside, the president discussed the possibility of removing him from command with Secretary of War Edwin Stanton. On December 13, Burnside, in an attempt to capture Richmond by crossing the Rappahannock River at Fredericksburg, launched a series of attacks against Lee's Confederate forces, all of them bloody, all of them fruitless. After losing a large part of his army, Burnside withdrew to the north bank of the Rappahannock. Unlike McClellan, Burnside took action, but not *decisive* action. And it came at a cost of 12,600 casualties, compared to fewer than 5,000 for the Confederates.[122]

Lincoln was beside himself with despair, but was at a loss for another general to replace him. It was during this period that the president found solace in an interview with Elizabeth Comstock and Rachel Grellett, traveling Quaker ministers. He had met them before to issue letters allowing them to visit army hospitals and camps for freed blacks in Maryland, Virginia, and Delaware to minister to the spiritual needs of wounded soldiers and former slaves. On this occasion, Lincoln welcomed them into his office and asked them to be seated, perhaps hoping that they had come to offer prayerful support.

Comstock explained that the two ministers felt called by the Lord to "come to him with a message of love and cheer and encouragement." "Well, if you have any encouragement for me," replied Lincoln, trying to force a smile across a forlorn face, "please give it. I need it. Be free to say whatever is on your minds." "Abraham, we believe we have a message from the Lord for thee," said Comstock. "He has laid a great burden upon thee and thou canst not bear it alone. It is too much for thee. He says be of good courage and I will be with thee. I will not leave thee nor forsake thee. Thou shall prevail. Cast all thy burdens upon Him. Nothing is too hard for Him. The destiny of this great nation is upon Him. Do not carry it thyself. Look to Him. He will guide thee. He will give thee wisdom and thou shall prevail." "May it not be that God has raised thee up, like Moses, to be the great emancipator of His people?" she continued. "To establish the nation united and free? As He said to Joshua, only be strong and of good courage."

After Comstock completed her message, the two Quaker ministers arose to leave, but Lincoln stopped them.

"Aren't you going to pray with me?" he asked.

"We hoped thee would ask for that," replied Grellett.
Taking their hands in his, Lincoln knelt down alongside them to pray.

Comstock later recalled that his hands "trembled like a leaf in the breeze," but that when she ended the prayer the president said "Amen, good and strong." "We felt as if we had helped him to roll the burden off his shoulders, and that Jesus was there to receive them."[123]

There is one other aspect of the Gurney, Comstock, and Grellett visits that deserves mentioning. Lincoln paid special attention to these Quaker ministers because they were women, though his interest in Comstock and Grellett may be attributed primarily to their ministerial activities in military camps and hospitals. He appreciated their efforts on behalf of the Union cause and giving them a few moments of his time was a token of his gratitude. Accordingly, William Stoddard, a White House secretary, observed that Lincoln's "manner with the softer sex was kindly and courteous" and that he displayed a "chivalrous deference to the ministering angels who went to and fro among our camps and hospitals."[124] There appears to be more to the president's interest in Eliza Gurney, though.

Lincoln could be charming to women, especially those who demonstrated sincerity and intelligence and were physically attractive like Gurney.[125] He was a great reader of human nature and an admirer of beautiful women.[126] At the same time, he was isolated from much social interaction with females by the jealousy of his wife, which became more intense as she struggled with her sanity.[127] As a result, Lincoln's potential to develop female friendships was extremely limited. Gurney, a 61-year-old widow, presented no threat to the 53-year-old president either because of age or marital status. Still, he may have felt as if he was compromising his emotional fidelity to Mary by carrying on an occasional correspondence with Gurney, thus the reason for having his secretary of agriculture, Isaac Newton, initiate the dialogue. That Gurney shared Lincoln's own spiritual leadings was of primary importance to him, but her gender and the sincerity of her actions were every bit as appealing to him. No doubt those attributes motivated his request to extend the interview as well as to conduct a correspondence.

For Quaker abolitionists who believed that slavery could be ended without bloodshed, the Civil War posed a painful dilemma. Now that Lincoln had made emancipation a major aim of the war, they struggled to find some way to support the Union effort without compromising their pacifist beliefs. Gurney, Comstock, and Grellett resolved the problem by offering the president the kind of spiritual support he needed to survive the fratricidal conflict while still maintaining their commitment to the Society of Friends' Peace Testimony. It would not be as easy for other Friends to reconcile their pacifist convictions with a war effort that aimed to end slavery, no matter how just the cause.

CHAPTER 3
Trials of War, 1863

At 11:00 a.m. on January 1, 1863, the Lincolns hosted a New Year's reception at the White House. The president stood for three hours greeting a long procession of several hundred diplomats, military officers, politicians, and members of the public. In the afternoon, he retired to his office with a few cabinet members to sign the final *Emancipation Proclamation*. Exhausted, his hand swollen from greeting others, Lincoln could hardly hold the gold pen he had chosen to sign the historic document. Realizing the importance of the moment, he put the pen down.

"If my name ever goes into history," he said, "it will be for this act." Lincoln worried that a feeble signature from a trembling hand would invite his critics to say, "he hesitated." That would not do, for "I never in my life felt more certain that I was doing right than I do in signing this paper ... and my whole soul is in it."

Lincoln then picked up the pen and with a firm hand signed the proclamation. "There," he said, "that will do."[1]

The *Emancipation Proclamation* represented a sea change in Lincoln's view of the Civil War. What began as a military conflict to preserve the Union now also became a struggle to free the slaves. The document transcended politics, its extensive provisions reflecting the vision of a truly moral leader. Not only did Lincoln declare the slaves free but he also ordered the Union army and navy to "recognize and maintain" that freedom and provided for the enlistment of blacks "into the armed forces of the United States."[2]

Lincoln anticipated the virulent attack from conservatives who accused him of caving in to the demands of the radical Republicans and for turning the war into an abolition crusade. They viewed the *Emancipation Proclamation* as the president's ultimate dictatorial action since he had vowed in his first inaugural address not to interfere with slavery where it already existed, acknowledging his constitutional duty to protect the "property of all U.S. citizens."[3] He also predicted the dissatisfaction of abolitionist extremists who were quick to point out that the proclamation provided only for the freedom of slaves under Confederate control and not for some 800,000 others who lived in the border states and other areas occupied by the Union army.[4] Some of the strongest criticism came from Quakers. Lucretia Mott viewed the *Emancipation Proclamation* as "only a half-way measure" and urged the members of her racially integrated Philadelphia Female Anti-Slavery Society to "keep on their armor in the struggle for the complete abolition of slavery."[5] Similarly, the editor of the *Friend*, in Philadelphia, regretted that the proclamation did not invite former slaves to enlist in the Union army.[6] Others took their case directly to Lincoln.

On March 26, Primitive Friends Thomas Lamborn and James D. Otis of New York Yearly Meeting, James Hopkins of New England Yearly Meeting, and Joseph Brinton of Pennsylvania General (Primitive) Meeting secured an interview with the president, who received the delegation "most sensibly and politely." Primitive Friends were a small group of ultraconservative Quakers who grew out of a series of obscure controversies concerning their relationship with other Wilburite Friends as well as with the Gurneyites.[7] Like the other schismatic groups in the Society of Friends, however, their concern over abolitionism involved *approach* rather than theology. Lamborn spoke for the group, emphasizing that they came "in gospel love" and did "not come to criticize the government or dictate to thee." Having issued the disclaimer, the Primitive Friend could now speak freely and proceeded to lecture the president on his responsibility "as an instrument of the Lord." "I have no sympathy with this great evil rebellion in support of a great wrong," said Lamborn, referring to the Confederate cause of slavery. "But this evil is not all in the South. This calamity ... is because of the sins of the whole people. Had the people of the North been faithful to the Lord, I believe the calamities caused by the sin of slavery would not have been felt in the North as it has been now, but the South would have felt it more exclusively." Accordingly, the *Emancipation Proclamation* did not go far enough in the view of these Primitive Friends, and they urged Lincoln to issue another "proclamation to show the people [both North and South] that they are chastised for their naughtiness and grievous rebellion against God and for their pride" in practicing the evil of slavery. Lamborn prophesized that the Lord, who "hath destroyed nations because of sin, will [continue] to punish the people until they learn righteousness" and that would only happen with universal emancipation.[8]

To be sure, Lincoln was not unmindful that the North had profited financially from slavery beginning with the founding of the colonies in the seventeenth century. Even after the institution was abolished above the Mason–Dixon Line, Northern merchants and manufacturers benefitted from cotton, rice, and sugar procured at the expense of slave labor.[9] Yet even as Lincoln restricted his proclamation to Confederate-controlled areas, his intention to affect universal emancipation was unmistakable. He had said as much four months earlier in his annual message to Congress when he declared that "in *giving freedom* to the *slave* we *assure freedom* to the *free*." This principle, so controversial in the divided nation, was fundamental to Lincoln, who considered the Declaration of Independence his political credo. For him, the abolition of slavery would bring to fruition the founders' belief that every American had a God-given right to "life, liberty, and the pursuit of happiness." It was a destiny, according to Lincoln, "we cannot escape." That destiny, however, would not come without sacrifice and a dramatic redefinition of American democracy, as he declared in his annual message to Congress the previous year:

> The fiery trial through which we pass, will light us down, in honor or dishonor, to the latest generation. ... The dogmas of the quiet past are inadequate to the stormy present. The occasion is piled high with difficulty, and we must rise with the occasion. As our case is new, so we must think anew, and act anew. We must disenthrall ourselves, and then we shall save our country. ... We shall nobly save, or meanly lose, the last best hope of earth. The way is plain, peaceful, generous, just—a way which, if followed, the world will forever applaud, and God must forever bless.[10]

Lincoln's messianic language not only mirrored the views of Primitive Friends but also revealed his belief that if the American people were willing to "disenthrall themselves" from the "dogmas of the past" in order to "think and act anew" that Providence would guide him in restoring the divided nation. There was a reason for the hundreds of thousands of lives that had been taken on the battlefields; a reason why families had been torn apart by those heart-wrenching deaths;

and a reason why the country and he, himself, had been subjected to such a "fiery trial." That reason was the monstrous evil of human slavery. Only by eradicating the injustice would he and the American people be able to purge the nation of sin and make it whole again in the eyes of the Almighty. Lincoln had tried earlier to resolve the personal tension between constitutional obligation and personal morality through gradual compensated emancipation in the border states. It was a futile effort. No longer would his conscience allow him to accommodate an institution that was constitutionally legal when he believed it was a deeply offensive moral wrong. Now, with the final *Emancipation Proclamation*, Lincoln proposed to make slavery a constitutional wrong as well. Essentially, he had come to believe, in a mystical sense, that emancipating the slaves was the reason he had been placed by God on this earth.

The *Emancipation Proclamation* also forced Lincoln to reconsider the role black troops might play in the war. Strong opposition in the North, as well as lingering prejudice that blacks were intellectually and socially inferior, limited most black involvement to driving supply wagons, burying the dead after battle, and building railroads for the war effort. Pressured by a series of costly Union defeats and a significant drop in white enlistments, Congress included a clause in the Second Confiscation Act authorizing Lincoln to "use as many persons of African descent" as he needed "for suppression of the Rebellion." At the same time, the lawmakers repealed the discriminatory provision of the 1792 Militia Act, which had barred blacks from serving in the army, and passed a new measure authorizing a militia draft within a state when it could not meet its quota with volunteers and allowing blacks to be used for military service. While the act referred only to those blacks who had been recently freed from bondage and did not intend to have them bear arms, it did provide for military training and opened the possibility for African Americans to fight.[11] The South Carolina Sea Islands, which came under Union control by August 1862, was the first to act on the new legislation, organizing two black regiments.[12] Still, Lincoln refused to raise a large black army on political grounds. "To arm the Negroes," he told his abolitionist critics, "would turn 50,000 bayonets from the loyal Border States against us that were for us."[13]

Free black leaders continued to urge the necessity of enlisting black troops, realizing that if the black man proved his patriotism and courage on the battlefield, the nation would be morally obligated to grant him first-class citizenship. No one expressed those sentiments more eloquently than Frederick Douglass. Attacking the inconsistency of Lincoln's position of making repeated calls for men only to let "Indo-Caucasian hands" fight, the famous black orator insisted that "once the black man gets upon his person the brass letters 'U.S.', a musket on his shoulder, and bullets in his pocket, there is no power on earth that can deny that he has earned the right to citizenship in the United States."[14] The debate continued until January 1, 1863, when the *Emancipation Proclamation* was made official. Having freed by executive order those slaves in the South, Lincoln could no longer deny the black man the opportunity to fight. Not only did Lincoln instruct the War Department to begin recruiting black soldiers, but he publicly authorized the enlistment of blacks. When some Northerners complained about Lincoln's change of heart, the president was swift in his response. "You say you will not fight to free Negroes," he shot back. "Some of them seem willing to fight for you. When victory is won there will be some black men who can remember that, with silent tongue and clenched teeth, and steady eye and well-placed bayonet, they have helped mankind on to this great consummation. I fear, however, that there will also be some white ones, unable to forget that with malignant heart and deceitful speech, they strove to hinder it."[15]

On February 13, 1863, Senator Charles Sumner of Massachusetts presented a bill in Congress proposing the "enlistment of 300,000 colored troops." Although the bill was defeated, the state's governor, John A. Andrew, requested and received permission from Secretary of War Edwin Stanton to organize a colored regiment of volunteers to serve for three years. In Massachusetts only 100 men volunteered during the first six weeks of recruitment. The state's black men were insulted by the fact that the regiment would be headed only by white officers and by the fact that black soldiers would receive lower pay than white ones. Disillusioned by the turnout, Andrew organized a committee of prominent citizens and black leaders to supervise the recruitment of black troops. Within two months' time, the committee collected $5,000 and established a line of recruiting posts from Boston to St. Louis. Soon the quota was raised, and 1,000 freedmen and former slaves from throughout the Union became part of the 54th Regiment Massachusetts Volunteer Infantry, Colored.[16] Commanded by Colonel Robert Gould Shaw, the 25-year-old scion of a wealthy and socially prominent Boston abolitionist family, all of the black volunteers understood the severe consequences of enlisting. Shortly after the 54th was mustered into service, the Confederate Congress passed an act declaring its intention to "put to death," if captured, "any

Negro" as well as "white commissioned officer [who] shall command, prepare or aid Negroes in arms against the Confederate States."[17]

By the spring of 1863, favorable reports of the black troops' training filtered back to Washington and into the Northern press. Lincoln read them with growing enthusiasm. He quickly became convinced that there was a psychological as well as purely military advantage to enlisting blacks in the Union army. "The colored population is the great available, yet unavailable, force for restoring the Union," he wrote to Governor Andrew Johnson of Tennessee. "The bare sight of fifty-thousand armed, and drilled black soldiers upon the banks of the Mississippi, would end the rebellion at once."[18] Black enlistment was authorized not a moment too soon, either.

With growing resistance to the Militia Act of 1862 and dwindling white enlistment, Congress, on March 3, 1863, passed the Enrollment Act, the first genuine national conscription law. The controversial act required the enrollment of every male citizen and those immigrants who had filed for citizenship between ages 25 and 45. Federal agents established a quota of new troops due from each congressional district. Still, men drafted could provide substitutes and until mid-1864 could even avoid service by paying a $300 commutation money. Many eligible men pooled their funds to cover the cost of any one of them drafted. Families used the substitute provision to select which member should go into the army and which would stay home. Of the 168,649 men procured for the Union army through the draft, 117,986 were substitutes, leaving only 50,663 who had their personal services conscripted.[19] In some cities, enforcement of the act sparked civil unrest as the war dragged on, leading to draft riots in the summer of 1863.[20]

Quakers were concerned that the new conscription law did not contain an exemption for conscientious objectors. Many Friends pled their conscience and refused to serve in the Union army, citing their belief in the Quakers' historic testimony on peace. The Peace Testimony was explicit even against voluntary payment of a fine or for a substitute, though Lincoln and Secretary of War Stanton offered to use the commutation fees for a freedmen's fund or hospitals. Both Philadelphia and Western Yearly Meetings reinforced this point in memorials to the president, insisting that to pay a fine or to hire a substitute "would be virtually admitting that God is not the sole and sovereign ruler of conscience" and that "human governments may control and coerce [conscience] or withhold the free exercise of it at their pleasure."[21] Primitive Friends from New York and New England were so strongly opposed to the new conscription law that they sent a delegation to meet with Lincoln. Realizing that Congress—not the president—"made the law," the delegation urged Lincoln to "use his influence to protect [our] peaceable people, who cannot fight even to save their own lives or property" and will not send others to do the same for them. They assured him of their religious commitment to pacifism, unlike others "who pretend to have conscientious scruples against war but are traitors at heart."[22] However, there were other young Friends who did pay the fee in order to escape military service. Still others, mostly new and near Quakers who sought the same conscientious objector status of birthright Friends, found themselves in the grasp of the Union army being denied an exemption by the federal government.[23] Together with those young Quakers who volunteered for military service, the variety of responses by pacifist Friends indicated a lack of consensus within the Society of Friends over its commitment either to the Union war effort or to the discipline of their religious body. Initially these contradictory responses raised questions within the War Department about the genuineness of the Friends' devotion to pacifism. In fact, the variety of Quaker responses to military service indicated the severe trial of principle and faith these young Friends were experiencing.

II

Lincoln's issuance of the *Emancipation Proclamation* intensified the Quaker dilemma of how to reconcile antislavery principles with pacifist religious beliefs. "There is a danger under present circumstances of allowing our testimony against war to be modified or lessened, from the fact that this war will certainly be the means of putting down slavery," wrote a concerned Hicksite Quaker in an October 3, 1863, letter to the *Friends Intelligencer*. "This war having been begun by slaveholders more firmly to secure themselves in their authority over slaves, we cannot be sorry to see that authority overthrown; yet it is done by a means of war that we, as Christians, cannot recommend or uphold."[24] In fact, there were those Quakers who wrote to Lincoln asking that he "let the South go peaceably" from the Union "without bloodshed."[25] From the beginning of the Civil War, Friends, regardless of their theological affiliation or geographical residence, emphasized their disdain of the Confederacy and their loyalty to the Union cause, though their pacifist principles precluded them from condoning the military means used to uphold that cause. Friends also pointed out the sharp distinction between their religiously inspired Peace Testimony and the politically motivated pacifism of the so-called "Peace Democrats," or "Copperheads," who opposed the war aims of the Lincoln administration.[26] There was nothing new about Quaker pacifism; it had been a fundamental article of religious discipline for two centuries.

Pacifism, like the other Quaker testimonies on simplicity, truthfulness, and equality, was inspired by the leading of the Inner Light, or Spirit of God within each person, as experienced individually or in group worship. Unlike the other testimonies, Friends' peace concerns evolved gradually from individual conscience to collective testimony to a uniform religious discipline. A uniform position did not exist in 1652, when George Fox, a religiously inspired English tradesman, founded the sect. Instead, the Peace Testimony can be traced to the decline of the Puritan Commonwealth in mid-seventeenth-century England.[27] After the death of Lord Protector Oliver Cromwell in 1659, radical Puritans in Parliament called on Quakers to serve as commissioners of the militia to prevent a takeover by the Crown. Most Friends refused, but a dozen or so took up posts in the militia. Despite their efforts, Royalists prevailed and the Commonwealth fell. When conservative Puritans restored Charles (Stuart) II to the throne in 1660, he promised to observe a policy of religious toleration outside the Church of England. Saddled with a heavily Anglican Parliament, however, Charles was unable to prevent lawmakers from restoring the Episcopal bishops and prayer books in the Church of England and requiring all clergy to follow these or lose their pulpits. Feeling betrayed, Puritan pastors abandoned their parish churches in droves rather than obey the edict.

While most Puritans chose to suffer in silence, a radical gang of "Fifth Monarchists" attempted to overthrow the government. Quakers struggled with all the violence. Initially they believed that the English Civil War was a manifestation of God's will, His desire to purge evil within human hearts and history. The early Friends dubbed this the "Lamb's War," meaning the fusing of personal experience and social ethic into a cosmic world-view through Christ, who is the Lamb in the Book of Revelation. Accordingly, there were those Friends who volunteered to fight in Cromwell's army in order to effect the Kingdom of God on Earth. By 1660, however, Quakers were confused by the constant warfare, violence, and religious intolerance of the restored monarchy. They were also suspected of being part of the effort to initiate a new civil war.[28] Friends, individually and collectively, turned to the Light for guidance. Realizing the need to declare their innocence, Friends, in 1660 and 1661, drafted statements to the king, Parliament, and England at large, stating that they rejected violence and could be relied upon to do so even under government persecution. "The Spirit of God by which we are guided is not changeable; the Spirit of Christ, which leads us into all Truth, will never move us to fight and war against men with outward weapons," they declared in a document that has come to be known as the *Peace Testimony*.[29]

During the seventeenth and eighteenth centuries, American Quakers expanded the meaning and scope of their peace concerns. Friends were one of five major denominations in colonial America. Quakers could be found in all 13 colonies and served as major political and economic forces in Pennsylvania, Rhode Island, and New Jersey. Organized into six yearly meetings and more than 300 monthly meetings across the eastern seaboard, Friends received nearly unconditional support from London Yearly Meeting in negotiating with the British government for exemption to serve in a militia. As a result, Friends, individually and collectively, maintained a strong consistency of conduct and behavior when their religious testimonies were threatened by secular affairs. While Quakers advocated obedience to government when its policies were consistent with their beliefs, they did not hesitate in adopting passive disobedience when it did not. Just as important, Friends were willing to suffer for their beliefs when the demands of secular government contradicted their religious testimonies.[30] Nowhere is this tendency as pronounced as with the Peace Testimony.

British North America witnessed constant warfare. Indian raids along the frontier as well as invasions by the armadas of enemy European powers were common. As a result, the militia often played a vital role in the defense of all the colonies except Pennsylvania, where strong Quaker influence and friendly relations with Native Americans exempted it from raising such a body. Elsewhere Quakers, unwilling to bear their share of the burden for military defense, were ostracized by the larger community. Maryland and New Jersey imposed fines on Friends who refused to serve in the colonial militia. On the other hand, New York (1755), Massachusetts (1757), Virginia (1766), and North Carolina (1770) recognized the religious scruples of Friends and exempted them from militia service.[31] Still, even in Pennsylvania, the French–Indian War posed a serious dilemma for Quakers between holding government office and obedience to their pacifist convictions. As a result of the stalemate, Friends, in 1756, withdrew en masse from the Pennsylvania Assembly and initiated a movement for spiritual revitalization that strengthened group solidarity through a stricter observance of their peculiar religious testimonies. Quakers made the Peace Testimony a fundamental article of faith, purging from membership those who dissented over pacifism in any way.[32] It was also at this time that Philadelphia Yearly Meeting established a Meeting for Sufferings, whose chief purpose was to care for Friends suffering from religious persecution. North Carolina and New York followed Philadelphia's lead and established similar bodies in 1757 and 1758, respectively. These Meetings for Sufferings—along with similar bodies that were established in New England, Maryland, and Virginia—were especially active during the War for American Independence when Quaker political influence came to an ignominious end throughout the colonies as Friends refused not only to pay war taxes but also to swear oaths of allegiance to the patriot government.[33]

By the beginning of the nineteenth century, Quaker differences with the federal government over the issue of pacifism were generally limited to the refusal of Friends to muster with state militias in strict accordance to their religious discipline. American society had become more accepting of Quakers because of their self-chosen role as keepers of the nation's conscience. Friends distinguished themselves through involvement a vast array of humanitarian reforms. Like the early Quakers of mid-seventeenth-century England, American Friends saw themselves as God's chosen instruments with a mission of bringing the rest of society into the orbit of their social testimonies and benevolent reforms, which included but were certainly not limited to the abolition of slavery. Quakers constantly looked for "openings" to be of service to their non-Quaker countrymen, to exert their influence without necessarily making converts.[34] In this way, Quakers, according to Sydney James, became "a people among peoples" in the nineteenth-century United States, able to "support the government and contribute to the national welfare in ways which would preserve and express their distinctive views" and doing so "without either sacrificing their strict fidelity to their distinctive code of behavior or compromising with worldliness."[35] Thus, secular society began to accept Quakers as one of several Protestant denominations, dominant in no state but tolerated in all despite popular suspicion of their pacifism and in the South of their antislavery position.

Friends had little difficulty maintaining this special niche in American society during the first half of the nineteenth century due to a relatively prolonged state of peace. In fact, the United States was involved in just two military conflicts—the War of 1812 and the Mexican War, which began in 1846—during this period. Neither conflict affected the patterns of daily life because of their brevity and, in the case of the Mexican War, because hostilities occurred outside U.S. borders. In both instances, Friends were careful to point out that their objection to war was based on religious principle, and they made sure to distance themselves from those political elements that opposed war. Beginning in the 1850s, however, Quakers discovered that their hatred of war and love of freedom were destined to result in a severe trial of principle and faith. Torn between two cherished principles, some Friends abandoned their pacifism altogether during the Civil War, others clung to it unconditionally, and still others resorted to a broad range of compliance or noncompliance with the Union war effort.[36]

Failing to understand or appreciate the dilemma, military officials and members of the non-Quaker public attacked those Friends who refused to support the Union war effort. Fortunately Lincoln, whenever he learned of the persecution, intervened. For example, Henry D. Swift, a New England Friend, refused to serve in the Union army unless it was in a camp hospital. Recruiters forced him to witness the execution of a deserter before he was tried by court martial and sentenced to be shot. When word reached Lincoln of his fate, he ordered the young man to be sent home on parole.[37] Another Friend from Lake Champlain, New York, was assigned to a regiment and sent off to Washington for training despite conscientious objection on religious grounds. Throughout the training period, the Friend, who continued to hold his ground, was severely punished and threatened with execution on the charge of treason. Finally, the colonel became so frustrated that he appealed to the president, explaining that the "refractory soldier" claimed to be a Quaker and refused to fight on religious principle. "Why that is plain enough," replied Lincoln after learning of the Quaker's courage to stand by his religious scruples. "There is only one thing to do. Trump up some excuse and send him home. They can't kill a boy like that you know. The country needs all her brave men wherever they are. Send him home."[38]

The Quakers of Richmond, Indiana, were excoriated in the press by their non-Quaker neighbors for refusing to fight. An editorial in *Quaker City Telegram* declared that "we love the 'Friends', but we do not love them when we've sent 40% of our sons and brothers to face the cannons, to pace the picket beat, make the long march, and bleed and die ... while they do nothing." The editorial also emphasized the Quaker inconsistency of wanting "justice and equality for all, including the Negro," while being unwilling to fight for a Union army "dedicated to the same cause."[39] Similarly, the Richmond Guards' Militia, in a letter to the editor of the *Broad Axe of Freedom*, insisted that the Civil War was being waged to "retain our liberties as bequeathed by the founding fathers" and if "Quakers would take up the gun instead of the pen, they would not only be worthy citizens of 'free America,' but would be following in the footsteps of Moses as it is written in Exodus."[40] Predictably, one Richmond Friend was harassed by a military recruiter when he refused to be conscripted or to pay $300 to hire a substitute on the grounds that it was "morally wrong to hire others to go to war." After the recruiting officer dismissed his explanation, he drafted bills for the public sale of the Friend's farm. Still the young man refused to go to war or to hire a substitute. Taking his leave, the recruiter posted the bills of sale on trees in the vicinity of the farm. A few days before the sale was to take place, the Quaker resistor learned that Governor Morton of Indiana informed the president of his dire situation and Lincoln ordered the public sale to be stopped.[41]

Perhaps the most famous case of Quaker conscientious objection was that of a Vermont Friend, Cyrus Pringle, and two others—Peter Dakin and Lindley Macomber—who did not qualify for exemption, having joined the Society of Friends shortly after the beginning of the war. Drafted on July 13, 1863, the three Friends decided to show their devotion to the Peace Testimony by rejecting exemption, payment of a commutation fee, or the hiring of a substitute. They were transported first to a Union military camp on Long Island in Boston Harbor and later to camps in Virginia near the battlefront, where they refused to participate in any military service or drills or even serve in a camp hospital. So strict was their adherence to the Peace Testimony that throughout their sojourn, officers tried to break them down by imposing severe punishments. On one occasion, Pringle, after being subjected to especially inhumane treatment, made the following entry in his diary:

> Two sergeants bid me to lie down on my back, and stretching my limbs apart tied cords to me wrists and ankles, and to these four stakes driven into the ground, somewhat in the form of an X. I was very quiet in my mind as I lay there on the ground soaked with the rain of the previous day, exposed to the heat of the sun, and suffering cruelly from the cords binding my wrists and

straining my muscles. If I dared the presumption, I should say that I caught a glimpse of heavenly pity. I wept, not so much from my own suffering as from sorrow that such things should be in our country where justice and freedom and liberty of conscience have been the annual boast of Fourth-of-July orators so many years. It seemed that our forefathers in the [Quaker] faith had wrought and suffered in vain, when the privileges they so dearly bought were so soon set aside. And I was sad that one endeavoring to follow our dear Master should be so generally regarded as a despicable and stubborn culprit.[42]

This and similarly harsh treatment earned Pringle the sympathy and respect of the ordinary soldiers who witnessed it but did little to weaken his resistance or to change the minds of the officers who meted out the punishments. Finally, in the autumn of 1863, Pringle's case was taken up by Isaac Newton, Lincoln's secretary of agriculture—and a member of the Society of Friends. The president, after learning the details of the case, informed Secretary of War Stanton of his "urgent wish to release [Pringle, Dakin, and Macomber] and send them home at once."[43]

To be sure, no Quaker suffered the penalty of death for his refusal to fight, though several were sentenced to death through court martial.[44] Lincoln respected Quaker resistors for their genuinely held religious convictions and believed that they could serve the Union cause far better at home than in the ranks of the military. Nor did he want to create martyrs; it would only increase political opposition among an already outspoken and growing peace movement. As a result, the president went to great lengths to accommodate the requests of Friends, even those who sympathized with the South. For example, Lincoln, in October 1863, agreed to exchange two Confederate spies imprisoned at Fort Delaware for the release of two Virginia Quakers, Robert Hollingsworth and William Williams, who had been seized by Confederate Colonel E. V. White as hostages. The president acted on a request of Samuel Janney, a Quaker minister of Loudoun County, Virginia, not at the demand of the Confederate colonel.[45]

Lincoln also acted on the requests of respected Friends he knew personally. For example, the president, in response to a request by Quaker parliamentarian John Bright, released Alfred Rubery, a Confederate sympathizer who was arrested in San Francisco in May 1863 for "giving aide to the existing rebellion." Rubery had plotted to seize a gunboat and turn it over to the Confederacy. Sentenced to 10 years imprisonment and a fine of $10,000, Rubery's parents enlisted the support of Bright to intercede on their son's behalf. Although the young Confederate was not a Quaker, Bright agreed to make the request. He communicated the situation to Lincoln, and the president immediately issued a pardon on the grounds that Rubery was "of the immature age of twenty years and of highly respectable parentage." Lincoln added that the pardon was "desired by John Bright, whose high character and steady friendship is held in high esteem by the United States." The pardon was issued on January 20, 1864, on the "condition that Rubery leaves the United States within thirty days."[46]

Isaac Newton, Lincoln's secretary of agriculture and a Quaker farmer from Pennsylvania, often acted as a liaison between the president and Friends.[47] Newton had endeared himself to the president because he befriended Mrs. Lincoln, preventing embarrassing public disclosures of her extravagant expenses.[48] He also comforted her after Willie's death by introducing her to some of Washington's spiritualists, who she believed could help her communicate with her dead son.[49] Although some members of Lincoln's inner circle considered Newton an "ignorant, credulous old gentleman" who indulged in gossip, no one doubted that he was "honest and kind," was fiercely loyal to the Society of Friends, and, for those reasons, had earned the president's trust.[50] In late July 1863, a delegation from the Meeting for Sufferings of Philadelphia Yearly Meeting enlisted Newton's aid in securing an appointment with Lincoln in order to secure the release of five southern Friends who had been forced to serve in the Confederate army against their wills and were taken prisoner by Union forces at the Battle of Gettysburg. Newton arranged an interview with the president through Secretary of War Stanton. Thomas Evans, the spokesman for the delegation, explained the extenuating circumstances to Lincoln, ending his plea by assuring the president that Friends "sympathized deeply with his trying circumstances in his honest efforts to terminate the bloodshed and restore the Union." After a few moments of silence, Lincoln expressed his gratitude for the visit and then reaffirmed his genuine respect for the Society of Friends as well as his sympathy for the trail of principle and faith they were experiencing:

> I understand very well the positions of your Society and do not at all doubt your loyalty. You cannot fight for the government because your religious principles forbid it, but you can pray for

it. I am thankful in believing that I have your prayers, the prayers of your religious Society, and the prayers of the God-fearing people throughout the land, and that I shall continue to have them.

This, gentlemen is what we must rely upon. If the Almighty be with us, we shall succeed, if He is against us, no human power can save us; but I cannot believe that He will suffer the enemies of our country to triumph and the great Christian principles we are contending for, to fall to the ground and be trampled under foot. These principles are as dear to you as they are to us, though we differ as to the mode of supporting and asserting them.[51]

The outcome of this particular interview is not known, though Lincoln's words are telling. His understanding of and appreciation for Quaker faith and practice assured Friends of his genuine sympathy for the trials they were experiencing. They felt comfortable corresponding with and visiting him at the Executive Mansion when they felt led by the Light to do so. The latter occasions also presented the opportunity for Friends to worship with Lincoln and assure him of their ongoing sympathy as he struggled with the heavy burdens of the war. In turn, the president's willingness to entertain their requests enabled Friends to establish a spiritual kinship with him, one that eased their own trial of principle and faith created by the war. This mutual trust is indicted in the correspondence Lincoln maintained with Eliza Gurney, a Quaker minister.

After their initial interview in October 1862, the president asked Gurney to write to him, the request being made through Secretary of Agriculture Newton. Having been moved by the Quaker minister's preaching and sensing her genuine sympathy for his plight, Lincoln's request reflected a need for spiritual support during a most difficult period.

To his pleasant surprise, she complied. "Many times, since I was privileged to have an interview with thee, nearly a year ago, my mind has turned towards thee with feelings of sincere and Christian interest," wrote Gurney in an August 18, 1863, letter to the president. "I felt inclined to give thee assurance of my continued hearty sympathy in all thy heavy burdens and responsibilities." Although she communicated her concern about the recent conscription act and its impact on Quaker resistors, Gurney also made sure to express her gratitude for the *Emancipation Proclamation*. "The prayers of many thousands" were answered by "thy successful efforts 'to burst the bonds of wickedness, and let the oppressed go free,'" she wrote of

Lincoln's executive order to free the slaves. Such a "praiseworthy act" confirmed Gurney's belief that the "Almighty Ruler of the Universe did design [him] to be instrumental in accomplishing His blessed purposes."[52]

Lincoln was moved by the letter. That he did not respond until more than a year later reflects the extraordinary demands of the war. According to the president's secretary, John Hay, Lincoln "wrote very few letters [and] ... did not read one in fifty that he received." Instead, he handed "the whole thing over to me, and signed without reading those letters I wrote in his name."[53] Thus, Lincoln's September 4, 1864, reply to Gurney reinforces the special emphasis he placed on their relationship. He acknowledged the Quaker minister's concern that the recent conscription act did not make sufficient allowance for those who opposed war on religious principle and sympathized with the "very great trial Friends have had and are having ... [being] opposed to both war and oppression." But Lincoln also recognized that he had a constitutional obligation to enforce the laws made by Congress. If he granted exemptions to those who were simply seeking to escape military service, he would earn the contempt of both legislators and his own War Department. Despite his precarious position, the president assured Gurney that "for those appealing to me on conscientious grounds, I have done, and shall do, the best I could and can, in my own conscience, under my oath to the law." Before closing, Lincoln expressed his hope that she would "believe this [promise]" and thanked her for her "earnest prayers to our Father in Heaven."[54] Lincoln remained true to his word as he valued the spiritual kinship he had established with the Quaker minister. Legend holds that Gurney's letter was found in Lincoln's coat pocket after he was assassinated at Ford's Theater on April 14, 1865.[55]

At the other end of the spectrum were the so-called Fighting Quakers who voluntarily participated in the Civil War, some in a combatant status. Their motives ranged from antislavery conviction to patriotism and from a naïve spirit of adventure to following the lead of peers caught up in the drama of war. Levi Coffin of Cincinnati, Ohio, refused to fight but was among the minority of Friends who actively supported the Union war effort. Like his pacifist brethren, Coffin viewed the conflict as God's punishment of a slaveholding nation. But he also believed that God sometimes sanctioned physical force for a just cause.[56] For Coffin, who was known as the "president" of the Underground Railroad's western line, there was no more just cause than the abolition of slavery. In fact, he was unapologetic about his belief that the radical abolitionist John Brown, who attempted to instigate a violent slave insurrection in 1859, may have been "an instrument in the hands of the Almighty to commence the great work of deliverance of the oppressed."[57] In 1861, with the outbreak of war, Coffin opened his house to armed volunteers assembling for enlistment and subsequently cared for wounded federal soldiers, his home serving as a makeshift hospital.[58] Nor was Coffin alone in his active support of the Union cause.

Some Quakers enlisted in the Union army because of strong abolitionist sentiments, believing that the means of warfare justified the end of emancipation. Among them was Edward M. Davis, Lucretia Mott's son-in-law. Prior to the war Davis was a fervent abolitionist and strong supporter of the New England Non-Resistance Society and helped to spread its radical ideas at the risk of offending more conservative Friends. But he was among the very first Quakers to enlist. Commissioned a captain, Davis was posted to General John C. Fremont, who was conducting the war in the West and freeing slaves in the territories he won. This, of course, was against the Lincoln administration's policies, but it sat well with Davis, who had "a good understanding with [his] commanding officer on emancipation."[59] Boston Quakers Norwood and Edward Hallowell also enlisted because of their strong antislavery convictions. Their parents had operated an Underground Railroad station, and early on they learned of the evils of human bondage. Both brothers accepted commissions in the 54th Massachusetts, the first African American regiment in the U.S. military. Their older brother, Richard, raised money for the black regiment and seized every conceivable opportunity to charge the Society of Friends with hypocrisy for abandoning its antislavery heritage.[60] Norwood, who trained and commanded the black troops, observed that there was "nothing quite so magnificent and so reliable as the colored volunteer." He "adapts himself more readily to the discipline of a camp," and "acquires drills in much less time than the average white soldier." In battle, the "colored troops fought well," demonstrating "not only courage, but dignity, self-respect and self-control."[61] Norwood's brother, Edward, echoed those sentiments in his report on the 54th's July 18, 1863, assault on Fort Wagner, a Confederate stronghold in Charleston, South Carolina. Commanding the left wing of the attack, Edward and his troops charged up the parapet in a valiant effort to seize the fort.

Exposed to the direct fire of cannon and rifles, the company "succeeded in driving the enemy from most of their guns, many following the enemy into the fort." The battle raged for "about an hour" with the 54th "holding the front until relieved by the Tenth Connecticut at about two o'clock A.M. of the 19th."[62] Although the 54th failed to capture Fort Wagner, the engagement proved the mettle of black soldiers and opened the ranks of the Union army to more than 180,000 African Americans who would infuse a new spirit into the war-weary North.[63]

Davis and the Hallowell brothers were impassioned abolitionists who viewed the Union army as an instrument of liberation for black slaves. Not only did antislavery activism inspire their enlistments, but it justified their involvement in the war after Lincoln issued the *Emancipation Proclamation* in 1863. Most non-Quakers respected their decision to fight, though they could not fully appreciate the rationale for their decision. As a result, there were those non-Friends who noted the irony of a "Fighting Quaker." Sarah Palmer, a Philadelphian, for example, remarked that some of city's "Quakers are drilling, contrary to all the peace principles of the sect." "May we suppose their hopes to end slavery are based on war!"[64]

Other Fighting Quakers were motivated by patriotism. Neal Dow, a birthright Friend and Maine politician, served as an officer in the Union army.[65] James Parnell Jones, another New England Quaker who served as a major and was later killed in the war, wrote to family and friends that the outbreak of the war offered an opportunity "for the country to be thoroughly aroused and strike the final blow for the destruction of the confederacy."[66] Daniel Wooten, an Indiana Quaker, wrote to his girlfriend shortly after he enlisted, trying to explain his decision to fight. "We all know the Bible says *thou shalt not kill*," he conceded. "But what are we to do with those persons who rebel against the laws of our country, are we to just lie down and let them have the reins of this republican government? No! Never! So long as God gives us he power to quell them by any means."[67]

Although there is no accurate estimate of Friends who enlisted in the Union army, their numbers were sufficient enough to cause alarm within the Society of Friends. At the beginning of the war, both Indiana and Western yearly meetings witnessed the defection of several members from the Society's pacifist principles. Insisting on absolute adherence to the Peace Testimony, those yearly meetings directed their members "under no circumstance [to] give way to a martial spirit, which your conscience condemns."[68] The radical abolitionist William Lloyd Garrison, visiting Philadelphia in 1861, observed that at least one of nearly every Quaker household was enlisting, much to the concern of his Quaker friends who lived in the city.[69] By 1865, the Hicksite Baltimore Yearly Meeting was "lamenting that so many of our precious young members, and some of more mature age, have been led to join the ranks of the warrior."[70] Some meetings responded by disowning recalcitrant members. Arch Street Meeting purged from its rolls 11 young men for serving in the Union army.[71] In New England, 43 Quakers had enlisted by 1863, and 27 of them were eventually disowned.[72] It would be mistaken to assume, however, that disownment was the Society's automatic response to such violations. While there is also no accurate estimate of the number of Friends who were disowned for fighting, it is clear that most meetings labored with members who deviated from the Peace Testimony. They were sensitive to the dilemmas these young Friends faced either between pacifist and abolitionist convictions, or pacifism and the liberty of conscience that had been a cornerstone of Quaker migration to the United States. "It is quite wrong to require a Friend to be disowned for acting up to his highest conviction of duty," wrote the editor of the New York *Friend*. "Warfare is horrible in the flesh—but it is heaven-born innocence by the side of a war upon conscience."[73] Thus, some meetings believed that those members who enlisted did so because they were following the Inner Light as it appeared to them, and it would be wrong to penalize conscience by disowning them. Peter Brock found that urban Hicksite and rural Orthodox meetings tended to embrace this thinking and were least prone to disown Fighting Quakers.[74] Similarly, Earlham College, sensitive to the pressures confronting their students, did not bar the entry of those who fought for the Union while still adhering to its testimony against war.[75] By June 1862, Joseph Moore, the college president, noted that several Union veterans returned to campus, some "on account of poor health," while others "regretted their past course," and still others were "striving to justify themselves for taking up arms."[76]

Regardless of their decision to comply or not to comply with the Union war effort, every Quaker was confronted with a painful trial that pitted the historic Peace Testimony against freedom from human oppression and, in some cases, the intolerance of non-Quaker neighbors who failed to understand the genuineness of their pacifist convictions. While Lincoln understood and appreciated the Friends' trial, he struggled with one of his own, specifically how to reconcile the unprecedented carnage of war with his belief in a benevolent God.

Not until the autumn of 1863 did he find a resolution, and it was inspired by a battle that took place in a small rural town in central Pennsylvania.

III

At 10:00 a.m. on the morning of November 19, 1863, Lincoln arrived on the town square in Gettysburg, Pennsylvania. Invited by a local commission to make a "few appropriate remarks" at the dedication of a national cemetery for the Union dead, the president mounted a black steed and took his place behind a military escort of color guard, staff officers, and ranks of infantrymen in preparation for the three-quarter-of-a-mile procession to the cemetery.[77] Other federal and state dignitaries would follow.

Early morning rain showers had dissipated, and the sun shone bright and clear. Thousands of people lined Baltimore Street. Bands played. Cannon were fired. Local entrepreneurs set up their tables along the parade route to sell cookies, lemonade, and relics of the battle that had taken place nearby just three months earlier.[78]

As the procession approached the outskirts of town, the new cemetery came into view. Graves fanned out in a semi-circular configuration in the middle of the boot-shaped piece of land that would serve as a final resting place for the Union dead. Not all of the work had been completed, and rows of stacked wooden coffins remained.

A three-foot-high speaker's platform, surrounded by federal marshals wearing bright yellow sashes and Union soldiers who stood side by side with rifles at the shoulder, became the focal point of the ceremony.

Shortly after 11:30 a.m., Lincoln and the primary speaker, Edward Everett, an ordained minister, former president of Harvard College, and the nations' most prominent orator, ascended the stage accompanied by Pennsylvania Governor Andrew G. Curtin. Prayers were offered and letters read from dignitaries who could not attend the dedication, including one from General George Meade, a native Pennsylvania and commander of the Army of the Potomac who led the Union forces at the Battle of Gettysburg. Finally, Everett was introduced.

For the next two hours, the Unitarian minister enthralled the audience with skillful gestures, clear diction, and his familiarity with the details of the Union victory at Gettysburg. Although he had placed a thick manuscript of the speech before him, Everett delivered the oration from memory, fixing the battle in the larger contextof the Civil War. Criticizing the Confederate army for their atrocities, he absolved Meade for allowing his counterpart, rebel commander Robert E. Lee, to escape. Then, evoking the imagery of ancient Greece, Everett "bid farewell" to the Union dead comparing them with the "great martyr-heroes" of Athens.[79]

Lincoln listened patiently to Everett's long oration, noting the powerful cadence of the delivery, the firm tone of voice, and the skillfully punctuated gestures. Then he rose, his lanky 6'4" frame casting a shadow over the lectern. Reaching into the pocket of his black frock coat, the president removed a single sheet of paper, and began his own address:

"Four score and seven years ago, our fathers brought forth on this continent, a new nation, conceived in liberty, and dedicated to the proposition that all men are created equal."

The crowd became silent, seemingly mesmerized by the resplendent figure before them. A young boy, intent on being as close as possible to the president, was impressed by Lincoln's face. Its "deep lines, the wrinkled brow, and deep-set brooding eyes, burned an indelible image in his memory."[80] Lincoln, completing just his third year in office, had aged dramatically because of the constant demands and overwhelming burdens of the war. Although he was 54 years old, the president looked as if he was 10 years older.

"Now we are engaged in a great civil war," he continued, "testing whether that nation, or any nation so conceived and so dedicated, can long endure. We are met on a great battlefield of that war. We have come to dedicate a portion of that field, as a final resting place for those who here gave their lives that that nation might live. It is altogether fitting and proper that we should do this."

A spontaneous applause broke out, the crowd sensing that he had completed the formal dedication of the cemetery. When the ovation subsided, however, Lincoln continued his address:

> But in a larger sense, we cannot dedicate—we cannot consecrate—we cannot hallow—this ground. The brave men, living and dead, who struggled here, have consecrated it, far above our poor power to add or detract. The world will little note, nor long remember what we say here, but it can never forget what they did here. It is for us, the living, rather to be dedicated here to the unfinished work which they who fought here have thus far so nobly advanced.

Again, there was a courteous applause. Lincoln was surpassing all expectations. His words were polished, his delivery emphatic[81]—nothing like the colorful stump speeches that had marked his earlier political career and that some feared would resurface at this most solemn occasion.[82] Waiting for the crowd to quiet, Lincoln paused before concluding his address:

> It is rather for us to be here dedicated to the great task remaining before us, that from these honored dead we take increased devotion to that cause for which they gave the last full measure of devotion; that we here highly resolve that these dead shall not have died in vain; that this nation, under God, shall have a new birth of freedom, and that this government of the people, by the people, and for the people shall not perish from the earth.[83]

Having completed the formal dedication, Lincoln turned and moved toward his chair. The crowd stood motionless and silent. The brevity of the address had taken them by surprise. Finally, there came applause. Lincoln interpreted the audience's response as disapproval and confided to his bodyguard, Ward Lamon, that the "speech was a flat failure, and the people are disappointed."[84] While Republican newspapers such as *Harper's Weekly* called the address "as simple and felicitous and earnest a word as was ever spoken," the Democratic press was especially vitriolic.[85] Calling Lincoln's dedication "a perversion of history so flagrant that the most extended charity cannot regard it as otherwise," Wilbur F. Storey of the *Chicago Times* insisted that "it was to uphold the constitution and the Union created by it that our officers and soldiers gave their lives at Gettysburg." "How dare he, then, standing on their graves, misstate the cause for which they died and libel the statesmen who founded the government? They were men possessing too much self-respect to declare that Negroes were their equals, or were entitled to equal privilege."[86] Similarly, the *New York World* accused Lincoln of "gross ignorance or willful misstatement," reminding the president that "this United States was not the product of the Declaration of Independence" but the "result of the ratification of a compact known as the Constitution, which said nothing about equality."[87]

Although Lincoln's *Gettysburg Address* lasted only two minutes, it had a profound impact on the nation. The message was too powerful for the general public to grasp its significance immediately. There were no details of the battle, no names of soldiers or sites. Instead, the president's words were distinguished by abstractness. Only in the following weeks would Americans begin to comprehend the significance of the speech, as did Edward Everett, who later admitted in a letter to Lincoln that "I should be glad if I could flatter myself that I came as near to the central idea of the occasion, in two hours, as you did in two minutes."[88] Contemporary scholars regard the Gettysburg Address as one of the greatest speeches in American history because of its eloquence, brevity, and enduring impact.[89] In just 272 words, Lincoln reiterated the principles of human equality espoused by the founding fathers in the Declaration of Independence and redefined the Civil War as not only a struggle for the preservation of the Union but a "new birth of freedom" that would bring true equality to all of its citizens.

What tends to be forgotten is that the Gettysburg Address also served as Lincoln's explanation and justification of the war's carnage. Until now, he had struggled mightily to reconcile the unprecedented bloodshed with his belief in a benevolent God. He had lost two of his closest friends—Elmer Ellsworth and Edward Baker—during the first year of the war. Those were deeply painful personal losses that enabled him to empathize with others who had lost close friends and family. As the war continued, the casualty lists grew to appalling proportions, and Lincoln assumed greater and greater personal responsibility for all the carnage. To be sure, the burden was painfully overwhelming. An estimated 620,000 Americans died in the Civil War, either in battle or from disease. Union losses totaled approximately 360,222, and Confederate losses 258,000. And Gettysburg was the costliest battle of all with a total of 51,112 casualties on both sides.[90]

The Battle of Gettysburg, which took place between July 1 and 3, 1863, marked a turning point in the Civil War. Confederate General Robert E. Lee had recently rallied his troops to a decisive victory at Chancellorsville. But the need to gain supplies, the fading hope of European recognition, and the possibility of striking a final blow against the Union persuaded him to launch an invasion of the North. In early June, Lee began maneuvering his army for the assault. After a hard-earned victory at Winchester, Virginia, the Confederates advanced across Maryland and into central Pennsylvania. Frustrated by General Joseph Hooker's timidity in halting the invasion, Lincoln replaced him with General George G. Meade to lead the Army of the Potomac. Four days later, on July 1, Meade met Lee almost by accident at Gettysburg. During the next three days, more than

163,000 men waged a vicious and costly fight. Lee attacked repeatedly but failed to dislodge the Union troops from their position, which extended along a four-mile front. The climax of the battle came on the afternoon of July 3 when Confederate General George E. Pickett led a heroic but fruitless charge against the center of the Union lines, losing 7,000 of his 15,000 men.

Meade's victory ended the most threatening Confederate invasion of the North, giving the Union an undisputed victory. The psychological impact of the battle was great for both armies. If Lee had won, he might have been emboldened to launch another invasion, this time on Washington or Philadelphia. Such an attack would have rejuvenated the confederacy, possibly bringing foreign support. Instead, Gettysburg became the "high tide" of the Confederacy. Lee's army never fully recovered from the defeat. Of the 75,000 men who marched into battle, the Confederates lost 28,063, losses that not only inflicted a severe blow to southern morale but would also prove to be irreplaceable. On the other hand, the Union victory boosted Northern morale, proving that the federal army could defeat the Confederacy if it had effective military leadership. But the victory came at a severe cost. Of the 82,289 men who fought for the Union at Gettysburg, 23,049 lost their lives.[91]

Lincoln, who always believed he was president of all the American people, both North and South, accepted the responsibility for those deaths. He understood that he was sending young men into harm's way to achieve his wartime policies. The only way he could accept that reality was to embrace the notion that the will of God prevailed. Determined that "these dead shall not have died in vain," Lincoln, in his Gettysburg Address, gave a higher meaning to the war and immortalized the dead soldiers by making them agents of political change.[92] Appealing to the reverence Americans had for the Declaration of Independence, the president redefined the document for future generations by calling for a rededication to the principle "that all men are created equal" so that "this nation, under God, shall have a new birth of freedom." It was a masterful stroke of oratory, insisting that the American people must, in consistency with the principles of the Declaration, accept the emancipation of black slaves if the great sacrifice of "those who here gave their lives that that nation might live" was to be duly honored. Lincoln had long believed that the Declaration was a pledge "to all people of all colors everywhere" and that that pledge was a permanent ideal to be distinguished from the federal Constitution, which was a constantly evolving testimony to human equality.[93] He had earlier insisted that the Framers avoided the use of the words *slave* or *slavery* because the "plain, unmistakable spirit of their age was hostility to that principle and toleration only by necessity."[94] At Gettysburg, Lincoln implicitly gave notice of his refusal to tolerate the institution of slavery any longer, placing the Constitution above the moral conventions of society that had once condoned human bondage. No longer would he allow political expediency to overrule his own moral judgment or spiritual conviction in the evils of slavery.

By linking the sacrifice of the Union soldiers at Gettysburg to the principles of the Declaration of Independence, Lincoln gave new meaning to the proposition that "all men are created equal." Now that proposition included African Americans as well as whites. If there was any doubt remaining that the president had made his original war aim of preserving the union synonymous with the moral objective of emancipation, it was now gone. No longer was the conflict solely about preserving the Union but to do so by achieving the moral cause of emancipation and extending the cherished principle of equality to the black man. In his dedication, Lincoln hallowed the nation by employing biblical cadences and by including the phrase "under God," which was not included in any of the written drafts.[95] In so doing, he revealed his awareness that the ideal of human equality could not be achieved without divine guidance. It was almost as if Lincoln had become an Old Testament prophet, attempting to rally a Christian nation around the higher ideal that the United States would be, from that day forward, united and eternally free. What gave force and meaning to the speech, however, was Lincoln's contention that emancipation was the higher purpose for which the Union dead had sacrificed their lives.

Quakers had registered this same point with the president ever since the war began. Individually and collectively, Friends appealed to Lincoln's view of a divine role in human affairs, drawing an important distinction between human agency and God's will. Progressive Friends, for example, reminded him that the "immediate and universal emancipation" of the slaves was a manifestation of "Divine guidance," and the war's "frightful effusion of blood" a direct consequence of man's "sins for [practicing] the un-Christian and barbarous system of slavery." Thus, if the war was to hold any meaning whatsoever, Lincoln would have to "decree the entire abolition of slavery throughout the land" or risk "the fiery judgments to be poured out, until the work of national destruction is consummated beyond hope of recovery."[96]

So, too, did individual Friends implore the president to transcend the human fallibility that gave rise to the war in favor of God's will in emancipating the slaves. Quakers were not insensitive to the principles of the Declaration of Independence. In fact, the Declaration was grounded in the very same belief in the liberty of conscience that motivated William Penn to resettle the Society of Friends in the New World in the 1680s. But there was a significant difference between Lincoln and the Society of Friends in their respective interpretations of Emancipation. For Lincoln, the complete abolition of slavery was a *political* necessity if the American people were to complete the "unfinished work" of the Union soldiers who died in battle. It was the cause that the Union dead had "so nobly advanced" and the "great task remaining" before the nation if democracy were to remain a viable form of government well into the future. Although Lincoln had come to that realization through a spiritual transformation, the only hint of divine inspiration he offered in the Gettysburg Address was the phrase: "this nation under God shall have a new birth of freedom." For Quakers, on the other hand, divine will was the most important factor in advancing the cause of emancipation and the only sure way to do God's work on this earth. Still, both Lincoln and the Quakers viewed the bloody carnage of the war as undeniable evidence that there was a higher purpose at work and that the dead should be remembered for the sacrifice they had made, whether that be to God, to country, or to both.

Drew Gilpin Faust argues that the Civil War transformed popular notions of death as well as the way in which Americans honored the dead and sought to explain it. On one hand, the war "transformed the mid-nineteenth century's growing sense of religious doubt into a crisis of belief that propelled many Americans to redefine or even reject their faith in a benevolent and responsive deity." On the other hand, the war also intensified doubt about the "human ability to know and to understand" why death on such a massive scale was taking place. That profound sense of doubt compelled Americans to ask, "What is death?" "Why is death?" "What is life?" and "Can we ever hope to know?"[97]

Lincoln, who also entertained such profound doubts, provided the American people with answers to those questions at Gettysburg. By equating national purpose with the sacrifice made by Union soldiers who died in battle, he gave justification of the war's carnage. Emancipation, now the purpose of the war, would immortalize the Union dead, creating an enduring inspiration for the nation and its people.

President-elect Abraham Lincoln, 1860. (Photograph by Alexander Hesler—Library of Congress)

Levi Coffin, ca. 1850. Coffin, a Quaker Underground Railroad agent, established Indiana Yearly Meeting of Anti-Slavery Friends in 1842. (Photograph by Library of Congress)

Lucretia Mott, ca. 1875. Mott, an outspoken pacifist, considered the Civil War divine punishment for slavery. (Photograph by F. Gutekunst —Library of Congress)

Isaac J. Wistar, 1861. Wistar left Haverford College to enlist in the Union army. He proved to be an inspirational leader and by war's end was promoted to Brigadier general. (Quaker Collection, Haverford College, Haverford, PA)

The Lincoln Family, ca. 1861. (Left to right): Mary Todd Lincoln, Willie, Robert, Tad, and President Abraham Lincoln. (Engraving by J. C. Buttre after a painting by Francis B. Carpenter—Library of Congress)

Pennsylvania Progressive Friends Meeting, located at Longwood, Chester County, Pennsylvania, sent a delegation to meet with Lincoln in June 1862 and urge emancipation. Those identified by number are: (1) Oliver Johnson, (2) Charles G. Ames, (3) William Lloyd Garrison, (4) Chandler Darlington, (5) Hannah Cox, (6) Thamsin Meredith, (7) Mary Baily, (8) Thomas Garrett, and (9) Rachel Garrett. (Chester County Historical Society, West Chester, PA)

Thomas Garrett, ca. 1856. Garrett, a radical Quaker abolitionist, operated an Underground Railroad station in Wilmington, Delaware. He is credited with assisting more than 2,300 fugitives to freedom, including Harriet Tubman. (Chester County Historical Society, West Chester, PA)

Gen. George B. McClellan, 1862. Commander of the Army of the Potomac, McClellan frustrated Lincoln by his reluctance to launch an attack against the Confederate army. (Photograph by Matthew Brady—Library of Congress)

Secretary of State William Seward was the most radical abolitionist in Lincoln's cabinet. (Photograph by Matthew Brady—Library of Congress)

Frederick Douglass, ca. 1870. Douglass, a former slave who became the most famous black abolitionist in the nation, criticized Lincoln's plans for colonization. (Photograph by John W. Hurn—Library of Congress)

Eliza P. Gurney, 1865. Lincoln was so moved by the genuine sympathy of the Quaker minister at their October 26, 1862, interview, that he established an ongoing correspondence with her. (Engraving by F. Gutekunst, Quaker Collection, Haverford College, Haverford, PA)

Lincoln's Cabinet at signing of the Emancipation Proclamation, January 1, 1863. (Left to right): Edwin M. Stanton, secretary of war; Salmon P. Chase, secretary of the Treasury; President Lincoln; Gideon Welles, secretary of the navy; Caleb B. Smith, secretary of the interior; William H. Seward, secretary of state; Montgomery Blair, postmaster general; and Edward Bates, attorney general. (Engraving by J. C. Buttre after a painting by Francis B. Carpenter—Library of Congress)

Secretary of War Edwin M. Stanton, ca. 1863–1864. The son of a Quaker physician, Stanton understood the Friends' concern about the federal conscription law and offered to use any commutation fee paid by Quaker resistors for the relief of freedmen rather than for the war effort. (Photograph by Matthew Brady—Library of Congress)

President Abraham Lincoln, November 8, 1863, two weeks before the Gettysburg Address. (Photograph by Alexander Gardner—Library of Congress)

Cyrus Pringle, ca. 1872. Pringle, a Quaker pacifist, was conscripted into the Union army because of his refusal to pay a commutation fee or hire a substitute. Subject to severe discipline for his refusal to participate in military drills, he was eventually pardoned by Lincoln. (Jepson Herbaria, University of California at Berkeley)

Edward N. Hallowell, 1862, served with distinction as an officer in the 54th Massachusetts Colored Regiment. (Quaker Collection, Haverford College, Haverford, PA)

John Greenleaf Whittier, ca. 1877. The Quaker poet and New England antislavery newspaper editor urged Friends to support the Union war effort by aiding the sick, wounded, and orphaned. (Engraving by J. E. Baker—Library of Congress)

"Underground Railroad" by Charles T. Weber. The painting, completed in 1893, celebrates the heroic activities of Levi Coffin, who assisted more than 2,000 fugitives between 1826 and 1846. (Cincinnati Art Museum, OH. Used by permission of Bridgeman Art Library)

Anna Elizabeth Dickinson, ca. 1862. On January 16, 1864, Dickinson, a Philadelphia Quaker, became the first woman to address the U.S. Congress. On that occasion, she excoriated Lincoln for his lenient amnesty proclamation for those who supported the Confederacy. (Library of Congress)

John Bright, 1870. An English Quaker and parliamentary reformer, Bright was an admirer of Lincoln. He was instrumental in preventing British aid to the Confederacy during the American Civil War. (Library of Congress)

President Abraham Lincoln, April 10, 1865, four days before his assassination. (Photograph by Alexander Gardner—Library of Congress)

Isaac and Sarah Harvey, 1878. The Quaker couple from Clinton County, Ohio, allegedly inspired Lincoln to emancipate the slaves in September 1862. (Frontispiece image from Friends with Lincoln in the White House: adapted from Nellie Blessing-Eyster's story by Henry W. Wilbur (Philadelphia: [s.n.], 1913, 2nd edition). Courtesy of Watson Library, Wilmington College, Ohio)

CHAPTER 4
Redemption, 1864–1865

At the outbreak of the Civil War, John Greenleaf Whittier, a New England Quaker and antislavery newspaper editor, urged Friends to find other ways to support the Union cause if they found themselves in a situation where the peace testimony and antislavery witness conflicted. "Steadily and faithfully maintaining our testimony against war, we owe it to the cause of truth, to show that exalted heroism and generous self-sacrifice are not incompatible with our pacifist principles," he wrote in an open letter addressed "To Members of the Society of Friends," on June 18, 1861. "Our mission is, at this time, to mitigate the sufferings of our countrymen, to visit and aid the sick and the wounded, to relieve the necessities of the widow and the orphan, and to practice economy for the sake of charity."

Whittier, second only to William Lloyd Garrison as the nation's leading antislavery propagandist, hated war, but he was also strongly devoted to the Union. Although past the age for military conscription, he was still acutely aware of the dilemma younger Friends faced, his poetry often expressing anguish over tensions between doubt and faith. At the same time, Whittier believed that Quakers had benefitted historically from the liberty of conscience afforded by their relocation from England to North American in the seventeenth century. Thus, he reminded Friends that "our Society is rich, and of those to whom much is given much will be required in this hour of proving and trial."[1]

Caught in the growing chasm between religious faith and patriotic duty, many Friends followed Whittier's advice and returned to their strength as humanitarian reformers. By alleviating the misery of sick and wounded soldiers and their families and providing for the material relief and education of freedmen, Friends achieved not only a resolution to their own spiritual trial but also redemption in the larger society that had criticized them for refusing to fight.

Initially, Friends responded by contributing to the comfort of sick and wounded soldiers as well as to the welfare of Union widows and orphans. Some distributed food, bandages, sheets, or warm clothing that they had collected or made themselves. Others ministered to the spiritual needs of Union soldiers and among Confederate prisoners of war.[2] Levi Coffin and his wife, Catharine, opened their home in Cincinnati, once an Underground Railroad station, to regiments of volunteers from Indiana and other northwestern states en route to the South. "We had so many boarders our house was like a military post," wrote Coffin in his *Reminiscences*. "It was not long until our services were needed in caring for sick and wounded soldiers brought here from Southern battlefields. We nursed them carefully until they were able to travel to their homes, feeling that it was our duty to do so."[3] In Philadelphia, Lucretia Mott preached at Camp William Penn, a training center for U.S. colored troops, though she stressed her belief that the time would come when war would be no more.[4] Mott's granddaughter, Maria Hopper, along with her aunt, Abby Hopper Gibbons, volunteered as nurses at Union army hospitals.[5] In Indiana, Friends formed the Richmond Sanitary Commission in 1862 to provide Union hospitals with much needed supplies, including bandages and blankets. Quaker farmers contributed 92 cords of wood, more than 2,000 pounds of flour, 40 bushels of corn meal, and 6 bushels of potatoes during the winter of 1863, all for the widows and orphans of Union soldiers.[6] A Michigan Friend, Laura Haviland, visited hospital camps in Cairo, Illinois, and Memphis, Tennessee, to administer medical care as did Martha Schofield of Darby Meeting in Pennsylvania.[7] Such humanitarian work earned pacifist Friends the respect and admiration of the military as reflected by the statement of one army chaplain who, after observing Quaker efforts, noted: "I saw the difference between talking Christianity and acting it."[8] While such benevolence also eased relations between Friends and government authorities, including Lincoln himself, it did not resolve the tension Quakers experienced over the federal conscription law, specifically the hiring of a substitute or the payment of a $300 commutation fee to secure an exemption from fighting.

For two years individual Quakers as well as committees from various Meetings for Suffering lobbied Lincoln and his secretary of war,

Edwin M. Stanton, to exempt those who objected to fighting on religious grounds. Lincoln was more accommodating than Stanton, tending to parole those Quaker resisters who appealed directly to him for an exemption.[9] In addition, the president often vetoed his secretary of war's efforts to make Friends accountable to the draft law, forcing Stanton to grant exemptions to Quaker resisters on a case-by-case basis.[10] Some were uncompromising pacifists who refused not only to pay money or hire a substitute but also to perform work that would further the war effort. The latter category included alternative service as a physician, nurse, or orderly because those efforts aimed at putting soldiers back on the battlefront, enabling them to take the lives of others.[11] Stanton, widely regarded as an arrogant, stubborn man, showed remarkable patience with these Friends, probably because he was the son of a Quaker physician himself.[12] But he also used his understanding of Quaker faith and practice to refute their arguments, insisting that service in a Union hospital constituted a "work of mercy" and was "in accordance with the commands of Christ."[13] Other, less rigid Friends agreed with Stanton and were receptive to the idea of alternative service. Apparently matters came to a head in November 1863 when a committee of Baltimore Yearly Meeting for Sufferings met with the secretary of war "on behalf of two conscripted Friends who [were] under arrest" for refusing military service. Stanton explained the "embarrassment the [Quaker] position caused the government and the Society of Friends, as well as himself personally, in his efforts to grant [Quakers] exemption." He also proposed that exemption be granted to those Friends who "pay $300 which would go into a special fund for the freedmen." The delegation, headed by James Carey, agreed to take Stanton's proposal before a special committee of the various Meetings for Suffering at Baltimore for their consideration and to return the following month with a response.[14]

In December, after the so-called Baltimore Conference, Carey and his delegation returned to Washington to meet with Stanton and reported that the Meetings for Suffering rejected his proposal. "As followers of the Prince of Peace," Carey informed him, "we cannot directly or indirectly pay money or render other service in lieu of requisitions for military purposes," including the relief of the freedmen. At the same time, Carey assured Stanton that Friends "have long labored for the relief and freedom of the bondsmen . . . and will continue and increase our efforts, whether relieved of military service or not." "Friends," he concluded, "can discharge the duties of good citizenship in this way without infringing upon our principles of peace."

Stanton listened attentively and, when Carey had finished, expressed his appreciation for the Friends' "liberal efforts" on behalf of the freedmen. But he also emphasized that the Friends' refusal to accept his proposal placed him—and them—in a difficult position. "If your liberal service to the freedmen or your caring for the sick and wounded released you from military conscription, the same cause would release nearly everyone and no soldiers could be found," he countered. "All sects and denominations and people of every class have shown an extended liberality" to the freedmen as well as to the sick and wounded. "If Friends have done more than others, it is because they are better able to do it." While Stanton stated that he had "great respect for the conscientious scruples of Friends" and would be "very sorry to oppress them," he emphasized that he was "responsible for executing the laws; not for making them." Repeating his earlier proposal, the secretary of war said that he would "hold the plan open to the Society of Friends, or any individual Friend," promising that the $300 payment would "not go into the general war fund, but be used to aid the destitute and suffering contrabands." There would be no changing his mind. Afterward, the Baltimore Conference issued an advice to all Meetings for Sufferings to urge their members to "maintain a meek and quiet spirit, avoid unprofitable discussions on the exciting topic of the day, and be not hasty in determining in advance what course you will pursue." Instead, "wait in patience, in faith and filial love and your Heavenly father will show you what you shall do."[15]

Two months later, in February 1864, Congress, persuaded by Lincoln, passed an amendment to the Enrollment Act based largely on Stanton's proposal. According to the provision,

> [m]embers of religious denominations, who shall by oath or affirmation declare that they are conscientiously opposed to the bearing of arms, and who are prohibited from doing so by the rules and articles of faith and practice of said religious denominations, shall, when drafted into the military service, be considered noncombatants, and shall be assigned by the Secretary of War to duty in the hospitals, or to the care of freedmen, or shall pay the sum of three hundred dollars ... to be applied to the benefit of the sick and wounded soldiers.[16]

The amendment represented the first federal provision of noncombatant service for religious objectors. It was a generous concession to the peace churches and satisfied the requirements of the Mennonites and Dunkards by providing two further alternatives to fighting: work in a military hospital and care of freedmen. Although the amendment stopped short of what the Baltimore Conference desired, most Quaker conscientious objectors complied with the measure.[17] In addition, the amendment allowed Lincoln to fulfill a promise he had made to many of the Quakers who had written and visited him, not the least of whom was Eliza Gurney.

Having recognized and sympathized with the Friends' "great trial of principle and faith," Lincoln had earlier vowed to do "the best I can in my own conscience [and] under my oath to the law ... for those appealing to me on conscientious grounds."[18] The president's sacrifice did not go unnoticed by the Quaker minister, either. On September 8, Gurney responded with a letter thanking Lincoln for his "very kind consideration for the religious scruples of the Society of Friends which has been so invariably and generously manifested by the government." Speaking on behalf of her co-religionists, Gurney "ventured to say that Friends are not less loyal for the leniency with which their honest convictions have been treated" and expressed her belief that "there are few among us who would not lament to see any other than Abraham Lincoln fill the presidential chair."[19] But even Gurney did not appreciate the extent of the sacrifice Lincoln had made by urging Congress to pass such generous terms for conscientious objection.

Just 46,000 men were conscripted into the federal army during the Civil War, and another 118,000 furnished substitutes. Collectively, these 164,000 men along with several thousand from earlier militia drafts made up barely 8 percent of Union troops.[20] Thus, the draft had never been very successful, and by the spring of 1864, volunteering had virtually ceased. War weariness had taken hold in the North. Many soldiers had volunteered for three-year terms, which would expire in 1864. Despite congressional inducements of bounties and furloughs to those who would re-enlist, at least 100,000 decided not to. The bloody Battle of the Wilderness, fought in early May 1864, resulted in another 17,000 casualties, further discouraging re-enlistment.[21] By allowing Quakers and the members of other peace churches to be exempt from the draft by a commutation fee or alternative service, Lincoln weakened the manpower of the Union army. Viewed in this light, Friends, for better and worse, registered a profound impact on Lincoln's prosecution of the war.

II

Levi Coffin was not a very patient man. Like many Quaker reformers, he was committed to social justice and human equality, but he carried the commitment to extremes. An obsessive compulsion to rescue runaway slaves prior to the Civil War became a fierce campaign to aid freedmen during and after it. Truth be told, Coffin could not help himself. His personal moral crusade against slavery began during his childhood near New Garden, North Carolina. Frequently exposed to the peculiar institution as a boy, Coffin became an abolitionist at age seven when he asked a slave who was in a chain gang why he was bound. Told that the shackles were meant to prevent him from escaping and returning to his wife and children, the youngster became disturbed by the thought of his own father being taken from him in a similar fashion. By age 15, he was violating the federal fugitive slave law on a regular basis, helping his family harbor runaway slaves on their Guilford County farm. Suffering persecution by local slaveholders, the Coffin family was forced to relocate to Newport, Indiana, in 1826.[22]

Once in free territory, Coffin opened his home as a station on the Underground Railroad and excelled as a local merchant and farmer, accumulating enough wealth to invest in the Richmond branch of the Bank of Indiana. During the 1830s, he served as director of the bank. His wealth and influence in the community allowed him to provide most of the funding necessary to supply food, clothing, and transportation for the region's clandestine—and illegal—operation.[23] Known as the "president of the Underground Railroad," Coffin and his wife, Catharine, are believed to have assisted more than 2,000 fugitives between 1826 and 1846.[24] Perhaps the most famous was Eliza Harris, who escaped across the Ohio River on a winter night when it was frozen over. Barefooted and carrying her baby, she was exhausted and nearly dead when she reached Coffin's home. He provided her with food, clothing, new shoes, and shelter before helping her to continue on her journey to freedom in Canada. The abolitionist writer Harriet Beecher Stowe, who was well acquainted with the Coffins, may have used them as the inspiration for the Quaker couple in her powerfully influential book *Uncle Tom's Cabin*.[25]

At the urging of fellow abolitionists, Coffin moved to Cincinnati in 1847 to operate a warehouse selling only goods produced by free labor. He also opened his house as a station on the Underground Railroad and, along with his wife, helped to organize a large network of safe houses in southwestern Ohio. Their own home at 3131 Wehrman Street was large enough to rent out rooms for boarders. With many guests coming and going, the home was an excellent place to hide fugitives without arousing suspicion. Catharine created costumes, and when runaways arrived they would be dressed as butlers, cooks, and other workers. Some of the mulattoes were even able to pass as white guests.[26] It was still a risky operation replete with dangers. Unlike his circumstances in Newport, Indiana, Coffin did not enjoy the same wealth or influence in Cincinnati. Neighbors could not be trusted to keep his secret. Some would be more than willing to reveal his illegal activities in return for the financial reward they would receive from federal authorities. If caught, Coffin faced stiff fines and imprisonment, which would easily bankrupt him. Years later, when asked why he jeopardized his financial success as well as his own safety by aiding fugitive slaves, the Quaker stationmaster pointed to the righteousness of following God's unerring law instead of those more fallible ones of civil society. "If by doing my duty and endeavoring to fulfill the injunctions of the Bible, I injured my business, then let my business go," he explained. "As to my safety, my life was in the hands of my Divine Master, and I felt that I had his approval."[27]

By 1864, Coffin had turned his attention to the relief of freedmen. The abrupt transition from human bondage to freedom and personal responsibility was extremely difficult for enslaved blacks. Once the Union army entered the South, thousands of former slaves wandered through the region in need of food, clothing, and shelter. Some of the contrabands worked for the army as laborers or farmers until July 1862, when the Lincoln administration allowed them to enlist in the military. Others, most notably women, children, and the elderly, were forced to fend for themselves. Most had to beg or steal scraps of food to survive and to seek shelter in abandoned warehouses, cellars, or makeshift camps behind Union lines.

Coffin recognized the need and immediately began to investigate ways to assist these destitute contrabands. "I wrote many letters to my friends in Ohio and Indiana, and they began to collect bedding, clothing and money and forward them to me," he recalled in his *Reminiscences*. "We had no facilities to send them to the various camps of the freedmen, or for properly distributing them. It seemed necessary to have some regular and responsible organization here on the border, to receive and forward the supplies."[28] To that end, Coffin helped form the Western Freedman's Aid Society to offer assistance to the slaves freed during the war. He also traveled to Great Britain to seek aid for the relief of the freedmen.[29] Impressed by Coffin's efforts, Lincoln, in December 1863, invited him and the leaders of similar freedmen's associations to meet in Washington in order to discuss the establishment of a federal Freedmen's Bureau by Congress. After meeting with the delegation, Lincoln "promised to send a message to Congress" and to "do all he could to promote the passage of a bill" creating such an organization.[30]

After the Civil War ended, Coffin raised $87,750 for the Western Freedman's Aid Society to provide aid to the free blacks, though he considered his efforts demeaning as if he was "begging for money."[31] He was also concerned about giving money freely to all blacks, some of whom he believed would never be able to care for themselves unless adequate education and farms were provided to them. Instead, Coffin felt that the society should distribute its limited resources only to those freedmen best able to benefit from them.[32] Nevertheless, he continued his involvement with the society until it disbanded in 1870, the same year blacks were guaranteed the right to vote by the Fifteenth Amendment. In April of that year, Coffin, age 72, publicly relinquished the title of "president of the Underground Railroad" that had been conferred upon him by Southern slave catchers. When asked to speak at a huge interracial rally in Cincinnati, the elder Quaker stationmaster stepped to the podium and delivered a fitting epitaph to his long and storied antislavery crusade. "Our underground work is done," he declared, "and as we have no more use for the road, I would suggest that the rails be taken up and disposed of, and the proceeds appropriated for the education of the freed slaves."[33]

Levi Coffin was only one of many Quakers involved in the relief of former bondsmen. Freedmen's aid committees and sewing groups existed in most American meetings regardless of theological orientation. In Philadelphia, the Friends Freedmen's Association was organized in 1863 by some of the most prominent Orthodox families, including the Copes, Cadburys, Shipleys, and Scattergoods. The following year, Hicksite Quakers established the Friends Association for the Aid and Elevation of the Freedmen. Even Lucretia Mott, famous for understatement, could not contain her enthusiasm for the effort. "We are really beginning to do something," she gushed, "the Biddles, the Parrishes, Whartons, and such like [are] alive to the subject!"[34] Both organizations provided both financial and material aid to former slaves, most notably in Virginia.[35] Philadelphia's Hicksite Friends formed the Women's Aid Society in April 1862, which later worked with the National Freedmen's Relief Association, raising $349,000 for work in camps near Vicksburg and at Helena, Arkansas.[36] Although Orthodox and Hicksite Friends tended to work separately, they did occasionally cooperate in aid to the freedmen.[37] In 1865, when newly freed slaves began to arrive in Philadelphia in record numbers, the two groups worked with the Pennsylvania Abolition Society in funding an office to find jobs and homes for the refugees.[38] New England Friends established the Washington Mission for Freedmen and raised $4,264 in 1867.[39] In the Midwest, Quaker efforts were more impressive. Indiana Yearly Meeting (Orthodox) provided financial and material aid to freedmen in Mississippi and Louisiana and sent a Quaker couple, Elkanah and Irena Beard, to monitor the distribution of supplies among the refugees.[40] "We stood almost baffled by the inroads of disease and death in the crowded camps," they reported, noting that there were more than 30,000 refugees without food, shelter, or medical care in just three of the contraband camps they visited.[41] Western Yearly Meeting, which encompassed parts of Indiana, Illinois, and Iowa, established the most extensive plan to provide food, blankets, and shelter for freedmen who had relocated nearby. In 1864 alone, they provided for the relief of 576 families and 3,242 individuals.[42] That same year, Laura Haviland was made a paid agent of the Michigan Freedmen's Aid Commission and traveled in Mississippi and Louisiana establishing aid stations and medical care for freed slaves.[43] Ohio Yearly Meeting donated about $6,000 worth of clothing to the freedmen of Jackson, Mississippi, and later raised more than $16,000 for their relief.[44]

Like Coffin, however, Quaker abolitionists were especially concerned that the freedmen not become dependent on aid but rather assume responsibility for themselves. Friends believed that education offered the most effective means to ensure not only personal responsibility but also financial independence for the freedman.[45] Just as important, education, according to Yardley Warner—the Quaker founder of several freedmen's schools in the South—would lessen white prejudice against African Americans. "An increase in the intelligence of the blacks engages the confidence of the white population, and wins them over to the good work," he insisted.[46] To that end, Quakers became instrumental in establishing freedmen's schools throughout the South, sometimes with the federally sponsored Freedmen's Bureau.

One of the early efforts was located at Port Royal, near Beaufort, South Carolina, where Union troops occupying the sea islands off the coast found themselves responsible for large numbers of slaves left behind when their plantation owners departed. Philadelphia Quakers assisted federal efforts by establishing the Port Royal Relief Committee in 1862. The committee set about finding teachers for these former slaves, many of whom were Quakers.[47] The very first school for freedmen—the Penn School on St. Helena Island, South Carolina—was also established in 1862 and sponsored by Philadelphia Friends. The Penn School, named after William Penn, was an important outgrowth of the federal government's "Port Royal Experiment" on South Carolina's Sea Islands. Designed to demonstrate that the freedmen were capable of self-sufficiency, the experiment paired government funding with private philanthropy to insure its initial success. Although the Penn School was not a Quaker institution per se, money and supplies came at various times from the Friends Freedmen's Association and individual Quakers, and a majority of the trustees were Friends. Within three years, the school was sending teachers of African descent into the surrounding area to open schools of their own.[48] In 1864 alone, the Friends Freedmen's Association of Philadelphia provided for the education of 3,700 pupils and another 21,200 Sunday school students in Virginia.[49] New York Yearly Meeting began a similar project in 1862 that eventually built a system of industrial and elementary schools in the South as far as Tampa, Florida, while New England Friends concentrated their efforts in the Washington, D.C., area and Tennessee.[50] Ohio Yearly Meeting operated a school for freedmen in Jackson, Mississippi, under the care of Beulah Henderson, Hannah Binns, and Emma Jones.[51] Western Yearly Meeting employed three teachers in Clarksville, Indiana, in 1865. A year later they opened nine new schools for Freedmen in Columbia, Mississippi, before expanding their educational outreach to Macon, Mississippi.[52]

Individual Friends also founded and taught schools for freedmen. Emily Howland and Julia Wilbur of New York Yearly Meeting taught at the Miner Normal School for Colored Girls in Washington, D.C., from 1857 to 1859. After 1862, Howland relocated to Arlington, Virginia, where she taught freed slaves in refugee camps to read and write.[53] Cornelia Hancock, a New Jersey Quaker, went south to Charleston, South Carolina, where she started a small school for freedmen in an abandoned church. She remained there until 1876.[54] In 1864, Indiana Friends Calvin and Alida Clark moved to Helena, Arkansas, where they opened an orphanage and a school, which later became Southland College, for some 80 needy black children. Alida was the "moving spirit" of the enterprise who ran the school and raised the money to keep it afloat, while Calvin "ably and faithfully supported his wife."[55] Sarah Smiley, a New England Friend, started freedmen's schools in Virginia and raised funds to establish others along the East Coast.[56]

It is important to note that virtually all of these relief and educational efforts were initiated and led by Friends prior to the establishment of a federal agency for the same purpose. Lincoln, already impressed by Quaker humanitarianism, urged Congress to establish the government's own "Bureau of Refugees, Freedmen and Abandoned Lands" to further such efforts. Approved by Congress in March 1865, the so-called Freedmen's Bureau was charged with the mission to feed and care for the thousands of refugees living in the South, to build schools and hospitals, to relocate refugees under the 1862 Homestead Act, to monitor the production of crops and the distribution of food and medicine, to find work for the freedmen, and to supervise labor contracts between them and their employers. Initially approved for just one year, Congress reauthorized the bureau for a second year and its educational programs for a third.[57] Providing financial and material assistance to Quaker and other relief organizations, the Freedmen's Bureau helped to establish 4,239 schools serving 274,000 students between 1865 and 1871.[58]

The Society of Friends' work for the relief of the freedmen represented a watershed in the history of American Quakerism. Compassion for the suffering of African slaves and a fierce commitment to social justice had thrust Friends into the forefront of the abolition movement in the late seventeenth century where they remained for nearly two centuries. At times, their efforts were praised. On other occasions, when their Underground Railroad activities violated federal law, Friends were denounced by the general public and, when caught, prosecuted by state and federal authorities. Humanitarian aid to freedmen, however, allowed Friends to express their loyalty to the Union in a practical way and one in which they had traditionally excelled. Instead of challenging government, Quakers were cooperating with it to further the cause of human freedom. Their relief work for freedmen had allowed Friends to redeem themselves for whatever criticism they had suffered in placing their peace principles above patriotism.

III

Quaker relief efforts for the freedmen anticipated—if not helped to inspire—the vital work of Reconstruction that lay ahead for Lincoln and the nation. Those efforts represented the kind of compassion and disinterested benevolence that the president hoped would guide the long, arduous process of restoring the Union.

Convinced of the eventual success of the federal army, Lincoln, as early as December 8, 1863, announced a generous plan of reconciliation. Hoping to restore the rebel states as soon as possible, the president not only offered to grant amnesty to those rebels who declared their loyalty to the Union but also stated his willingness to recognize the reconstituted governments of former Confederate states that formally abolished slavery and where at least 10 percent of eligible voters took a loyalty oath.[59] Congress repudiated Lincoln's lenient 10 percent plan, demanding a slower and harsher readmission process. In the summer of 1864, they passed the Wade–Davis bill, calling for the president to appoint a provisional governor for each conquered state. When the majority of white males in each state swore allegiance to the Union, the governor could call a state constitutional convention whose delegates were elected by voters who had not fought for the Confederacy. The new state constitutions would be required to abolish slavery, disenfranchise Confederate civil and military leaders, and repudiate debts accumulated by state governments during the war. Only then would Congress readmit the states to the Union.[60] Lincoln vetoed the measure.

What plan he might have passed is not known, though his *second inaugural address*, delivered on March 4, 1865, urged generosity and goodwill. "With malice toward none and charity for all," Lincoln declared, "let us strive on to finish the work we are in; to bind up the nation's wounds; to care for him who shall have borne the battle, and for his widow, and his orphan—to do all which may achieve and cherish a just, and a lasting peace, among ourselves, and with all nations."[61] The speech, according to historian Ronald White, was a "blueprint for tolerance." Appealing to the high ideals of the American people, Lincoln hoped that his speech would "lay the groundwork for a reconstruction of compassion and reconciliation."[62]

Lincoln had impressed at least one Southern Friend, John B. Dutton, who had "not favored his elevation to the presidency four years ago." But Lincoln had "changed [his] opinion." Dutton now believed that the president was "the most suitable man for putting down the rebellion and establishing a nation of free men" and that emancipation would allow the United States to "rise to a pinnacle of greatness never attained by a nation since the creation of the world."[63] Then there was Philadelphia Quaker Lucretia Mott, who believed that Lincoln had not gone far enough. "How good the late *Inaugural* was, and how determined the colored people are to have their own right to vote," wrote Mott, referring to the final conciliatory paragraph of Lincoln's address.[64] Mott, never satisfied with the status quo, was a step ahead of Lincoln, interpreting his appeal to "strive on to finish the work we are in" as a desire to achieve black voting rights. That battle would have to wait. Only recently had the president secured congressional passage of a constitutional amendment abolishing slavery for all time. It had not been an easy task, either.

Lincoln had been a polarizing leader during his first four years in office. The Democratic opposition excoriated him as "King Abraham Africanus the First" for stretching his war powers to their constitutional limits. At the same time, the conservative wing of his own Republican Party ridiculed him as too liberal, while the liberal wing criticized him for not being liberal enough.[65] There were even some Quakers who excoriated the president. Perhaps the most famous was Anna Elizabeth Dickinson of Philadelphia, a strikingly attractive novelist and abolitionist who rose to fame as a much admired lecturer against slavery in 1860 at the age of 18. Shortly after Lincoln's first inaugural address in March 1861, Dickinson, a radical abolitionist who was put off by the president's assurance to the South that he would not interfere with the institution of slavery where it already existed, told a gathering of Boston abolitionists that he was "not so far from a slave catcher after all." In private, she was even more insulting, ridiculing Lincoln as "an Ass for the slave power to ride."[66]

Dickinson's youth, gender, diminutive size, and forceful delivery made her unique on the lecture circuit where she crusaded for a vindictive reconstruction policy and justice to the freed slave.[67] She became such a popular speaker that Republicans enlisted her to campaign in New Hampshire, Connecticut, and New York in 1863 and persuaded her to address Congress the following year.[68] Accordingly, on January 16, 1864, the small Quaker orator addressed federal legislators in the House of Representatives. While in the midst of a violent attack on Lincoln's lenient amnesty proclamation, the president and the First Lady entered the House chamber. "Let no man prate of compromise," she declared. "Defeated by ballots, the South appealed to the bullet. Let it stand by the appeal. There is no arm of compromise long enough to stretch over the sea of blood, and the mound of fallen heroes, to shake hands with their murderers." The audience applauded her sentiments as well as the courage she demonstrated in expressing them. Although Dickinson went on to advocate Lincoln's reelection in order "to complete the grand and glorious work left for a second term in office," her criticism clearly registered with the president, who "sat with his head bowed, rarely looking at Miss Dickinson."[69]

That spring, the radical abolitionist visited Lincoln at his request. When she began to urge a more vigorous enforcement of the *Emancipation Proclamation*, the president tried to divert her by telling a humorous story. According to her own account of the interview, Dickinson was annoyed by the diversion and snapped: "I didn't come here to listen to stories. I can read better ones in the newspapers than you can tell me!"

Lincoln relented. Instead he shared some letters indicating the progress of Reconstruction in Louisiana. But Dickinson remained unmoved. "These plans are all wrong," she allegedly said. "They are as bad as can be."

The president had heard enough. "If the radicals want me to lead, let them get out of the way and let me lead," he declared as he ushered the brash Quakeress out the door.[70]

It is highly doubtful that Anna Dickinson would have been this insulting toward Lincoln. Her recollection of the interview, published in Boston's *Daily Courier*, was probably designed to maintain her high standing among radical abolitionists who, generally, believed that Lincoln was moving too slowly on emancipation. An alternative account of the interview, provided by J. M. McKim, is perhaps more accurate. McKim was a mentor of Dickinson and one who maintained close ties to several legislators on Capitol Hill. One of his confidants was Congressman William D. Kelley of Pennsylvania, who supposedly attended the interview with the radical Quaker abolitionist and provided McKim with the following account: Dickinson "said but very few words," being "more a witness than a party." When she did voice an opinion, it was "foolish, according to her own acknowledgement" and she "burst into tears, begging the president to excuse her." Lincoln was extremely considerate and assuaged her feelings.[71] Regardless of the version, Dickinson remained opposed to the president and withdrew her endorsement for Lincoln's reelection later that year.[72]

To be sure, few predicted that Lincoln would win reelection in 1864. He was not the unanimous choice of the Republicans for the nomination since a mix of radicals, abolitionists, and disappointed office-seekers favored General John C. Fremont. They hoped to divide the Republican Party with a platform calling for a constitutional amendment ending slavery.[73] Only after several prominent Republican businessmen and professionals, including Quaker newspaper editor John G. Whittier, convinced Fremont to "stand aside for the greater number in the party" did he agree to withdraw his candidacy.[74] Even then, Lincoln's reelection was far from certain, in spite of the fact that he secured the dissenters' desired constitutional amendment in his party's platform. The president was running against his former commanding general, the highly popular George B. McClellan, who was nominated by the Democrats. Nor was the war going well, with Union forces unable to make any significant gains during the spring and summer of 1864.[75] It was during these dark days that artist F. B. Carpenter, a frequent guest at the Executive Mansion, noted, "Mr. Lincoln had the saddest face I ever painted." Carpenter added that on one occasion, he found the president "alone, pacing up and down a narrow passage, his head bent forward upon his breast, heavy black rings under his eyes revealing sleepless nights." Such a "careworn and troubled appearance," he added, "was enough to bring tears of sympathy into the eyes of his most violent enemies."[76]

Although Lincoln's bid for reelection was threatened by his detractors, he also enjoyed a solid base of supporters, including many Friends. In addition to Whittier, who discouraged Fremont's candidacy, Lincoln enjoyed the ongoing support of Quaker minister Eliza Gurney, who, by September 1864, was addressing her letters to him, "Esteemed Friend." Gurney spoke to the president's spiritual needs during this time, assuring him that "in thy time of trouble a gracious God who comforts all that mourn will continue to sustain and strengthen, uphold and comfort thee." Urging Lincoln to find solace in his Christian faith, the Quaker minister reminded him that the "believer in Jesus will have a holy calm, peace with God, a deep, still undercurrent of soul-satisfying happiness which even the rudest storms of time cannot fail to disturb." She repeated her firm belief that the president was chosen by God "to fulfill the important trust of achieving an unbroken Union where the oppressed are set free." Gurney concluded the letter by assuring the president that most Quakers felt that he was "conscientiously endeavoring to fulfill the solemn duties of his high and responsible office according to his own convictions of right" and that he would enjoy their support in the "next Presidential election."[77] Similarly, Lincoln, meeting with the female officers of the Philadelphia Sanitary Commission to thank them for their service, was consoled by a Quaker member. She could see the heavy toll the war had taken on him and, taking his hand in hers, she said, "Friend Abraham, thee need not think thee stands alone. We are all praying for thee. All our hearts, the hearts of all people, are behind thee and three cannot fail. The Lord has appointed thee and He will sustain thee. Take comfort, friend Abraham, God is with thee." Noticeably moved by her words, Lincoln admitted that it had been a "bad day," and that he had "almost forgotten that the hearts of all loyal people are with me." "If I didn't have that knowledge," he added, "and the knowledge that God is sustaining and will sustain me until my appointed work is done, I could not endure it. My heart would have broken long ago." Thanking the Quakeress for her kindness, he turned to the other women and said, "God bless you all."[78]

Support of other Friends came from political considerations. The English parliamentarian and Quaker John Bright had long admired Lincoln's efforts at restoring the Union and aided those efforts abroad whenever possible. As the election of 1864 neared, Bright wrote a letter to Horace Greeley, editor of the *New York Tribune*, endorsing a second term for Lincoln. Bright stated his "fervent hope that Mr. Lincoln may be placed at the head of your Executive for another term" due to his "grand simplicity of purpose, and a patriotism which knows no change, and which does not falter." Bright counted himself among those British subjects "who deplored the calamities which the [Confederate] leaders of secession have brought upon your country, who believe that slavery weakens your power and tarnishes your good name throughout the world, and who regard the restoration of your Union as a thing to be desired and prayed for by all good men." He was also aware that some Americans found fault with Lincoln but surmised that "it would be strange indeed, if, in the midst of difficulties so stupendous and so unexpected, any administration should wholly avoid mistakes." Bright concluded his endorsement with this perspective: "To us, looking on from this distance, and unmoved by the passions from which many of your people can hardly be expected to be free, regarding his Presidential path ... we see in it an honest endeavor faithfully to do the work of his great office, and, in the doing of it, a brightness of personal honor on which no adversary has yet been able to fix a stain."[79] In the United States, Lincoln enjoyed almost uniform backing from Midwestern Friends, who believed that a second term for the president represented the best chance for a constitutional amendment abolishing slavery as well as the restoration of the Union.[80] Although Lincoln did not enjoy as strong support among Friends in the East, he had, by 1864, won over some of his fiercest critics, like Lucretia Mott. Writing to her sister, Martha Coffin

Wright, Mott, who flattered herself a "watchful critic of the administration," begrudgingly admitted that Lincoln "has done well for the colored people" and that it was "doubtful if one could have been elected who would have done more."[81]

Lincoln's fortunes changed as the presidential campaign unfolded. McClellan, who supported a continuation of the war and restoration of the Union, was forced to repudiate the Democratic Party's platform, which called for an immediate cessation of hostilities and a negotiated settlement with the Confederacy. The act divided the Democrats and made McClellan's success at the polls remote at best.[82] Union military success in the autumn of 1864, highlighted by the fall of Atlanta, also boosted Northern support for Lincoln's prosecution of the war. Thus, the president won reelection easily with 212 electoral votes to McClellan's 21 and a popular vote margin of 403,000, or 55 percent[83] Armed with such a popular mandate, Lincoln was determined to complete the work of emancipation.

Although he had freed the slaves by executive order, it was done as a "wartime necessity" implemented by his ill-defined powers as commander-in-chief. Thus, the *Emancipation Proclamation* was a temporary measure that could easily be overturned by the courts after the war ended. "A question might be raised whether the proclamation was legally valid," Lincoln feared in early February 1865. "It might be added that it only aided those who came into our lines ... or that it would have no effect on the children of slaves born hereafter." The passage of a constitutional amendment abolishing slavery once and for all would be a "King's cure for all the evils."[84] If, on the other hand, the Civil War ended without a constitutional amendment ending slavery, the very purpose of the war would be undermined and the Union soldiers who sacrificed their lives would die in vain. The Senate had already passed such an amendment the previous spring, but there were not enough Republicans in the House to provide the two-thirds majority required for passage in that branch of Congress.[85] The main obstacle was the proslavery Democrats, who would eagerly embrace a peace settlement realizing that it would undermine the campaign for emancipation. If Lincoln could secure 20 votes from the opposition party before the war ended, he would finally abolish slavery for all time. To this end, he enlisted the support of James Ashley, an Ohio Republican and the House floor manager, who persuaded several Democrats to back the measure.[86] Lincoln also relied on Secretary of State William Seward to persuade reluctant representatives, many of whom were lame ducks, having been voted out of office in the previous year's congressional elections. To give Lincoln plausible deniability, Seward assembled a team of lobbyists to do the heavy arm-twisting and promises of patronage.[87]

On January 31, 1865, the U.S. House of Representatives narrowly reached the two-thirds majority needed to pass the bill by a vote of 119 to 56.[88] Afterward, the amendment was sent to the state legislatures, where the Northern states quickly ratified it. Although the formal adoption of the amendment would not come until December 6, 1865, Lincoln had redeemed himself in the eyes of African Americans and secured his place in history as the "Great Emancipator."[89]

IV

On the evening of Good Friday, April 14, 1865, President Lincoln and his wife attended Ford's Theater on Tenth Street in Washington, D.C., to see *Our American Cousin*, a popular farce about the visit of an awkward, boorish American to England, where he goes to claim the family estate from his aristocratic relatives. Lincoln was exceptionally happy. Five days earlier, Confederate General Robert E. Lee had surrendered his massive army at Appomattox Court House, Virginia, effectively ending the American Civil War. With the bloody carnage behind him, the president looked forward to the business of Reconstruction. It was a time for celebration.

At 10:15 p.m., John Wilkes Booth, a famous actor and Confederate sympathizer, quietly slipped into the presidential box intent on seeking revenge. Just three days earlier, Booth had attended a speech in which Lincoln voiced his support for enfranchising the former slaves. Furious at the thought of "nigger citizenship," the Maryland actor swore that it would be the president's "last speech" and that he would "put [Lincoln] through."[90] Booth went unnoticed, inching toward the president. Suddenly he fired his .44-caliber single-shot derringer into the back of Lincoln's head.

As the president slumped forward in his seat, mortally wounded, Booth leapt onto the stage. Although he broke his leg in the fall, the assassin still managed to escape out the back door of the theater. Lincoln was immediately examined by a doctor in the audience and then carried across the street to William Petersen's boardinghouse and into the first-floor bedroom. He never regained consciousness. The next morning, at 7:22 a.m., the president was pronounced dead. Upon learning of Lincoln's death, Secretary of War Edwin Stanton uttered the words, "Now he belongs to the ages."[91]

No American president had ever before been murdered. The tragedy triggered an outpouring of grief beyond anything the United States had ever witnessed. People turned out by the thousands to pay their last respects in every city where Lincoln's funeral train stopped en route from Washington, D.C., to Springfield, Illinois, where he was laid to rest. After the train arrived at Philadelphia on April 22, the president's coffin was placed inside the Assembly Room of Independence Hall, the same room in which the Declaration of Independence had been signed and in which Lincoln spoke four years earlier en route to Washington to take office. A public viewing began at 6:00 a.m. on Sunday, April 23, and lasted 20 hours, ending at 1:17 a.m. the following morning. An estimated 128,640 mourners filed past the open casket to offer their last respects to the martyred president.[92]

Between April 15, when news of the assassination reached Philadelphia, and April 23, when Lincoln's coffin arrived in the city for a public viewing, thousands of people mourned the martyred president. Public buildings were draped in mourning. Women pinned crepe bows to their dresses with Lincoln's image and the red, white, and blue colors of the American flag. Philadelphia's Quakers had been conducting their own memorial services since learning of Lincoln's death and continued to do so throughout the following week.[93] Friends were overwhelmed with emotion, some unable to perform their daily routines. Philadelphia Monthly Meeting (Hicksite) suspended its business and adopted a minute expressing their grief over the death of the "chief magistrate of our nation," who "manifested the most friendly feelings toward us as Society, always respecting, as far as lay in his power, our conscientious convictions."[94] Green Street Monthly Meeting's memorial was more poignant, reflecting the spiritual and emotional bonds Friends shared with Lincoln:

> The president's death has filled our hearts with great sorrow and appreciation of the many virtues in his character as well as the great loss sustained by the people of this nation, especially the freedmen, who truly looked up to him as a father. We hold in grateful remembrance the consideration with which he regarded our conscientious scruples in relation to military enactments, and believe he did for us in this respect, all that his position allowed. Yielding to the holy promptings of "Love to God and love to man," he was instrumental in measurably redeeming our country from the dark stain of slavery; saying to the Bondmen,

"be ye free." His integrity of purpose, Christian charity and acknowledgement of the Divine Spirit are forcibly expressed in his late Inaugural Address ... While we deplore the loss of so good and great a man, because he loved righteousness and hated inequity, we remember the source whence wisdom is derived and believe if we are sufficiently humbled to seek for it, in the confiding faith becoming a Christian People "our house shall not be left unto us desolate" but in the mercy and goodness of our all-wise Providence the future will be brighter than the past.[95]

Many of Philadelphia's monthly meetings—both Hicksite and Orthodox—adopted similar minutes expressing their high regard for the fallen president as well as their appreciation for his sympathy for their religious principles during the war and for his commitment to human freedom.[96]

At Haverford College (Orthodox), "neither professors or students felt like going on with the usual recitations." Samuel Gummere, the president, canceled classes and scheduled a memorial service for April 19. As students took their seats in Founders' Hall, "there was not a dry eye in the room." Former college president Thomas Chase began the service by reading "some appropriate passages from the Bible." He was followed by Professor William Wetherald, who urged students to "emulate the virtues of the departed, his modesty, his humility and his uprightness."[97]

Individual Friends also paid homage to the fallen president. On April 20, Martha Schofield, a Philadelphia Quaker school teacher, closed and shuttered her schoolhouse. Inside, she hung five flags draped in black outside along with two photographs of Lincoln. "Never do I want to forget this impressive time," she recorded in her journal, "and I want to impress the children with the weight of it." Schofield also wore a crepe bow on her dress commemorating the dead president for a total of 90 days. On the afternoon of April 23, when Lincoln's coffin arrived in the city, she watched the somber procession to Independence Hall. At 6:00 a.m. the next morning, Schofield and her sister stood in line outside for four hours waiting to pay their final respects to the martyred president as he lay in state inside the Hall. Later that day, she recorded in her journal that her visit was "not for show" as was the case with so many curiosity seekers who came to view the body, "but because Abraham Lincoln had grown into the hearts of the people." "His truth, integrity, honesty and great works winning for him a love that no other man living or dead ever before enjoyed," she added.[98] Quaker minister Rachel Wilson Moore memorialized Lincoln as "the right man in the right place at the right hour." In "letting the oppressed go free," she wrote in her journal, "the president ushered in a wonderful era in the history of the world. Sad indeed is the thought that his useful and valuable life was sacrificed to pay for his devotion to the cause of humanity."[99]

There were even those Quakers living in the South who were quick to voice their sorrow. Samuel Janney, a prominent Friends of Loudoun County, Virginia, observed that the members of his Goose Creek Monthly Meeting also "feel the sad bereavement which has brought deep and universal distress upon the people of the loyal states." Janney had reason to be especially saddened by the president's death. He had met with him on several occasions regarding a partnership between the federal Freedmen's Bureau and Quaker relief efforts in the war-torn South. "For myself," he wrote in an April 19 journal entry, "I can say that I felt for him an affection and reverence that I never felt for any other statesman, and having had some acquaintance with him, I mourn the loss of a personal friend." At the same time, Janney "dreaded the rigid [Reconstruction] measures [he] anticipated from [Lincoln's] successor, [Andrew Johnson]."[100] Nor was he alone in this concern.

Rebecca Williams, also a Quaker resident of Loudoun County, was filled with doubt about the nature of Reconstruction under another president. In an April 23 journal entry, she evokes the language of the Old Testament, writing that while "Lincoln, like Moses, led his countrymen through many trials," the nation must find "a Joshua to lead on until we can reach the consummation of peace and a restored union."[101] On the other hand, J. M. Walker, a Waterford, Virginia, Quaker, believed it possible that Providence played a role in Lincoln's passing and would also find the right person to lead the nation through Reconstruction. "Are the ways of Providence past finding out?" he wrote in an April 25 letter to Janney. "Can it be that Abraham Lincoln, having fulfilled his mission and duty so well ... is now removed in order that another man of different temperament may take the helm of state to conduct it through the difficult process of Reconstruction?"[102]

These memorials indicate the special bond Quakers felt with Abraham Lincoln. Their shared virtues, which included a firm respect for the liberty of conscience and human equality, allowed them to work together during the Civil War, respecting the problematic circumstances each other faced. Although Friends may have disagreed with Lincoln's prosecution of the fratricidal conflict, they could not help but respect his difficult position as president charged with defending of the federal constitution. As a result, they were most grateful for the consideration he gave them in matters regarding emancipation and conscientious objection. What's more, Lincoln's integrity of purpose, Christian charity, and acknowledgment of the divine spirit were at the core of Quaker faith and practice. These shared qualities not only allowed both parties to achieve a spiritual kinship with each other but also enabled them to weather the near-impossible challenges of the Civil War and overcome a similar trial of principle and faith.

Conclusion

Abraham Lincoln was a complex, private person. He may have prosecuted the Civil War in a seemingly arbitrary manner, but he was wracked by guilt over the terrible carnage he helped to create. What's more, Lincoln suffered the loss of a favored son and the erratic and often embarrassing behavior of a wife who was growing insane, while tolerating the haughtiness of a commanding general and the constant bickering of a divided cabinet. Still, he managed to preserve the Union and redefine the American experiment in democracy by abolishing slavery forever. Through it all he maintained a humility that was truly exceptional among wartime leaders, most of whom assume their cause is favored by God. Lincoln simply did not possess that kind of arrogance.

In April 1864, Lincoln was asked why he had been compelled to make such a dramatic shift in policy from preserving slavery in the areas where it already existed to complete emancipation. "I claim not to have controlled events, but confess plainly that events have controlled me," he explained. "Now, at the end of three years struggle, the nation's condition is not what either party or any man devised, or expected. God alone can claim it."[1] Lincoln repeated this belief a year later on March 4, 1865. "We cannot expect God to serve our purposes," he declared in his second inaugural address, "we serve His. Fondly do we hope that war passes, but if God wills it continues, God has His purposes."[2] These modest statements of human limitation grounded in a firm conviction in the doctrine of necessity are perhaps the clearest expressions of Lincoln's belief in God's role in shaping his actions on Earth. They also echo the same sentiments he expressed to the various Quaker groups and individuals he interviewed during the war and endeared the president to the Society of Friends.

While it is impossible to determine the exact degree of influence Quakers may have had on Lincoln's decision-making and wartime policies, their relationship was based on a mutual trust inspired by a common belief in the doctrine of necessity and the understanding that human beings are instruments of the divine will. Lincoln and the Quakers supported each other throughout the Civil War in seeking a resolution to a similar trial of principle and faith, specifically how to achieve emancipation while ending the bloody carnage of war. Friends met with the president and wrote to him constantly, offering their prayers, urging emancipation, and assisting with the education and relief of freed slaves. This Quaker influence played an important role in the president's evolving spirituality as well as his wartime policies.

Lincoln's thinking on emancipation changed over the course of his presidency, and those changes coincided with his correspondence and interviews with Quaker groups and individual Friends. When Lincoln took office in April 1861, he was morally opposed to slavery but respected his constitutional obligation to protect the institution in the states where it already existed. Within the next year, however, he initiated a voluntary program of gradual, compensated emancipation in Delaware, believing that the other border states would follow its example.[3] As a result, Confederate leaders would recognize the futility of their cause, putting an end to war and eventually paving the way for emancipation in the South. That Lincoln chose Delaware for this plan is no coincidence. The state was home to a considerable Quaker population with a strong antislavery tradition and an active Underground Railroad network that assisted an increasing stream of fugitive slaves after the passage of the federal Fugitive Slave Act in 1850.[4]

When the plan for gradual compensated emancipation followed by colonization in Africa or the Caribbean was rejected by the border states, Lincoln planned to end slavery in Confederate-controlled areas by executive order.[5] His thinking was encouraged on June 20, 1862, when he was visited by a delegation of progressive Friends, including Thomas Garrett, Oliver Johnson, William Barnard, Eliza Agnew, Dina Mendenhall, and Alice Hambleton. The delegation urged Lincoln to pursue a policy of "immediate and universal emancipation."[6] Although the request was more radical than the subsequent *Emancipation Proclamation*, issued on September 22, 1862, it did anticipate Lincoln's ultimate goal for a constitutional amendment forever banning slavery in the United States and the assimilation of the freedmen into American society. Between September 22, when the preliminary *Emancipation Proclamation* was issued, and April 14, when the president was assassinated, Quakers continued to press Lincoln for that goal, insisting that it was in accordance with God's will. Among the most persuasive abolitionists were Quaker ministers Elizabeth Comstock, Rachel Grellett, and Eliza Gurney, all of whom appealed to Lincoln's firm belief in the doctrine of necessity. Comstock and Grellett, who visited Lincoln in December 1862, urged him to surrender his soul to God's will. "May it not be that God has raised thee up, like Moses, to be the great emancipator of His people?" they asked. "To establish the nation united and free?"[7] Gurney was apparently more persuasive.

In her October 1862 visit, Gurney, quoting from 1 Peter 4:12, evoked the "fiery trail" experienced by the early Christians who were facing persecution for their faith. She compared Lincoln's circumstances to "God's chosen people," recognizing the "trials and persecutions" he would have to confront because of his recent decision to emancipate the slaves. Gurney urged the president to "commit his way unto the Lord by prayer" whenever those trials emerged. If he did so, she believed that "the peace of God" would "keep the president in heart and mind." She then knelt and offered a prayer "that light and wisdom might be shed down from on high, to guide our President," bringing Lincoln to tears.[8] He was so moved, he wrote to her admitting that both the Quakers and himself were "indeed going through a great trial—a fiery trial." He also shared his belief that God "for some wise purpose of His own, allows the war to continue" and that he might be an "instrument in the hands of our Heavenly father."[9] Lincoln's letter to Gurney represents the most complete expression of his belief in the doctrine of necessity to that point in time, a theme that began with the "Meditation on the Divine Will" a month earlier and reached its fullest expression in his second inaugural address of March 4, 1865.

Similarly, Friends pressed Lincoln to establish a conscription policy that would acknowledge conscientious objection based on religious principles. Having been approached by many Quakers on this subject since the outbreak of war in April 1861, Lincoln, despite his precarious position, pardoned those Friends who "appeal[ed] to [him] on conscientious grounds," and did so "the best [he] could, in [his] own conscience, under [his] oath to the law."[10] To that end, Congress, persuaded by Lincoln, in February 1864, passed an amendment to the Enrollment Act allowing "[m]embers of religious denominations, who ... are conscientiously opposed to the bearing of arms" to be considered "non-combatants, and assigned ... to duty in hospitals, or to the care of freedmen, or to pay three hundred dollars ... to be applied to the benefit of the sick and wounded soldiers."[11]

Finally, Quakers influenced Lincoln's thinking on Reconstruction by providing material aid and education to freedmen. Lincoln, impressed by Quaker humanitarianism, urged Congress in spring 1865 to establish the government's own Freedmen's Bureau to further such efforts. Approved by Congress in March 1865, the federal agency provided material aid, education, and relocation for the thousands of refugees living in the South. It also provided financial and material assistance to Quaker relief organizations in establishing schools for freedmen.[12]

Lincoln's association and cooperation with Quakers became so common during the war that many Friends felt as if they enjoyed a special relationship with the president, so special that they addressed him as "friend." When he was assassinated, Quakers felt as if they had lost one of their own. Not before or since Lincoln's administration has the Religious Society of Friends been as devoted to a U.S. president, this in spite of the fact that two of his successors were Quakers.[13]

With the passage of time, Lincoln's relationship with the Quakers assumed mythological proportions. One story involves the influence of a Quaker couple—Isaac and Sarah Harvey of Clinton County, Ohio—on Lincoln's decision to emancipate the slaves. The Harveys felt themselves "called" to pay a visit to the president in the late summer of 1862. They arrived in Washington, D.C., on September 18, just as news of the Union victory at Antietam reached the capitol. The two Friends happened to meet Salmon Chase, a fellow Ohioan and the secretary of the treasury, who arranged an interview for them with the president and escorted them to the Executive Mansion the following day. The Harveys told Lincoln that he could end slavery as well as the Civil War if the federal government agreed to pay $300 per slave to every slaveholder. After hearing the idea, the president allegedly informed them of his similar plan for compensated emancipation and then wrote a brief note to the Harvey's monthly meeting certifying that the couple had fulfilled their mission:

> I take pleasure in asserting that I have had profitable intercourse with friend Isaac Harvey and his good wife, Sarah Harvey. May the Lord comfort them as they have sustained me.
> Abraham Lincoln
> September 19, 1862

Conclusion 123

Three days later, Lincoln, in a sudden shift of policy, issued the preliminary draft of the *Emancipation Proclamation*.

The story first appeared in *Harper's New Monthly Magazine* in September 1870. Titled "A Day among the Quakers," the essay was authored by Nellie Blessing-Eyster, who had interviewed Isaac and Sarah Harvey two years earlier.[14] The essay was republished, in revised form, in New York's *New Voice* in 1889 under the title "Mr. Lincoln and the Crazy Quaker."[15] Afterward, the story gradually worked its way into the history books. In 1912, Henry W. Wilbur adapted the story in his work *Friends with Lincoln in the White House*.[16] Twenty-seven years later, Carl Sandburg repeated the account in his seminal book on Lincoln, titled *The War Years*, giving it credibility among historians.[17]

Not until 1952 was the accuracy of the Harvey visit challenged by Quaker historian Henry J. Cadbury, who noted the absence of any primary source documentation of it. According to Cadbury, Lincoln's alleged written acknowledgment of the meeting with Isaac and Sarah Harvey, penned on September 19, 1862, has never been found. In addition, Roy Basler, editor of the Lincoln papers, cited just three documents from the president's collection that identify the Quaker couple: (1) a letter of introduction from Governor Richard Yates of Illinois, dated September 3, 1861; (2) a letter of introduction from Governor Oliver P. Morton of Indiana, dated September 23, 1861; and (3) a letter to Lincoln from Isaac Harvey himself, dated July 25, 1864, asking the president "when it would be convenient to receive a short call from my wife and self in a little matter of business." Harvey also writes, "I will be prepared to present a letter of introduction from Governor Brough [of Ohio], endorsed by Governor [Andrew] Curtin [of Pennsylvania]." Although Isaac Harvey appears to have had some influential contacts among the war governors, Cadbury concludes that any claim of an 1862 visit as well as any claim about his influence over Lincoln's decision to free the slaves is fictitious.[18] But Cadbury's conclusion is too severe for this writer.

The existence in the *Lincoln Papers* of three letters of introduction suggests that Isaac Harvey took the time to plan his visit with the president, not that it was a spontaneous event as suggested by Blessing-Eyster's account. While there may be some question as to the actual date of the interview, it does appear that the Harveys and Lincoln met sometime between 1861 and 1864. It is possible that Blessing-Eyster embellished the story by placing the Harvey's visit in September 1862, a few days before Lincoln issued the first draft of the *Emancipation Proclamation*, in order to suggest a connection between the two events. What is important is that the visit actually took place, reinforcing the unique relationship the Quakers enjoyed with Lincoln. Descendants of the Harvey family have made painstaking efforts to ensure the credibility of such a visit.[19] As a result, Wilmington College, a Quaker institution in Clinton County, Ohio, felt strongly enough about the accuracy of the event that it raised $84,000 to cast and erect life-sized bronze statues of Isaac and Sarah Harvey on its campus. Dedicated on September 20, 2009, the statues, titled "Who Sends Thee?," depict the local Quaker couple on their way to Washington, D.C., to speak with President Lincoln about emancipation. While the actual date of the Harvey's interview with Lincoln is debatable, the couple's intentions are not and, like the statues, reflect the Quaker testimonies of peace, integrity, and equality, which are among the core values of Wilmington College.[20]

Another story involves Quaker minister Eliza P. Gurney's August 18, 1863, letter to Lincoln, which was allegedly found in the president's coat pocket after he was assassinated on April 14, 1865. To be sure, Lincoln valued Gurney's friendship and expressed his great appreciation for her spiritual support and prayers in a subsequent September 4, 1864, letter to her.[21] But there is no indication that Gurney's letter was among his personal belongings on the night he was killed. Instead, the legend was fabricated by the Quaker minister's friends, probably to enhance her stature and influence after her death in 1881. Joseph Bevan Braithwaite, the biographer of Eliza's husband, Joseph John Gurney, was the first to make the claim in an obituary published the following year. On that occasion, Braithwaite wrote, "E. P. Gurney had the mournful satisfaction of learning that her letter to the president written nearly two years before, had been carefully treasured by him and was in his pocket when [John Wilkes Booth's] fatal shot reached him."[22] Richard F. Mott, a Burlington, New Jersey, neighbor, repeated the story in almost identical wording in his edited work *Memoirs and Correspondence of Eliza P. Gurney*, which was published in 1884.[23] From there, the legend proliferated being exaggerated each time it appeared in print. In 1895, for example, Augustus J. C. Hare, another Gurney biographer, included Eliza's photograph, writing, "A letter to President Lincoln from Mrs. J. J. Gurney, an intimate friend, was found in his pocket, with her photograph, after his death."[24] Fifteen years later, Amelia Mott Gummere, the daughter of Richard F. Mott, suggested that Lincoln had always kept the letter in his possession after receiving it. "Eliza Gurney's letter was discovered in President Lincoln's breast pocket," she wrote, "where, much worn and read, it had been constantly carried even to the moment when the fatal shot was fired."[25]

However, Lincoln scholar F. Lauriston Bullard found no trace of Gurney's letter among the contents of Lincoln's pockets after they were donated by the president's granddaughter, Mary Lincoln Isham, to the Library of Congress in the 1940s. The contents had been placed in a box that had been in the possession of Robert Lincoln, the president's eldest son, since the death of his father. While Bullard admitted that the absence of Gurney's letter was "not conclusive" since "all that was in Lincoln's pockets may not have been kept with the box," it did cast doubt over the accuracy of the story.[26]

At the same time, it is important to note that the absence of Gurney's letter in Lincoln's coat pocket does not eliminate the fact that the president and the Quaker minister had interacted. That Lincoln initiated a two-year correspondence with the Quakeress suggests that he felt a degree of intimacy with her that was exceptional and one that, if made public, would be embarrassing for a married man. Thus, if, in fact, Lincoln was carrying Gurney's August 18, 1863, letter in his coat pocket on the night of his assassination, his son Robert may have quietly removed it in order to spare his mother and the family any humiliation.

These stories make an important statement about historical memory and how Quakers viewed their relationship with Abraham Lincoln. There is no doubt that Lincoln valued his association with Eliza P. Gurney, for it provided him with a spiritual and perhaps emotional solace that he enjoyed with few, if any, family, friends, or cabinet members. On the other hand, the president's association with Isaac and Sarah Harvey was fleeting but still reflects the special relationship Friends believed they enjoyed with Lincoln.

These accounts of Lincoln and the Quakers, regardless of their authenticity, remind us that the presidency, if occupied by one who genuinely seeks to serve the interests and needs of the American people, is not so much an office as a trust. Just as important, Lincoln and the Quakers remind us that it is possible for individuals as well as religious groups to work together with those they elect to public office to further the ideals upon which our nation was founded. For Quakers, those ideals include the liberty of conscience and the freedom of all human beings. That Lincoln, our nation's greatest president, struggled with the same spiritual trial in securing those ideals endeared him to the Society of Friends, one of the country's most respected humanitarian and religious groups.

Notes

INTRODUCTION

1. Eliza P. Gurney, *Memoir and Correspondence of Eliza P. Gurney*, edited by Richard F. Mott (Philadelphia: J. B. Lippincott, 1884), 309–312. The original memoir of Lincoln's interview with the Quaker delegation is in the collections of the Historical Society of Pennsylvania, Philadelphia.

2. Gurney, *Memoir and Correspondence of Gurney*, 312–313.

3. John M. Whitall quoted in Gurney, *Memoir and Correspondence of Gurney*, 309.

4. Letter, Abraham Lincoln to Eliza P. Gurney, Washington, DC, October 26, 1862, quoted in *The Collected Works of Abraham Lincoln*, edited by Roy P. Basler (hereafter, *CW*), 8 vols (New Brunswick, NJ: Rutgers University Press, 1953–1955), Vol. 5, 478.

5. See Thomas D. Hamm, *The Transformation of American Quakerism: Orthodox Friends, 1800–1907* (Bloomington: Indiana University Press, 1988), 21, 49.

6. Gurney replied to Lincoln on August 8, 1863, at the request of a fellow Quaker, Agriculture Commissioner Isaac Newton. Newton served as a back channel between Lincoln and the Quakers throughout the Civil War. [See Letter, Eliza P. Gurney to President Abraham Lincoln, "Earlham Cottage," Atlantic City, NJ, August 8, 1863, *Memoir and Correspondence of Gurney*, 315–316]. For other accounts of Lincoln's relationship and correspondence with Eliza Gurney, see: F. Lauriston Bullard, "Lincoln and the Quaker Woman," *Lincoln Herald*, Vol. 46, No. 2 (June 1944): 9–12; D. Elton Trueblood, "The Widow's Might," *Christian Herald* (July 1965): 24–27; and Max L. Carter, "Elizabeth Kirkbride Gurney's Correspondence with Abraham Lincoln: The Quaker Dilemma," *Pennsylvania Magazine of History and Biography*, Vol. 133, No. 4 (October 2009): 389–396.

7. Letter, Gurney to Lincoln, August 8, 1863.

8. Letter, Abraham Lincoln to Eliza P. Gurney, Washington, DC, September 4, 1864, *CW*, Vol. 7: 535–536.

9. Thomas E. Drake, *Quakers and Slavery in America* (Gloucester, MA: Peter Smith, 1950), 6–15, 196–197.

10. Sydney V. James, *A People Among Peoples: Quaker Benevolence in Eighteenth-Century America* (Cambridge, MA: Harvard University Press, 1963), 291–299, 316–334; Jack D. Marietta, *The Reformation of American Quakerism, 1748–1783* (Philadelphia: University of Pennsylvania Press, 1984), 272–279; Margaret H. Bacon, *The Quiet Rebels: The Story of Quakers in America* (New York: Basic Books, 1969), 94–121; and Drake, *Quakers and Slavery in America*, 167–175.

11. For primary source accounts that detail Quaker involvement on the Underground Railroad, see: Pennsylvania Yearly Meeting of Progressive Friends, *Proceedings, 1853–1862* (New York: Oliver Johnson, 1862); William Still, *The Underground Railroad* (1872. Reprinted by Johnson Publishing Co., Chicago, 1970); Levi Coffin, *Reminiscences of Levi Coffin: The Reputed President of the Underground Railroad* (Cincinnati, OH: Robert Clarke, 1876). For secondary source material, see: Charles L. Blockson, *The Underground Railroad in Pennsylvania* (Jacksonville, NC: Flame International, 1981); Larry Gara, *The Liberty Line: The Legend of the Underground Railroad* (Lexington: University of Kentucky Press, 1961); William C. Kashatus, *Just over the Line: Chester County [Pennsylvania] and the Underground Railroad* (University Park, PA: Penn State Press, 2002); James A. McGowan, *Station Master on the Underground Railroad: The Life and Letters of Thomas Garrett* (Jefferson, NC: McFarland, 2005); Wilbur H. Siebert, *The Underground Railroad from Slavery to Freedom* (1898. Reprinted by Arno Press, New York, 1968); and R. C. Smedley, *History of the Underground Railroad in Chester and the Neighboring Counties* (Lancaster, PA: Lancaster Journal, 1883).

12. See Peter Brock, *The Quaker Peace Testimony, 1660 to 1914* (York, England: William Sessions, Ltd., 1990); H. Larry Ingle, *First Among Friends: George Fox & the Creation of Quakerism* (New York: Oxford University Press, 1994), 191–196; and Hugh Barbour, *The Quakers in Puritan England* (New Haven, CT: Yale University, 1964), 196, 202–207, 221.

13. Rufus M. Jones, *The Later Periods of Quakerism* (London: Macmillan & Co., 1921), 728–729, 737–738; Bacon, *Quiet Rebels*, 116–117; Charles C. Moskos and John Whiteclay Chambers, editors, *The New Conscientious Objection: From Sacred to Secular Resistance* (New York: Oxford University Press, 1993), 30–31; Edwin B. Bronner, "A Time of Change: Philadelphia Yearly Meeting, 1861–1914," in John M. Moore, editor, *Friends in the Delaware Valley: Philadelphia Yearly Meeting, 1681–1981* (Haverford, PA: Friends Historical Association, 1981), 112–114; and Christopher Densmore and Thomas Bassett, "Quakers, Slavery and the Civil War," in Hugh Barbour, et al., *Quaker Crosscurrents: Three Hundred Years of Friends in the New York Yearly Meetings* (Syracuse: Syracuse University Press, 1995), 191–192.

14. Donna McDaniel and Vanessa Julye, *Fit for Freedom, Not for Friendship: Quakers, African Americans, and the Myth of Racial Justice* (Philadelphia: Quaker Press, 2000), 150–156; Linda Selleck, *Gentle Invaders: Quaker Women Educators and Racial Issues During the Civil War and Reconstruction* (Richmond, IN: Friends United Press, 1995); Henrietta S. Jaquette, "Friends' Association of Philadelphia for the Aid and Elevation of the Freedmen," *The Bulletin of the Friends Historical Association*, Vol. 46, No. 2 (Autumn 1957): 68–73; Thomas H. Smith, "Ohio Quakers and the Mississippi Freedmen: 'A Field to Labor,' " *Ohio History*, Vol. 78, No. 3 (Summer 1969): 160–167; and Susan T. Hatcher, "North Carolina Quakers: The Freedmen's Friends," *Southern Friend* (Spring 1981): 32–38.

15. For Lincoln's reference to his Quaker ancestry, see *The Chester County Times* (West Chester, PA, February 11, 1860). For Lincoln's Quaker genealogy, see Waldo Lincoln, *History of the Lincoln Family* (1923); M. D. Learned, *Abraham Lincoln: An American Migration* (1909); Ida Tarbell, *In the Footsteps of the Lincolns* (1924); David S. Keiser, "Quaker Ancestors for Lincoln," *Lincoln Herald*, Vol. 63 (1961): 134–137; and Henry J. Cadbury, "The Hunt for Lincoln's Quaker Ancestors," *Friends Journal* (February 1, 1966): 12. Each of these accounts identifies Mordecai Lincoln, the great-great-grandfather of the president, as having settled in Exeter Township, Berks County, Pennsylvania, in 1733. Mordecai's sons, Abraham and John, married into the Quaker religion. Abraham (born 1736) married Ann Boone, a Quaker, in 1760. John (born 1716) married Rebecca Flower, a third-generation Quaker.

16. Lincoln's "Quaker" traits are identified in Joseph E. Suppinger, "The Intimate Lincoln," *Lincoln Herald*, Vol. 85, No. 3 (Fall 1983): 161.

17. Allen C. Guelzo, *Abraham Lincoln: Redeemer President* (Grand Rapids, MI: Wm. B. Eerdmans Publishing Company, 1999), 151. During the 1860 presidential campaign, Lincoln's political supporters, in order to avoid controversy, found it useful to describe him as "a regular attender" and "liberal supporter of the Presbyterian Church in Springfield." In fact, Mary Lincoln was a regular attender and pewholder in that church. As president, Lincoln often did attend the New York Avenue Presbyterian Church but was not a member. [See Mark A. Noll, "The Ambiguous Religion of Abraham Lincoln," in *A History of Christianity in the United States and Canada* (Grand Rapids, MI: William B. Eerdmans, 1992), 51–52].

18. William Herndon, *Herndon's Lincoln: The True Story of a Great Life* (2 vols, New York, 1917), Vol. 2, 156. Herndon claimed that he never heard Lincoln "utter an expression which remotely implied the slightest faith in Jesus as the Son of God and the Savior of men." Similarly, Ward Hill Lamon, Lincoln's bodyguard and a gruff man with lowbrow humor, cast doubt on the strength of the president's religiosity. Lamon, who loaned his name to a biography of Lincoln written by his daughter, recalls the president imitating a camp revival preacher and joking with him while visiting Antietam after the bloody Union victory. See Lamon, *Recollections of Abraham Lincoln:*

1847–1865, edited by Dorothy Lamon Teillard (Lincoln: University of Nebraska Press, 1994), 151, 156.

19. William Barton, *The Soul of Abraham Lincoln* (1920. Reprinted by University of Illinois Press, Urbana, 2005), 260–291; Nathaniel Stephenson, *An Autobiography of Lincoln* (New York: Blue Ribbon Books, 1926), 264; J. G. Randall, *Lincoln the President: Last Full Measure* (New York: Dodd, Mead and Co., 1955), 375–377; William J. Wolf, *The Almost Chosen People: A Study of the Religion of Abraham Lincoln* (Garden City, NY: Doubleday & Co., 1959), 117; G. Frederick Owen, *Abraham Lincoln: The Man and His Faith* (Carol Stream, IL: Tyndale House Press, 1976); Douglas L. Wilson, *Honor's Voice: The Transformation of Abraham Lincoln* (New York: Vintage, 1999), 76–85, 186–187, 309–312; William Lee Miller, *Lincoln's Virtues: An Ethical Biography* (New York: Vintage, 2003), 83–90; Michael Burkhimer, *Lincoln's Christianity* (Yardley, PA: Westholme Publishers, 2007), 154–155; Richard Carwardine, *Lincoln: A Life of Purpose and Power* (New York: Alfred A. Knopf, 2006), 191–248; and Eric Foner, *The Fiery Trial: Abraham Lincoln and American Slavery* (New York: W.W. Norton, 2010), 35–37.

20. Guelzo, *Redeemer President*; Harold Holzer, *Lincoln President-Elect: Abraham Lincoln and the Great Secession Winter 1860–1861* (New York: Simon & Schuster, 2008); and Stephen Mansfield, *Lincoln's Battle with God: A President's Struggle with Faith and What It Meant for America* (Dallas, TX: Thomas Nelson, 2012). Guelzo, in particular, argues that Lincoln's thinking on "Providence and free will was much more reflective of his Calvinist background, rather than any Quaker influence." What is more, he insists that it is "very hard to penetrate the complications in Lincoln's thinking." Most historians want him to be "linear and consistent, when he was really only curious and opportunistic." To that end, the "real difficulty lies in identifying any influences—including Quaker—on Lincoln, since he was peculiarly resistant to being in anyone's debt, much less asking anyone's opinion." (See author's interview of Allen Guelzo, Gettysburg, PA, December 14, 2012.)

21. Several scholars identify Lincoln's acceptance of the doctrine of necessity, including: Barton, *Soul of Lincoln*, 292–302; Guelzo, *Redeemer President*, 102–142; Carwardine, *Life of Purpose and Power*, xii; and David Herbert Donald, *Lincoln* (New York: Simon & Schuster, 1996 paperback), 514.

22. D. Elton Trueblood, *Abraham Lincoln: Theologian of American Anguish* (New York: Harper & Row, 1973).

23. Daniel Bassuk, *Abraham Lincoln and the Quakers* (Wallingford, PA: Pendle Hill Publications, 1987).

24. See Otto E. Neuburger, "Quaker Documents in the Lincoln Collection," *Friends Intelligencer*, Vol. 105, No. 33 (August 14, 1948): 467. The 18,350 papers cover the period 1824 to 1865 and were published by Roy P. Basler between 1953 and 1955. See Basler, *Collected Works of Lincoln*. There does not appear to be any written correspondence between Lincoln and the Quakers prior to his election to the presidency in 1860.

25. Some of the primary sources appeared in an exhibit curated by Christopher Densmore at the Friends Historical Library of Swarthmore College, Swarthmore, Pennsylvania. Titled "Lincoln and the Quakers," the exhibit opened on January 6, 2009, in celebration of the 200th anniversary of Lincoln's birth. It can still be viewed online at http://www.swarthmore.edu/library/exhibitions/lincoln/.

CHAPTER 1: ANTISLAVERY KINSHIP, 1861

1. Bradley R. Hoch, *The Lincoln Trail in Pennsylvania: A History and Guide* (University Park, PA: Penn State Press, 2001), 4. Lincoln had seen Independence Hall in 1848 when he attended the Whig National Convention in Philadelphia. That year there had been a Whig political rally in Independence Square to ratify the nominations of Zachary Taylor as presidential candidate and Millard Fillmore as the vice-presidential candidate, but this was Lincoln's first opportunity to go inside the building.

2. In all 11 states seceded from the Union. Four of these (Virginia, Arkansas, North Carolina, and Tennessee) did not secede until after the Battle of Fort Sumter, which occurred on April 12, 1861. Five additional states were Border Slave States that did not secede from the Union: Missouri, Kentucky, West Virginia, Maryland, and Delaware. [See James M. McPherson, *Ordeal by Fire: The Civil War and Reconstruction* (New York: McGraw-Hill, 2001, third edition), 139–165.]

3. Abraham Lincoln (hereafter "AL") "Speech at New Haven, CT," March 6, 1860, *CW*, Vol. 4: 16; and AL, "First Inaugural Address," March 4, 1861, *CW*, Vol. 2: 215.

4. McPherson, *Ordeal by Fire*, 136–138.

5. AL, "Speech in Independence Hall, Philadelphia, PA," February 22, 1861, *CW*, Vol. 4: 240–241.

6. Donald, *Lincoln*, 277–279; Norma B. Cuthbert, ed., *Lincoln and the Baltimore Plot, 1861* (San Marino, CA: Huntington Library, 1949); and Daniel Stashower, *The Hour of Peril: The Secret Plot to Murder Lincoln before the Civil War* (New York: Macmillan, 2013). The assassination plot was hatched by Cypriano Ferrandini, a Baltimore barber who, along with other pro-secessionist allies, intended to kill Lincoln when he transferred trains from the city's Calvert Street Station to the Camden Street Station. Although Lincoln refused to alter his original plans to visit Independence Hall and to address the Pennsylvania state legislature on February 22, 1861, he did agree, after returning to Philadelphia from Harrisburg, to travel to Washington, incognito. Thus, Lincoln boarded an 11:00 p.m. train to Baltimore, passing unrecognized through that city at about 3:30 a.m. and arriving unannounced at Washington two and a half hours later.

7. Foner, *Fiery Trial*, 70–71. Lincoln repeatedly used the *Declaration of Independence* to defend his antislavery convictions beginning in a January 27, 1838, address he delivered before the Young Men's Lyceum of Springfield, Illinois. Other speeches in which he referenced the Declaration to defend his antislavery beliefs include: "Eulogy of Henry Clay," delivered at Springfield, Illinois on July 6, 1852; "Speech on Kansas-Nebraska Act," delivered at Peoria Illinois on October 16, 1854; and the "House Divided Speech," delivered at Springfield, Illinois, on July 16, 1858. Each time he was highly selective in the reference, preferring to ignore the fact that the founding fathers' antislavery beliefs were ambiguous at best as they did little, as a group, to extend freedom to African Americans.

8. Letter, AL to Joshua Speed, Springfield, IL, August 24, 1855, *CW*, Vol. 2: 320.

9. AL, *CW*, Vol. 1: 74–75.

10. Foner, *Fiery Trial*, 8–9, 52–60.

11. Michael Burlingame, *The Inner World of Abraham Lincoln* (Chicago: University of Illinois Press, 1994), 21.

12. AL, "Speech on Kansas-Nebraska Act," Peoria, Illinois, October 16, 1854, *CW*, Vol. 2, 247–281.

13. Foner, *Fiery Trial*, 68–84.

14. Frances Daniel Pastorius, "Germantown Protest, 1688," quoted in Drake, *Quakers and Slavery*, 12. Original manuscript is in the Records of Philadelphia Yearly Meeting (Orthodox), Vol. N24, at the Quaker Collection, Haverford College Library, Haverford, PA.

15. Roberts Vaux, *Memoirs of the Lives of Benjamin Lay and Ralph Sandiford* (Philadelphia, Solomon W. Conrad, 1815), 17, 25–28.

16. John Woolman, "Some Considerations on the Keeping of Negroes" (1754) in *The Journal and Major Essays of John Woolman*, edited by Philip Moulton (New York: Oxford, 1971), 198–209.

17. Jack Marietta, *The Reformation of American Quakerism, 1748–1783* (Philadelphia: University of Pennsylvania Press, 1984), 46–72, 150–168.

18. Philadelphia Yearly Meeting (hereafter, "PYM"), *Minutes*, 1754. Quaker Collection, Haverford College, Haverford, PA.

19. PYM, *Minutes*, 1758.

20. Jean R. Soderlund, *Quakers and Slavery: A Divided Spirit* (Princeton, NJ: Princeton University, 1985), 98–100.

21. See Arthur J. Mekeel, *The Quakers and the American Revolution* (York, UK: William Sessions, 1996), 232–310. Mekeel points out that the persecution of Quakers by the new American government and the Continental army was widespread and included Quakers throughout the 13 colonies. The most severe case was the forcible exile of a group of Philadelphia Quakers to Winchester, Virginia, in 1777, on the suspicion of loyalty to the British Crown.

22. Marietta, *Reformation of American Quakerism*, 267–279; Richard Bauman, *For the Reputation of Truth: Politics, Religion, and Conflict Among the*

Pennsylvania Quakers, 1750–1800 (Baltimore: Johns Hopkins Press, 1971), 227–229; and Sydney V. James, *A People Among Peoples: Quaker Benevolence in Eighteenth-Century America* (Cambridge, MA: Harvard University, 1963), 268–285.

23. Drake, *Quakers and Slavery*, 80–84. Philadelphia Yearly Meeting was the first to disown slaveholding members in 1776, followed shortly thereafter by New York Yearly Meeting. Within the next eight years, all the yearly meetings in North America adopted the discipline in the following order: Baltimore Yearly Meeting (1778); North Carolina Yearly Meeting (1781); New England Yearly Meeting (1782); and Virginia Yearly Meeting (1784).

24. Henry J. Cadbury, "Negro Membership in the Society of Friends," *Journal of Negro History*, 21 (1936), 151–213. Cadbury examines the late 18th and early 19th century Monthly and Quarterly Meeting records of PYM's constituent meetings, which reveal a conspicuous absence of African American members. Cadbury concludes that black membership was discouraged among Friends because of a fear of assimilation and/or miscegenation. More recently, Ryan P. Jordan identified the existence of segregated seating within many Quaker meetinghouses after 1776. He claims that the so-called "Negro pews" were located "toward the back of the meetinghouse" and indicated that "large numbers within the Society of Friends were unable to imagine African Americans as equals within their spiritual fellowship." When a more radical minority of Quaker abolitionists began to raise arguments over ending the segregated seating in the early 1840s, the Society of Friends ignored their pleas choosing to "frame efforts at racial equality as a dangerous and public politicization of the Quakers' private anti-slavery testimony." [See Jordan, *Slavery and the Meetinghouse: The Quakers and the Abolitionist Dilemma, 1820–1865* (Bloomington: Indiana University Press, 2007), 67, 72.] Similarly, Donna McDaniel and Vanessa Julye identify a pattern of racism among Friends that began in the seventeenth century and persists to the present day. [See McDaniel and Julye, *Fit for Freedom, Not for Friendship: Quakers, African Americans, and the Myth of Racial Justice* (Philadelphia: Quaker Press, 2000).]

25. Hugh Barbour & J. William Frost, *The Quakers* (Westport, CT: Greenwood Press, 1988), 173.

26. Philadelphia Yearly Meeting of Ministers and Elders, *Minutes*, 1806; Philadelphia Yearly Meeting, *Minutes*, 1806. Microfilm copy. Quaker Collection, Haverford College.

27. Robert W. Doherty, *The Hicksite Separation: A Sociological Analysis of Religious Schism in Early Nineteenth Century America* (New Brunswick, NJ: Rutgers University, 1967); and H. Larry Ingle, *Quakers in Conflict: The Hicksite Reformation* (Knoxville: University of Tennessee, 1986).

28. Barbour & Frost, *Quakers*, 194.

29. Walter Edgerton, *A History of the Separation in Indiana Yearly Meeting* (Cincinnati, OH: Western Tract Society, 1856), 37–39; David S. Heidler

and Jeanne T. Heidler, *Henry Clay: The Essential American* (New York: Random House, 2010), 373–374; and Drake, *Quakers and Slavery*, 164–165.

30. Thomas D. Hamm, *The Transformation of American Quakerism: Orthodox Friends, 1800–1907* (Bloomington: Indiana University Press, 1988), 32–33.

31. Levi Coffin, *Reminiscences of Levi Coffin* (Cincinnati, 1876; Reprinted by Aro Press and The New York Times, 1968), 230–233, 246.

32. Edgerton, *Separation of Indiana Yearly Meeting*, 171–175; and Hugh Barbour and J. William Frost, *The Quakers* (Westport, CT: Greenwood Press, 1988), 197.

33. Hamm, *Transformation of American Quakerism*, 32–35.

34. Drake, *Quakers and Slavery*, 134; Hamm, *The Transformation of American Quakerism*, 61; and Barbour & Frost, *Quakers*, 192.

35. Barbour & Frost, *Quakers*, 192.

36. James, *A People Among Peoples*, 291–299, 316–334; Marietta, *Reformation of American Quakerism*, 272–279; Drake, *Quakers & Slavery*, 167–185; R. C. Smedley, *History of the Underground Railroad in Chester and the Neighboring Counties of Pennsylvania* (Lancaster, PA: Lancaster Journal, 1883. Reprinted by Stackpole Books, Mechanicsburg, PA, 2005 paperback); and Margaret H. Bacon, *The Quiet Rebels: The Story of Quakers in America* (New York: Basic Books, 1969), 94–121.

37. Drake, *Quakers and Slavery*, 166; Ryan P. Jordan, *Slavery and the Meetinghouse: The Quakers and the Abolitionist Dilemma, 1820–1865* (Bloomington, IN: 2007), 6–10; William C. Kashatus, *Just Over the Line: Chester County and the Underground Railroad* (West Chester, PA: Chester County Historical Society, 2002), 35–67.

38. AL, "Reply to Governor Andrew J. Curtin at Harrisburg, Pennsylvania," February 22, 1861, *CW*, Vol. 4: 243–244.

39. AL, "Address to the Pennsylvania General Assembly at Harrisburg," February 22, 1861, *CW*, Vol. 4: 244–246.

40. John G. Whittier, "The Quakers Are Out," in *Life and Letters of John G. Whittier* (2 vols., London: Sampson Low, Marston & Company, 1895), Vol. II, 431–432. Whittier, a New England Quaker abolitionist, published the campaign song in October 1860 in a leaflet titled "A Voice from John G. Whittier." The words reflect his anxiety over the outcome of the Pennsylvania election:

> Not vainly we waited and counted the hours,
> The buds of our hope have all burst into flowers.
> No room for misgiving—no loop-hole of doubt,
> We've heard from the Keystone! The Quakers are out!

> The plot has exploded—we've found out the trick;
> The bribe goes a-bogging; the fusion won't stick.
> When the wide-awake lanterns are shining about.
> The rogues stay at home, and the true men are out!

> The good state has broken the cords for her spun;
> Her oil springs and water won't fuse into one;
> The Dutchman has seasoned with freedom his krout,
> And slow, late, but certain, the Quakers are out!
>
> Give the flags to the winds! Set the hills all aflame!
> Make way for the man with the Patriarch's name!
> Away with misgiving—away with all doubt,
> For Lincoln goes in when the Quakers are out!?

41. Hamm, *Transformation of American Quakerism*, 61–62; and Drake, *Quakers & Slavery*, 194–195.

42. Barbour & Frost, *Quakers*, 162–163; and Rufus Jones, *Later Periods of Quakerism* (London: Macmillan, 1921), Vol. I, 406–408. Quaker ministers from Philadelphia, London, and New England who traveled to the South encouraged the migration of Friends to the Old Northwest Territory where there was no slavery.

43. For statistics on decline of Southern Quakerism, see: William Medlin, *Quaker Families of South Carolina and Georgia* (Columbus, SC: Ben Franklin Press, 1982), 33; Stephen Weeks, *Southern Quakers and Slavery* (Baltimore: Johns Hopkins Press, 1896), 271–272.

44. Louis T. Jones, *The Quakers of Iowa* (Iowa City, 1914), 145, 183, 192.

45. Eric Foner, *Free Soil, Free Labor, Free Men: The Ideology of the Republican Party before the Civil War* (New York: Oxford University Press, 1995, revised edition).

46. Barbour & Frost, *Quakers*, 196.

47. AL, "Speech at Cincinnati, Ohio, September 17, 1859," *CW*, Vol. 3: 459–463; and *Collected Works' First Supplement, 1832–1865*, edited by Roy F. Basler (New Brunswick, NJ: Rutgers University, 1974), 43.

48. Foner, *Fiery Trial*, 116.

49. *The New York Times*, March 4, 1861.

50. AL quoted in Trueblood, *Theologian of Anguish*, 248.

51. Jean H. Baker, *James Buchanan* (New York: Times Books, 2004), 140.

52. *New York Herald*, March 4, 5, 1861; *New York Times*, March 5, 6, 1861; and Julia Taft Bayne, *Tad Lincoln's Father* (Lincoln: University of Nebraska, 1931, 2001 reprint), 6–10.

53. AL, "First Inaugural Address: March 4, 1861," *CW*, Vol. 4: 267–268.

54. AL, "First Inaugural Address: March 4, 1861," *CW*, Vol. 4: 271.

55. Letter, Elizabeth Newport to Abraham Lincoln, Philadelphia, PA: March 1, 1861. Friends Historical Library, Swarthmore College, Swarthmore, PA.

56. Martha Schofield, *Journal*, November 6, 1860, quoted in Katherine Smedley, *Martha Schofield and the Re-education of the South, 1839–1916* (Lewiston, NY: Edwin Mellen, 1987), 44.

57. *The Friend* (Philadelphia), Vol. 34, No. 27, March 9, 1861.

58. Letter, Lucretia Mott to Martha Coffin Wright and Eliza Wright Osborne, "Roadside," [Cheltenham, Pennsylvania], March 19, 1861 quoted in *Selected Letters of Lucretia Coffin Mott*, edited by Beverly W. Palmer (Chicago: University of Illinois Press, 2002), 308.

59. Carol Faulkner, *Lucretia Mott's Heresy: Abolition and Women's Rights in Nineteenth Century America* (Philadelphia: University of Pennsylvania, 2011), 177.

60. Margaretta Walton, *Journal, 1860–1861*. Margaretta Walton Papers, Friends Historical Library, Swarthmore College.

61. Harold M. Hyman, "War Powers in Nineteenth-Century America: Abraham Lincoln and His Heirs," in *This Constitution: Our Enduring Legacy* (Washington, DC: Congressional Quarterly Inc., 1986), 249–260; and Mark E. Neely, Jr., *The Fate of Liberty: Abraham Lincoln and Civil Liberties* (New York: Oxford University Press, 1992).

62. Philadelphia Yearly Meeting for Sufferings (Orthodox), "Epistle" quoted in *The Friend*, April 27, 1861.

63. "Advice," Minutes of New England Yearly Meeting (Orthodox) (Providence, R.I.), 1861.

64. "An Address," Minutes of the Representative Meetings of Western Yearly Meeting Held at Plainfield, Indiana, 5 mo.- 2-1861. Transcription in William H. S. Wood Collection, 1860–1887. Quaker Collection, Haverford College, Haverford, PA.

65. "Epistle of Counsel and Caution," Indiana Yearly Meeting for Sufferings, May 30, 1861.

66. "Epistle," Indiana Yearly Meeting (Orthodox) Minutes, 1860–1869, August 1, 1862. Quaker Archives. Earlham College, Richmond, IN.

67. Philip C. Garrett, editor, *A History of Haverford College* (Philadelphia: Porter & Coates, 1892), 325; and Norwood P. Hallowell, *Reminiscences* (Privately published manuscript, West Medford, MA, 1897). Although there is no record of the numbers of Haverford students who enlisted in the Union army, there is evidence that Lincoln enjoyed strong support at the Quaker college. When the president-elect's train passed through Haverford en route to Harrisburg on Friday morning, February 22, 1861, he was "cheered by successive groups of boys" who "rushed down to the tracks in hopes of catching a sight of Lincoln." Acknowledging his well-wishers, " 'Old Abe' appeared on the rear platform [of the train], hat in hand, and bowed graciously to each group." [See Letter, Thomas J. Battey to George T. Thomas, Haverford, PA, April 5, 1929. Quaker Collection Haverford College, Haverford, PA.]

68. Pat B. Reed, *Westtown: In Word & Deed, 1799–1999* (Westtown, PA: Westtown School, 1998), 89.

69. Letter, Sgt. Philip Price, 30th Pennsylvania Regiment, to Elizabeth Taylor Pratt, Langley, VA, November 10, 1861. Archives, Westtown School, Westtown, PA. Sgt. Price wrote to his friend Elizabeth Pratt to assure her

that her son, Joseph, would be "safer in the Army than on his own in a big city like Philadelphia." Joseph Pratt was killed at the Battle of Fredericksburg in December 1862.

70. Letter, William L. Jefferis to Father, Westtown, December 27, 1861. Archives, Westtown School.

71. Letter, Margaret Gummere to Mother, Westtown, June 1863. Archives, Westtown School.

72. Letter, Margaret Gummere to Mother.

73. Letter, John Harvey to Hannah Harvey, Richmond, IN, April 21, 1861 quoted in Opal Thornburg, *Earlham: The Story of the College, 1847–1962* (Richmond, IN: *Earlham* College, 1963), 105.

74. Thornburg, *Earlham*, 106.

75. Letter, Daniel Wooten to Miriam Green, Richmond, IN, May 1, 1861. Miriam Green Papers, Indiana Historical Society, Indianapolis, IN.

76. Letter Daniel Kind to Walter Carpenter, July 8, 1862. President's Papers, Quaker Archives, Earlham College, Richmond, IN.

77. Letter, Cyrus Green to Miriam Green, October 17, 1862. Green Papers.

78. See Michael S. Mangus, " 'A Cruel and Malicious War': The Society of Friends in Civil War Loudoun County, Virginia," *Quaker History*, Vol. 88, No. 1 (Spring 1999), 43–44.

79. Jones, *Later Periods*, 728–729.

80. Brock, *Quaker Peace Testimony*, 166–170.

81. Jacquelyn S. Nelson, *Indiana Quakers Confront the Civil War* (Indianapolis: Indiana Historical Society, 1991), 34–39.

82. Hamm quoted in McDaniel and Julye, *Fit for Freedom, Not for Friendship*, 147.

83. Edward N. Wright, *Conscientious Objectors in the Civil War* (Philadelphia, 1931); and Drake, *Quakers and Slavery*, 197.

84. Letter, Lucretia Mott to Martha Coffin Wright, Roadside, August 18, 1861, quoted in Carol Faulkner, *Lucretia Mott's Heresy: Abolition and Women's Rights in Nineteenth Century America* (Philadelphia: University of Pennsylvania Press, 2011), 179.

85. Margaret Hope Bacon, *Valiant Friend: The Life of Lucretia Mott* (New York: Walker & Co., 1980, paper), 180.

86. Letter, Mott to Editor, *National Anti-Slavery Standard*, Roadside, July 13, 1861, in Palmer, *Letters of Mott*, 312.

87. Foner, *Fiery Trial*, 176–177; and Frederick J. Blue, *No Taint of Compromise: Crusaders in Anti-Slavery Politics* (Baton Rouge, Louisiana, 2005), 256. Fremont was relieved of his duty by Lincoln on November 2, 1861 both for his belligerence in refusing to modify his order and for allegations that he had been giving business contracts to his own staff, one of whom was Mott's son-in-law, Edward M. Davis. [See Lincoln, *CW*, Vol. 4: 506, 518.]

88. Letter, Mott to Martha Coffin Wright, Roadside, November 6, 1861 in Palmer, *Letters of Mott*, 313; and Bacon, *Valiant Friend*, 180.

89. Letter, Henry H.G. Sharpless to George Sharpless, Philadelphia: November 23, 1861. Quaker Collection, Haverford College.

90. *New York Times*, September 16, 1861.

91. Goodwin, *Team of Rivals*, 393–394.

92. Daniel W. Hamilton, *The Limits of Sovereignty: Property Confiscation in the Union and the Confederacy during the Civil War* (Chicago, 2007), 86–92.

93. *New York Times*, September 16, 1861; and *Congressional Globe*: 37th Congress, 1st Session, 412.

94. Foner, *Fiery Trial*, 169.

95. Foner, *Fiery Trial*, 173.

96. Foner, *Fiery Trial*, 181.

97. Foner, *Fiery Trial*, 182–184.

98. McPherson, *Ordeal by Fire*, 239; and Bill Cash, *John Bright: Statesman, Orator, Agitator* (London: I.B. Tauris, 2012), 151. On May 8, 1861, Lord John Russell made a statement supporting the Confederate government in the House of Commons, which met with broad approval.

99. McPherson, *Ordeal by Fire*, 239.

100. Goodwin, *Team of Rivals*, 396–401.

101. *Morning Call* (London) quoted in Cash, *John Bright*, 155.

102. Palmerston quoted in Kevin Periano, *Lincoln in the World: The Making of a Statesman and the Dawn of American Power* (New York: Crown Publishers, 2013), 125.

103. Periano, *Lincoln in World*, 131, 151.

104. Periano, *Lincoln in World*, 125–129.

105. *John Bright*, "Speech to House of Commons," (May 28, 1861) quoted in Cash, John Bright, 151–152.

106. John Bright, "Speech to House of Commons," (December 4, 1861) in W. Robertson, *The Life and Times of the Right Honorable John Bright* (2 vols., London: Christian Age Office, 1884), II: 281–288.

107. Cash, *John Bright*, 145. For the most complete treatment of Bright's relationship with Lincoln, see Chapter 5. "Lincoln and Bright: Fighting Against Slavery and for America."

108. Bright quoted in Herman Ausubel, *John Bright: Victorian Reformer* (New York: Wiley, 1966), 125.

109. Palmerston quoted in Jasper Ridley, *Lord Palmerston* (New York: Dutton, 1970), 286, 495.

110. Cash, *John Bright*, 157–158.

111. Periano, *Lincoln in World*, 151.

112. Letter, John Bright to Senator Charles Sumner, London, December 5, 1861 quoted in Robertson, *Life & Times of Bright*, II: 289–290.

113. Periano, *Lincoln in World*, 125.

114. Donald, *Lincoln*, 322–323.

115. Bright quoted in John Bigelow, *Retrospections of an Active Life* (4 vols., New York: Baker & Taylor, 1909), I: 441–442.

116. Bright quoted in Ephriam D. Adams, *Great Britain and the American Civil War* (2 vols., New York: Russell & Russell, 1924), I: 232.
117. Donald, *Lincoln*, 323.
118. Letter, John Bright to Richard Cobden, London, December 9, 1861 quoted in Robertson, *Life & Times of Bright*, II: 292.
119. Cash, *John Bright*, xxii.
120. Cash, *John Bright*, 145. Once, after receiving a letter from Bright, Henry Janney, a Quaker merchant in Washington D.C., told Lincoln, who asked to see it. Janney quotes Lincoln: " 'I love to read the letters of Mr. Bright'. I complied when he read carefully every word, then remarked to those around him, '[M]y friend has shown me a letter from Mr. Bright. I believe he is the only British statesman who has been unfaltering in his confidence in our ultimate success.' " [See Letter, Henry Janney to John Bright, Washington, D.C.: April 24, 1865, John Bright Papers, British Library, London, England].
121. "Memorial," London Yearly Meeting of the Religious Society of Friends to Viscount Palmerston, First Lord of the Treasury, and Earl Russell, Principal Secretary of State for Foreign Affairs, London, England, December 1, 1861 in *Minutes of the Meeting for Sufferings, 1857–1862* (London: Friends House Library, 1862). The memorial was signed by Josiah Forster, Richard Foster, Samuel Fox, and John Hodgkin for the Meeting for Sufferings, London Yearly Meeting.
122. Letter, Abraham Lincoln to Francis T. King, Washington DC, January 7, 1862. Wood Papers, Quaker Collection, Haverford College.
123. AL quoted in Gordon H. Warren, *Fountain of Discontent: The Trent Affair and Freedom of the Seas* (Boston: Northeastern University Press, 1981), 171.
124. Mathew Stanley, James Kersey, and John Pinson, "Memorial to the President of the United States," *Minutes of Western Yearly Meeting of the Society of Friends*: 1 mo.-10-1862. Wood Papers, Quaker Collection, Haverford College.
125. Letter, Samuel Boyd Tobey, clerk, New England Yearly Meeting of Friends to President Abraham Lincoln, Providence, Rhode Island: February 5, 1862 quoted in *Friends Review*: August 2, 1862.
126. Letter, Lincoln to Samuel B. Tobey, Washington, DC, March 19, 1862 in *CW*, 5: 165.
127. Cash, *John Bright*, 159–163.
128. McPherson, *Ordeal by Fire*, 239–240.

CHAPTER 2: JUSTIFYING EMANCIPATION, 1862

1. Goodwin, *Team of Rivals*, 426–427.
2. See James McPherson, *Battle Cry of Freedom: The Civil War Era* (New York: Oxford University Press, 1988), 348–350; and William C. Kashatus,

"The Rise and Fall of 'Young Napoleon,' " *Pennsylvania Heritage* (Winter 2011): 6–15.

3. Goodwin, *Team of Rivals*, xvi–xvii, 394–396

4. Ruth Painter Randall, *Lincoln's Sons* (Boston: Little, Brown, 1955), 61–62.

5. Julia Taft Bayne, *Tad Lincoln's Father* (Lincoln: University of Nebraska Press, 2001; originally published 1931), 3.

6. Randall, *Lincoln's Sons*, 91–93.

7. Michael Burlingame, *The Inner World of Abraham Lincoln* (Chicago: University of Illinois, 1994), 57–72; Philip B. Kunhardt, Jr., Philip B. Kunhardt III, and Peter W. Kunhardt, *Lincoln: An Illustrated Biography* (New York: Alfred A. Knopf, 1992), 6–7; and Geoffrey C. Ward, Ric Burns and Ken Burns, *The Civil War: An Illustrated History* (New York: Alfred A. Knopf, 1990), 94.

8. Jerrold M. Packard, *The Lincolns in the White House: Four Years That Shattered A Family* (New York: St. Martin's Press, 2005), 75–78; and Doug Wead, *All the Presidents' Children: Triumph and Tragedy in the Lives of America's First Families* (New York: Atria Books, 2003), 91.

9. Lincoln quoted in Ruth Painter Randall, *Mary Lincoln: Biography of a Marriage* (Boston: Little, Brown & Co., 1953), 101.

10. Nineteenth-century United States discouraged emotional intimacy between fathers and their children. The economic and social changes spurred by industrialization and urbanization stifled a man's relationship to his offspring. Women, who were nurturers by nature, dominated the domestic realm, being primarily responsible for childrearing. Men, who were defined by the authority to govern and the power to control, were drawn away from their families toward income-producing work in the public sphere. As a result, Victorian-era fathers assumed the distant roles of provider and disciplinarian for their children. [See Shawn Johansen, *Family Men: Middle Class Fatherhood in Early Industrializing America* (New York: Routledge, 2001), 3–15; Robert L. Griswold, *Fatherhood in America: A History* (New York: Basic Books, 1993), 13–17; and John Demos, *Past, Present, and Personal: The Family and the Life Course in American History* (New York: Oxford University Press, 1986), 51–52.] Lincoln's own parenting style was strongly influenced by the emotional and physical abuse he suffered as a child. His father, Thomas, was a farmer and carpenter living on the frontier. Though his frustration and poverty can be attributed to his difficult circumstances, they also fostered resentment in his son. After his wife died in 1819, Thomas left nine-year-old Abraham and his eleven-year-old sister to fend for themselves in the Indiana wilderness. Six months later, he returned with a new wife to care for his children. During his adolescence, when Abraham assumed greater work responsibilities, his father abused him. Never fully understanding his son's desire to read and learn, Thomas berated Abraham as "lazy" and was known to "knock him over" whenever he caught him reading books. Predictably, Abraham

rebelled against those things that were most important to his father—his Baptist religion and his pro-slavery politics. [See Doug Wead, *The Raising of a President* (New York: Atria Books, 2005), 11–12, 99–103, 112–113, 125.]

11. Randall, *Lincoln's Sons*, 72–75.
12. Donald, *Lincoln*, 336.
13. Goodwin, *Team of Rivals*, 415–419.
14. Packard, *Lincolns in the White House*, 119.
15. Elizabeth Keckly, *Behind the Scenes, or, Thirty Years a Slave and Four Years in the White House* (New York: Oxford University Press, 1988; originally published 1868), 103.
16. Lincoln quoted in Helen Nicolay, *Lincoln's Secretary: A Biography of John G. Nicolay* (New York: Longman, Green, 1971), 132–133. Lincoln continued to be deeply scarred by the loss of his favorite son. After Willie's casket was placed in a vault at Georgetown's Oak Hill Cemetery, the president would often visit the tomb and gaze upon his dead son's face. Once, he asked the Union officer who accompanied him, "Do you ever find yourself talking with the dead?" When the officer said "yes," Lincoln, sobbing and shaking with emotion, replied, "So do I dream of my boy Willie. Since his death, I catch myself every day involuntarily talking with him as if he were still with me." [See Shenk, *Lincoln's Melancholy*, 197; and Lincoln quoted in "Mary's Charlatans" (The Lehman Institute, 2000), http://www.mrlincolnswhitehouse.org]
17. Randall, *Mary Lincoln*, 284–289.
18. Justin G. Turner and Linda L. Turner, *Mary Todd Lincoln: Her Life and Letters* (New York: Alfred A. Knopf, 1972), 147; Randall, *Mary Lincoln*, 260; and Wead, *All the Presidents' Children*, 92.
19. Keckly, *Behind the Scenes*, 104. In 1875, Robert Lincoln assembled an army of lawyers and experts to swear in court that his mother was insane. The jury found her insane and she was committed to a mental asylum for a year. [See Mark E. Neeley, Jr. and R. Gerald McMurty,*The Insanity File: The Case of Mary Lincoln* (Carbondale: Southern Illinois University Press, 1986).]
20. Jean H. Baker, *Mary Todd Lincoln: A Biography* (New York: W.W. Norton, 1989), 217–222. Michael Burlingame contends that Mary Lincoln possessed many of the symptoms associated with "borderline personality disorder." Among her most defining characteristics were impulsiveness, intense jealousy, excessive vanity, emotional instability, and a lack of tactfulness and discretion. [See Burlingame, *Inner World of Lincoln*, 313.]
21. For works on Lincoln as a victim of chronic depression, see: Nathaniel Stevenson, *Lincoln: An Account of His Personal Life* (1922); L. Pierce Clark, *Lincoln: A Physcho-Biography* (New York: Scribner, 1933); Milton H. Shutes, *Lincoln's Emotional Life* (Philadelphia: Dorrance, 1957); Charles Strozier, *Lincoln's Quest for Union: Public and Private Meetings* (New York: Basic Books, 1982). These works argue that Lincoln's chronic depression can be traced to two emotional crises he experienced as a young man: the death of his first

true love, Ann Rutledge; and the breaking of his engagement to Mary Todd Lincoln on the eve of their wedding.

22. AL quoted in Anna L. Boyden, *Echoes from Hospital and White House: A Record of Mrs. Rebecca R. Pomroy's Experience in War-Times* (Boston: D. Lothrop, 1884), 56.

23. Among the first Lincoln scholars to make the important distinction between "chronic depression" and "melancholy" were: Burlingame, *Inner World of Lincoln*; Douglas Wilson, *Honor's Voice: The Transformation of Abraham Lincoln* (New York: Knopf, 1998); and Allen C. Guelzo, *Abraham Lincoln: Redeemer President* (Grand Rapids, Michigan: Erdmans, 1999). Burlingame argues that "bereavement in childhood is one of the most significant factors in the development of depressive illness in later life." He speculates that Willie's death "probably reminded Lincoln of the death of his own mother, which was a devastating blow to him as a child." [See Burlingame, *Inner World of Lincoln*, 93–94, 104]. Joshua Wolf Shenk has authored the most complete work on Lincoln's melancholy, offering a compelling argument on how it shaped his leadership, personality and presidency. [See Shenk, *Lincoln's Melancholy: How Depression Challenged a President and Fueled His Greatness* (Boston: Houghton Mifflin, 2005).]

24. Isaac N. Arnold, *The Life of Abraham Lincoln* (1880. Reprinted by Chicago: A.C. McClurg & Co., 1909), 6.

25. Bassuk, *Lincoln and the Quakers*, 24; and Emanuel Hertz, *Lincoln Talks* (New York: Viking, 1939), 582–583.

26. Stanton and Lincoln quoted by Douglas Wilson in Lincoln (DVD Produced by Vikram Jayanti for History Channel), 2008. Attorney General Edward Bates observed that Lincoln's story-telling also served the purpose of "illustrating the point he wished to enforce," something that gave the point "a strength and clearness impossible in abstract discussion." [See Bates quoted in F.B. Carpenter, "Personal Impressions of Abraham Lincoln," *Friends Intelligencer*, Vol. 22, No. 11 (May 20, 1865): 171].

27. Shenk, *Lincoln's Melancholy*, 126, 142, 156 179, 190.

28. William Wolf, *The Almost Chosen People: A Study of the Religion of Abraham Lincoln* (New York: Doubleday, 1959), 51, 131, 179–180.

29. AL quoted in Henry C. Deming, *Eulogy of Abraham Lincoln delivered before the General Assembly of Connecticut, June 8, 1865* (Hartford: A. N. Clark & Company, 1865), 42.

30. Ward Hill Lamon, Lincoln's bodyguard, insisted that the president "did not, to my knowledge, in any way change his religious ideas, opinions or beliefs, from the time he left Springfield till the day of his death." [See Lamon, *Recollections of Abraham Lincoln, 1847–1865* (Lincoln: University of Nebraska Press, reprint 1994).] John Nicolay, Lincoln's personal secretary, also claimed that Lincoln "gave no outward indication of his mind having undergone any change in [religion] where here [in Washington]." [See Nicolay quoted in Guelzo, *Redeemer President*, 313].

31. Lincoln quoted in Carpenter, *Six Months*, 189.

32. Randall, *Lincoln's Sons*, 101.

33. Reverend Phineas D. Gurley quoted in Shenk, *Lincoln's Melancholy*, 197.

34. *Lincoln* scholars agree that his spiritual transformation began with the death of his son, Willie, in February 1862. They include: Donald, Lincoln, 336–337; Ronald White, *Lincoln's Greatest Speech* (New York: Simon & Schuster, 2002), 134; Stephen Oates, *With Malice Toward None: A Life of Abraham Lincoln* (New York: Harper & Row, 1977), 70; Sandburg, *Abraham Lincoln: The War Years*, III: 379–380; Shenk, *Lincoln's Melancholy*, 197; Trueblood, *Theologian of American Anguish*, 30–31; and Guelzo, *Redeemer President*, 328–330.

35. Trueblood, *Theologian of Anguish*, 31–32.

36. Several scholars identify Lincoln's acceptance of the doctrine of necessity, including: Barton, *Soul of Lincoln*, 292–302; Guelzo, *Redeemer President*, 102–142; Carwardine, *Life of Purpose and Power*, xii; Donald, *Lincoln*, 514.

37. Lincoln quoted in Oates, *With Malice Toward None*, 293.

38. Nathanial W. Stephenson, *Abraham Lincoln and the Union* (New Haven, CT: Yale University Press, 1918), 261.

39. Carl Sandburg, *Lincoln: The War Years* (New York: Harcourt, Brace & Co., 1939), Vol. I: 501.

40. Longwood Progressive Friends Meeting, "Memorial to the President," June 5–7, 1862 in *Proceedings of the Pennsylvania Yearly Meeting of Progressive Friends Held at Longwood, Chester County* (New York: Oliver Johnson, 1862), 15–16.

41. Congressman William D. Kelley (R-Pa.) quoted in Allen Thorndike Rice, editor, *Reminiscences of Abraham Lincoln by Distinguished Men of His Time* (New York: North American Review, 1888), 284–285.

42. Lincoln treated all self-serving ministers and religious delegations with equal contempt. On September 15, 1862, for example, he was visited by an interdenominational group of Chicago Christians who insisted that God wanted him to emancipate the slaves immediately. Although it was only a week before Lincoln issued the draft *Emancipation Proclamation*, he lectured his visitors on the limits of his power to end slavery and quickly ended the interview. [See AL, *CW*, Vol. V: 419–425.]

43. The Longwood Progressive Friends Meeting's deviation from the Peace Testimony is reflected in the following minute: "We have no hesitancy in declaring that the government—measuring it by its constitutional obligations—had no alternative but to seek to suppress this treasonable outbreak by all the means and forces at its disposal, or else to betray the sacred trusts committed to it by the people; and therefore, throughout this fearful struggle, it has had our sympathy, and desire for its success." [See PYMPF, *Proceedings*, 1862, 11.]

44. "Presentation of the Memorial to the President": June 20, 1862 in *Proceedings of Longwood Progressive Friends Meeting*, 17–19.

45. Richard Carwardine, "Abraham Lincoln, the Presidency, and the Mobilization of Union Sentiment," *The American Civil War: Explorations and Reconsiderations*, edited by Susan-Mary Grant and Brian Holden Reid (New York: Longmans Publishing, 2000), 87–88.

46. Ward Hill Lamon, *Recollections of Abraham Lincoln*, 91–92.

47. Earl Shenk Miers, *Lincoln Day by Day: A Chronology, 1809–1865* (Dayton, OH: Morningside, 1991); and the website "Lincoln Log: A Daily Chronology of Abraham Lincoln's Life," which is largely based on Roy Basler's *Collected Works of Abraham Lincoln*. The website can be accessed at www.the lincolnlog.org. The author's study proved to be inconclusive as each of these sources identified half a dozen or less contacts with each of the following religious denominations: African Methodist Episcopalians, Baptists, Congregationalists, Disciples of Christ, Episcopalians, Jews, Methodists, Moravians, Presbyterians, Quakers, Roman Catholics, and Unitarians. Clearly, Lincoln had much more contact with some of these denominations since his own bodyguard, Ward Lamon Hill, claimed that he "was meeting on almost a daily basis with clergymen" during the first few years of his presidency. [See Hill, *Recollections of Abraham Lincoln*, 91–92.]

48. E-mail, James M. Cornelius to the author: October 31, 2013.

49. The 16 Progressive Friends Meetings in the United States were: Yearly Meeting of Congregational Friends, Waterloo, Seneca County, New York; Yearly Meeting of Friends of Human Progress, North Collins, Erie County, New York; Milton Yearly Meeting of Friends, Milton, Ulster County, New York; Yearly Meeting of Congregational Friends, Genesee County, New York; Cortland Meeting of Progressives, Cortland, Cortland County, New York; Green Plain Yearly Meeting of Congregational Friends, Green Plain, Clark County, Ohio; Ohio Yearly Meeting of Progressive Friends, Salem, Columbiana County, Ohio; Goshen Half Yearly Meeting of Congregational Friends, Logan County, Ohio; Wabash Yearly Meeting of Congregational Friends, Wabash County, Indiana; Indiana Yearly Meeting of Friends of Human Progress, Richmond, Wayne County, Indiana; Half Yearly Meeting of Congregational Friends, Dublin, Wayne County, Indiana; Fountain County Meeting of Congregational Friends, Fountain County, Indiana; Michigan Yearly Meeting of Friends of Human Progress, Battle Creek, Michigan; Yearly Meeting of Progressive Friends, Eden, Clinton County, Iowa; Pennsylvania Yearly Meeting of Progressive Friends, Longwood, Chester County, Pennsylvania; and Philadelphia Association of Progressive Friends, Philadelphia, Pennsylvania. [See Albert J. Wahl, "The Congregational or Progressive Friends in the Pre-Civil War Reform Movement." (PhD dissertation, Temple University, 1951): 332–333.]

50. Jordan, *Slavery and the Meetinghouse*, 93–94.

51. Albert J. Wahl, "The Progressive Friends of Longwood," *Friends Historical Society Bulletin*, Vol. 42, No. 1 (Spring 1953): 14–16. For names of the founding members of the Longwood Progressive Friends Meeting, see:

Wahl, "Progressive Friends in Pre-Civil War Reform," 344. Christopher Densmore argues that "because many active agents of the Underground Railroad were associated with Progressive Friends, some people have interpreted the 1852–1853 separation of activist, anti-slavery Friends from Kennett Monthly Meeting as connected with the question of involvement with the Underground Railroad. This was not the case." Densmore points out that both the main body of Kennett Monthly Meeting (Hicksite) as well as the separatists Progressive Friends submitted to the Philadelphia Yearly Meeting's (Hicksite) 1851 directive to resist complying with the 1850 Fugitive Slave Law and be willing to "suffer the penalties" rather than obey a law that was "so clearly unjust." [See Densmore, "Introduction," R.C. Smedley, *History of the Underground Railroad in Chester and the Neighboring Counties of Pennsylvania* (Lancaster, PA: Lancaster Journal, 1883. Reprinted by Stackpole Books, Mechanicsburg, PA, 2005 paperback), xvi–xvii.

52. Pennsylvania Yearly Meeting of Progressive Friends (hereafter, "PYMPF"), *Proceedings* (1853): 5.

53. Letter, Thomas Garrett to Samuel May, Jr., Wilmington, DE, November 24, 1863 quoted in James A. McGowan, *Station Master on the Underground Railroad: The Life and Letters of Thomas Garrett* (Jefferson, NC: McFarland & Company, Inc., 2005), 189–190.

54. PYMPF, *Proceedings* (1853): 5.

55. Wahl, "Congregational or Progressive Friends," 141–142.

56. Jordan, *Slavery and the Meetinghouse*, 96.

57. *American Republican* (West Chester, PA), September 25, October 21, 1855.

58. PYMPF, *Proceedings* (1853): 5.

59. PYMPF, *Proceedings* (1858): 11–17.

60. PYMPF, "Slavery," *Proceedings* (1856): 43–44.

61. Foner, *Fiery Trial*, 212–213, 223–224; and Goodwin, *Team of Rivals*, 459–460.

62. See Edward A. Miller, *Lincoln's Abolitionist General: The Biography of David Hunter* (Columbia: University of South Carolina Press, 1997), 96–104; and Mark Grimsley, *The Hard Hand of War: Union Military Policy Toward Southern Civilians, 1861–1865* (New York, 1995), 127.

63. James M. McPherson, *Ordeal by Fire: The Civil War and Reconstruction* (New York: McGraw-Hill, 2001), 257–272; and Goodwin, *Team of Rivals*, 431–432, 436–444. Grant, Union commander of the Department of the West, often achieved victory at the expense of appalling casualty rates. On April 6–7, 1862, for example, Grant's forces launched a bloodbath against Confederate troops under the command of General Albert Sidney Johnston at Shiloh, Tennessee. In two days of fighting, there were more than 3,000 dead, over 20,000 wounded or missing in action out of the 80,000 soldiers from both sides. Critics pressed for Grant's firing after the battle, but Lincoln refused, saying, "I can't spare this man. He fights." [See Philip B.

Kunhardt, Jr., et al. *Lincoln: An Illustrated Biography* (New York: Alfred A. Knopf, 1992), 178.]

64. Philip L. Ostergard, *The Inspired Wisdom of Abraham Lincoln* (Carol Stream, IL: Tyndale House Publishers, 2008). Ostergard identifies by date and substance dozens of interviews Lincoln conducted with delegations from many Christian denominations.

65. AL quoted in Francis Carpenter, *Six Months at the White House*, 20, 22.

66. Quakers Isaac and Sarah Harvey of Clinton County, Ohio, also paid a visit to Lincoln to discuss emancipation. Although one writer has identified the date of the interview as September 1862 and suggests that the Harveys inspired the president's decision to free the slaves, no documentary evidence exists to support either the specific date or the couple's connection to the *Emancipation Proclamation*. [See Nellie Blessing-Eyster's interview of Isaac and Sarah Harvey originally published in *Harper's Magazine* about 1874; and Henry W. Wilbur, *Friends with Lincoln in the White House* (Philadelphia, 1912).] However, documentary evidence does suggest that the Harveys visited Lincoln sometime during his presidency. [See Henry J. Cadbury, "Another Quaker Legend of Lincoln," *Friends Intelligencer*, Vol. 109, No. 6 (February 9, 1952): 75–76].

67. Allen C. Guelzo, *Lincoln's Emancipation Proclamation: The End of Slavery in America* (New York: Simon & Schuster, 2004), 112; and Foner, *Fiery Trial*, 217–218.

68. Kunhardt, *Lincoln*, 184.

69. Foner, *Fiery Trial*, 212–213.

70. Foner, *Fiery Trial*, 215–216.

71. Goodwin, *Team of Rivals*, 462–463.

72. AL quoted in Gideon Welles, *Diary of Gideon Wells, Secretary of the Navy Under Lincoln and Johnson* (3 vols. Boston: Houghton Mifflin, 1911. Reprinted 1960), Vol. I: 70–71.

73. Goodwin, *Team of Rivals*, 462.

74. Welles, *Diary*, Vol. I: 70–71.

75. Goodwin, *Team of Rivals*, 461–463.

76. Lerone Bennett, Jr. *Forced Into Glory: Abraham Lincoln's White Dream* (Chicago: Johnson Publishing Company, 2000).

77. Henry Louis Gates, Jr., editor, *Lincoln on Race & Slavery* (Princeton: Princeton University Press, 2009), xx–xxi.

78. Foner, *Fiery Trial*, 216.

79. John Hope Franklin, *The Emancipation Proclamation* (New York: Doubleday, 1965 paperback edition), 36–38; Richard Striner, *Father Abraham: Lincoln's Relentless Struggle to End Slavery* (New York: Oxford University, 2006), 169–170; Foner, *Fiery Trial*, 218; Guelzo, *Lincoln's Emancipation Proclamation*, 118–119.

80. AL, "Emancipation Proclamation–First Draft," (July 22, 1862), *CW*, Vol. 5: 336–337.

81. See Gideon Welles, "History of Emancipation," *Galaxy* (1872): 841; Guelzo, *Lincoln's Emancipation Proclamation*, 120–123; Goodwin, *Team of Rivals*, 465–468; Foner, *Fiery Trial*, 219–220; Franklin, *Emancipation Proclamation*, 38–40; Striner, *Father Abraham*, 171.

82. AL quoted in Carpenter, *Six Months at the White House*, 21–22; and Guelzo, *Lincoln's Emancipation Proclamation*, 123; and Goodwin, *Team of Rivals*, 467–468.

83. AL, "Address on Colonization to a Deputation of Negroes," August 14, 1862, *CW*, Vol. 5: 370–375.

84. E. M. Thomas quoted in ibid., 375.

85. James Oakes, *The Radical and the Republican: Frederick Douglass, Abraham Lincoln, and the Triumph of Antislavery Politics* (New York: W.W. Norton & Co., 2007), 193–194.

86. *New York Times*, August 15, 1862.

87. Letter, Reverend E. M. Thomas to President Abraham Lincoln, August 17, 1862 quoted in Foner, *Fiery Trial*, 225.

88. Frederick Douglass, "Douglass' Monthly: September 1862," in *The Life and Writings of Frederick Douglass*, edited by Philip S. Foner (5 vols; New York, 1950–1973), 4: 313.

89. Oakes, *Radical and Republican*, 195.

90. Horace Greeley, "The Prayer of Twenty Millions," in *Dear Mr. Lincoln: Letters to the President*, edited by Harold Holzer (Reading, MA: Addison-Wesley, 1993), 156–161.

91. Letter, AL to Horace Greeley," Washington, DC, August 22, 1862, *CW*, Vol. 5: 388–389.

92. AL, "Meditation on the Divine Will," September, 1862, *CW*, Vol. 5: 404. According to Lincoln's secretary John Hay, the "Meditation" was "not written to be seen of men," but for some reason, he left it on his desk where Hay discovered it and copied it.

93. Ronald C. White, Jr., *A. Lincoln. A Biography* (New York: Random House, 2009), 625.

94. Wolf, *Almost Chosen People*, 30–31.

95. Longwood Progressive Friends Meeting, "Memorial to the President," June 5–7, 1862.

96. Letter, Lydia Longstreth to AL, Philadelphia, September 21, 1862. Longstreth-Noble Family Papers, Friends Historical Society, Swarthmore College.

97. Letter, Mary J. Schofield to AL, Bucks County, PA, September 16, 1862. Ash-Schofield Papers, Friends Historical Society, Swarthmore College.

98. Trueblood, *Theologian of Anguish*, 9.

99. McPherson, *Ordeal by Fire*, 303–311.

100. Foner, *Fiery Trial*, 230–231; and Guelzo, *Emancipation Proclamation*, 155–156.

101. Donald, *Lincoln*, 378–379.

102. See *New York Tribune*: September 23, 1862; and *Chicago Tribune*: September 23, 1862.

103. Donald, *Lincoln*, 377–378.

104. Cash, *John Bright*, 160–162.

105. Rachel Wilson Moore, *Journal, 1863–1864*, edited by George Truman (Philadelphia: T. Ellwood Zell, 1876), 228–238.

106. Letter, Caleb Russell and Sallie A. Fenton, Prairie Grove Monthly Meeting, to President Abraham Lincoln, Prairie Grove, Iowa: December 27, 1862 quoted in *Friends Intelligencer*, Vol. 20, No. 1, March 14, 1863.

107. Letter, AL to Caleb Russell and Sallie A. Fenton, Washington, DC, January 5, 1863, Friends Historical Library, Swarthmore College, Pennsylvania; and *CW*, Vol. 6: 39–40.

108. F. Lauriston Bullard, "Lincoln and the Quaker Woman," *Lincoln Herald*, Vol. 46, No. 2 (June 1944): 9–12; and Barbour & Frost, *Quakers*, 324.

109. Bullard, "Lincoln and the Quaker Woman," 10.

110. Eliza Gurney had ties to both London Yearly Meeting and Philadelphia Yearly Meeting. In fact, Lincoln initially mistook her as an *English* Quaker minister, though she was born and raised in America. [See Trueblood, *Theologian of American Anguish*, 43.] James Carey was a Quaker merchant from Baltimore and an assistant clerk of Baltimore Yearly meeting at the time of the visit. He had also been strongly influenced by the theology of Joseph John Gurney, Eliza's late husband. [See *The Friend* (Philadelphia), Vol. 68 (1895): 120]. The author could not find any information on the backgrounds of the group's other members, John M. Whitall, Hannah B. Mott.

111. Eliza P. Gurney, *Memoir and Correspondence of Eliza P. Gurney*, edited by Richard F. Mott (Philadelphia: J.B. Lippincott, 1884), 309–312. The original memoir of Lincoln's interview with the Quaker delegation is in the collections of the Historical Society of Pennsylvania, Philadelphia.

112. Gurney, *Memoir and Correspondence of Gurney*, 312–313.

113. John M. Whitall quoted in Gurney, *Memoir and Correspondence Gurney*, 309.

114. Letter, John G. Nicolay to Therena Bates, Washington, DC: October 26, 1862 quoted in *With Lincoln in the White House: Letters, Memorials& Other Writings of John G. Nicolay, 1860–1865*, edited by Michael Burlingame (Carbondale: Southern Illinois University Press, 2006), 90.

115. Joshua Zeitz, *Lincoln's Boys: John Hay, John Nicolay, and the War for Lincoln's Image* (New York: Viking, 2014), 2–3. William Stoddard, an assistant secretary, once observed that Nicolay was "decidedly German in his manner of telling men what he thought of them. People who do not like him ... say he is sour and crusty." [See Stoddard,*Inside the White House in War Times* (New York: n.p., 1890), xi, 57.]

116. Letter, AL to Eliza P. Gurney, Washington, DC, October 26, 1862, *CW*, Vol. 5: 478.

117. White, *A. Lincoln*, 523.
118. AL, "Annual Message to Congress," (December 1, 1862) *CW*, Vol. 5: 537.
119. AL, "Second Inaugural Address," (March 4, 1865) *CW*, Vol. 8: 332–333.
120. Letter, AL to Eliza P. Gurney, Washington, DC, September 4, 1864, *CW*, Vol. 7: 535–536.
121. The complete Lincoln-Gurney correspondence can be found in Mott, *Memoir and Correspondence of Gurney*, 307–318.
122. McPherson, *Ordeal by Fire*, 327–328.
123. Elizabeth Comstock, *The Life and Letters of Elizabeth L. Comstock*, edited by C. Hare (London: Headley Brothers, 1895), 180.
124. William O. Stoddard, "White House Sketches, No. 10," *New York Citizen*: October 20, 1866.
125. For testimony of Eliza Gurney's intelligence and beauty, see: Bullard, "Lincoln and the Quaker Woman," 9–10; and Augustus J. C. Hare, *The Gurneys of Earlham* (2 vols., London, 1895), Vol. 2: 325–328.
126. Some historians argue that Lincoln was extremely awkward or did not like women unless they were the wives of old friends. Those married women provided him with congenial company outside the arena of courtship. [See: Oates, *With Malice Toward None*, 57; Wilson, *Honor's Voice*, 109, 111; and Donald, *Lincoln*, 55.] Others claim that Lincoln's problematic and distant relationship with women stood in marked contrast to his warmer relations with several men in his life and that two of those relationships had homosexual overtones. The two male relationships in question were with: Joshua Speed, a Springfield shopkeeper, which took place between 1837 and 1842; and David Derickson, a captain of the Pennsylvania Bucktails who served as Lincoln's bodyguard between September 1862 and April 1863. [See C. A. Tripp, *The Intimate World of Abraham Lincoln* (New York: The Free Press, 2005).] Still others maintain that Lincoln had a strong but controlled passion for women. [See Burlingame, *Inner World of Lincoln*, 123; and John Y. Simon, "Abraham Lincoln and Ann Rutledge." *Journal of the Abraham Lincoln Association* 11 (1990): 13–34.]
127. According to Elizabeth Keckley, who served as a seamstress and friend to the First Lady, "Mrs. Lincoln's love for her husband sometimes prompted her to act very strangely. She was extremely jealous of him, and if a lady desired to court her displeasure, she could select no surer way to do it than to pay marked attention to the President." [See Elizabeth Keckley, *Behind the Scenes, or, Thirty Years a Slave, and Four Years in the White House* (New York: Oxford University Press, 1988; orig. 1868), 124]. Several accounts exist of the negative influence Mary Todd Lincoln exercised on her husband, beginning with William Herndon's *Lincoln: The True Story of a Great Life* (Chicago, 1890). Later historians tended to rely on this source for their assessment of the marriage, most notably Michael Burlingame's

Inner World of Lincoln and Douglas Wilson's *Honor's Voice*. In recent years, however, more sympathetic accounts of Mary Lincoln have emerged, painting a positive light on the marriage and her contributions to Lincoln's personal life and career. Among these sympathetic treatments are: Justin G. Turner and Lina Levitt Turner, *Mary Todd Lincoln: Her Life and Letters* (New York: Alfred A. Knopf, 1972); Jean H. Baker, *Mary Todd Lincoln: A Biography* (New York: W.W. Norton, 1987); and Jennifer Fleischner, *Mrs. Lincoln and Mrs. Keckley: The Remarkable Story of the Friendship Between a First Lady and a Former Slave* (New York: Broadway Books, 2003).

CHAPTER 3: TRIALS OF WAR, 1863

1. AL quoted in Frederick W. Seward, editor. *Seward at Washington, as Senator and Secretary of State: A Memoir of His Life, with Selections from His Letters, 1861–1872* (New York, 1891), 151. The account of Lincoln's signature on the final Emancipation Proclamation is also told in Foner, *Fiery Trial*, 240; and Guelzo, *Lincoln's Emancipation Proclamation*, 240.
2. AL "Final Emancipation Proclamation" (January 1, 1863), *CW*, 6: 28–31.
3. T. Harry Williams, *Lincoln and the Radicals* (Madison: University of Wisconsin Press, 1960), 216–217; and Ralph Korngold, *Thaddeus Stevens: A Being Darkly Wise and Rudely Great* (Westport, CT: Greenwood, 1974), 195–196. By 1863, Lincoln had already shredded habeas corpus in Maryland, closed down newspapers, and imprisoned those for lukewarm sympathy for the South under the guise of the Executive's constitutional war powers.
4. Foner, *Fiery Trial*, 241–242; Williams, *Lincoln and the Radicals*, 216–217. The *Final Emancipation Proclamation* provided freedom primarily to slaves in areas that were still under Confederate control, specifically those 3.9 million bondsmen residing in the states of Alabama, Arkansas, Florida, Georgia, Louisiana, Mississippi, North Carolina, South Carolina, Texas, and Virginia. With the exceptions of Union-held parts of the Carolinas, Arkansas, and Mississippi, the *Proclamation* did not apply to the nearly 800,000 slaves that lived in the border states as well as other areas occupied by the Union army, which included 7 counties in Tidewater, Virginia; 13 parishes in southern Louisiana; and the entire state of Tennessee.
5. Speech, Lucretia Mott to Philadelphia Female Anti-Slavery Society, "29th Annual Report" (1863) quoted in Dana Greene, *Lucretia Mott: Her Complete Speeches and Sermons* (New York: Edward Mellon, 1980), 265.
6. The *Friend* (Philadelphia), Vol. 35 (1863), 151.
7. Hamm, *Transformation of American Quakerism*, 99.
8. Thomas Lamborn quoted in Joseph Brinton, *Journal*: April 14, 1863 in Eileen Waring, "Four Friends Drop in on Lincoln," *Friends Journal*. Vol. 11, No. 10 (May 15, 1965): 253–255. Joseph Brinton's journal can be found at

Friends Historical Library of Swarthmore College, Swarthmore, Pennsylvania.

9. See Christopher Densmore, "Abraham Lincoln, the Civil War and Chester County Quakers," (Unpublished paper delivered at Unionville High School, January 15, 2010), 6–7. It is interesting to note that Lamborn urged Lincoln to include the nation's apostasy in his upcoming proclamation for a day of national fasting, which he did four days later on March 30, 1863.

10. AL, "Annual Message to Congress, December 1, 1862," *CW*, 5: 537.

11. Benjamin Quarles, *The Negro in the Civil War* (New York: Da Capo Press, 1989. Originally published 1953), 200.

12. James M. McPherson, *The Negro's Civil War. How American Blacks Felt and Acted During the War for the Union* (New York: Ballantine Books, 1991), 167.

13. AL, "Speech to Indiana delegation, August 4, 1862," *CW*, 5: 357.

14. Frederick Douglass, *Douglass' Monthly*, V (August 1862), 852.

15. Letter, AL to James C. Conkling, Washington, DC, August 26, 1863, *CW*, 6: 407–410.

16. Luis F. Emilio, *A Brave Black Regiment. History of the 54th Massachusetts Regiment* (Salem, NH: Ayer Company, 1990. Originally published, 1894), 1–10.

17. Congress of the Confederate States of America, "An Act of Congress, Section IV," (May 1, 1863) quoted in Emilio, *Brave Black Regiment*, 7.

18. Letter, AL to Governor Andrew Johnson, Washington DC: March 26, 1863, *CW*, 5: 149–150.

19. James W. Geary, *We Need Men: The Union Draft in the Civil War* (Northern Illinois University Press, 1991); and McPherson, Ordeal by Fire, 384–386. Still, the vast majority of Union troops were volunteers. Of the 2,100,000 Union soldiers, about 2 percent were draftees, and another 6 percent were paid substitutes.

20. Iver Bernstein, *The New York City Draft Riots: Their Significance for American Society and Politics in the Age of the Civil War* (New York: Oxford University Press, 1990).

21. For quotations, see: "Memorial to President Lincoln," Minutes of Philadelphia Yearly Meeting: February 24, 1863. See also: "Memorial to Chief Executive of the United States and those in authority in the Army and Navy," Meeting for Sufferings, Western Yearly Meeting: July 21, 1863.

22. "Four Friends Drop in on Lincoln," *Friends Journal*, Vol. 11, No. 10 (May 15, 1965): 253–255.

23. Peter Brock, *The Quaker Peace Testimony, 1660–1914* (York, England: William Sessions, 1990), 168–173. Southern Quakers experienced similar problems. In April 1862, the Confederate Congress passed a conscription act that allowed able-bodied men exemption only on the condition of furnishing a substitute. After the peace churches lobbied the Congress, a supplementary act was passed in October permitting an exemption for

conscientious objectors who paid a fine of $500. But even this exemption was withdrawn late in the war when the Confederate army suffered a severe shortage of manpower. Under these circumstances, many Southern Friends escaped conscription by hiding, deserting, or even crossing enemy lines. [See Brock, *Peace Testimony*, 168–169, 172].

24. Letter, September 15, 1863, *Friends Intelligencer* (Philadelphia) Vol. 20, No. 30 (October 3, 1863), 474.

25. Letter, Mary H. Child to AL, Philadelphia, February 27, 1861, Ash-Schofield Papers, Friends Historical Library, Swarthmore College.

26. Brock, *Peace Testimony*, 167.

27. Divided opinion exists on the exact origins of Quaker pacifism. Some scholars argue that pacifism was an important element in the Quaker outlook from 1652 when George Fox founded the sect. They point to converted Quaker soldiers who had fought in Cromwell's army as evidence. Among these converted pacifists was James Nayler, who articulated the "Lamb's War" ethic of fighting an inward spiritual struggle to purge oneself of the pride and vanity, which gave rise to war, instead of an outward, carnal battle against other human beings. [See Meredith Weddle, *Walking in the Way of Peace* (New York: Oxford University, 2001); Hugh Barbour, *The Quakers and Puritan England* (New Haven, CT: Yale University Press, 1964); Geoffrey F. Nuttall, *The Holy Spirit in Puritan Faith and Experience* (Oxford, 1947); and Mabel R. Brailsford, *A Quaker from Cromwell's Army: James Nayler* (London, 1927)]. Other scholars acknowledge that while there were "premature pacifists" among the earliest Friends, Quakers, as a sect, adopted the peace principle only after the Restoration and that even Fox had not committed himself to pacifism before that time. [See Christopher Hill, *The World Turned Upside Down: Radical Ideas during the English Revolution* (Harmondsworth (Middlesex), 1975; and BarryReay, *The Quakers and the English Revolution* (New York: Palgrave Macmillan, 1985)].

28. William C. Braithwaite, *The Beginnings of Quakerism* (Cambridge, 1961), 461–463; and Barbour & Frost, *Quakers*, 33–35.

29. "Declaration of the Society of Friends to King Charles II, November 21, 1660–1661, in George Fox, *A Journal* (1694), edited by John L. Nickalls (Cambridge, 1952), 234.

30. Arthur J. Mekeel, *The Quakers and the American Revolution* (York, England: William Sessions, 1996 reprint), 1–2.

31. Brock, *Peace Testimony*, 47–51.

32. Jack Marietta, *The Reformation of American Quakerism, 1748–1783* (Philadelphia: University of Pennsylvania Press, 1984), 51–80; and Sydney V. James, *A People Among Peoples: Quaker Benevolence in the Eighteenth Century* (Cambridge, MA: Harvard University Press, 1963), 169–192. Some Friends who were disowned by Philadelphia Yearly Meeting and New England Yearly Meeting for complying with the patriot war effort established the Free Quaker Society. Their discipline was identical to the Religious Society of

Friends with the exception that the liberty of conscience was given equal weight to pacifism. [See William C. Kashatus, *Conflict of Conviction: A Reappraisal of Quaker Involvement in the American Revolution* (Lanham, MD: University Press of America, 1990), 108–112].

33. Mekeel, *Quakers and American Revolution*, 5–8, 148–182; Brock, *Peace Testimony*, 142–154; Arthur J. Worral, *New England Quakerism, 1656–1830* (Ann Arbor, 1970), 56–58.

34. James, *A People Among Peoples*, 268–286; and Richard Bauman, *For the Reputation of Truth: Politics, Religion and Conflict Among Pennsylvania Quakers, 1750–1800* (Baltimore: Johns Hopkins Press, 1971), 228–229.

35. James, *A People Among Peoples*, 333.

36. Brock, *Peace Testimony*, 157, 163.

37. Margaret E. Hirst, *The Quakers in Peace and War* (London: Swarthmore Press, 1923), 433.

38. "Lincoln and the Lake Champlain Quaker," *The Friend* (Philadelphia, 1905), Vol. 78: 306.

39. "Friends and the Draft," *Quaker City Telegram* (Richmond, IN), October 11, 1862.

40. "Letter to Society of Friends," *Broad Axe of Freedom* (Richmond, IN), May 11, 1861.

41. Emmanuel Hertz, *Lincoln Talks* (Viking Press, 1939), 538–539.

42. Cyrus Pringle, *The Record of a Quaker Conscience: Cyrus Pringle's Civil War Diary, 1863* (New York: Macmillan Company, 1918), 76–77.

43. Pringle, *Civil War Diary*, 90–93.

44. Brock, *Peace Testimony*, 178.

45. John E. Divine, editor. *"To Talk Is Treason": Quakers of Waterford, Virginia, on Life, Love, Death and War in the Southern Confederacy* (Waterford, VA: Waterford Foundation, 1996), 57–60.

46. Henry J. Cadbury, "1863 Bright: Letter from the Past–No. 202," *Friends Journal*, Vol. 9, No. 14 (July 15, 1963): 311–312.

47. Bassuk, *Lincoln & Quakers*, 23.

48. Tyler Dennett, *Lincoln and the Civil War in the Diaries and Letters of John Hay* (New York: Dodd, Mead & Company, 1939), 273–274.

49. Margaret Leech, *Reveille in Washington, 1860–1865* (New York: Harper & Brothers, 1941), 301.

50. See John Hay quoted in Dennett, *Lincoln in Diaries of Hay*, 273–274; Edward Bates quoted in Howard K. Beale, editor, *The Diary of Edward Bates, 1859–1866* (Washington, DC: United States Government Printing Office, 1933), 228; Ben Perley Poore, *Perley's Reminiscences* (2 vols., New York: Hubbard Brothers, 1886), II: 124; and Leech, *Reveille in Washington*, 301.

51. Letter, Joseph J. Lewis to Eli K. Price, West Chester, PA, October 11, 1889 in *The Friend* (Philadelphia), Vol. 54 (1880): 101–102.

52. Letter, Eliza Gurney to President Abraham Lincoln, Burlington, NJ: August 18, 1863 in *Memoirs and Correspondence of Eliza P. Gurney*, edited by

Richard F. Mott (Philadelphia, 1884), 314. The original letter is in the collection of the Historical Society of Pennsylvania, Philadelphia, PA.

53. Letter, John Hay to William Herndon, September 5, 1866 quoted in Zeitz, *Lincoln's Boys*, 159.

54. Letter, AL to Eliza P. Gurney, Washington, DC, September 4, 1864, *CW*, Vol. 7: 535–536.

55. Henry J. Cadbury, "The Letter in Lincoln's Pocket–Letter from the Past No. 47," *Friends Intelligencer*, Vol. 101, No. 7 (February 12, 1944): 102.

56. Coffin, *Reminiscences*, 600–606.

57. Letter, Levi Coffin to Daniel Huff, Cincinnati, OH, December 1, 1859, Huff Family Papers, Earlham College.

58. Coffin, *Reminiscences*, 605.

59. Brock, *Peace Testimony*, 180; and Bacon, *Valiant Friend*, 180.

60. Emilio, *Brave Black Regiment*, 6; and Norwood P. Hallowell, *The Negro as a Soldier in the War of the Rebellion* (Boston: Little, Brown and Co., 1897), 25.

61. Hallowell, *Negro as a Soldier*, 9–10, 16, 34–35, 40.

62. Letter, E. N. Hallowell to Brigadier General T. Seymour, Morris Island, SC: November 7, 1863 in Emilio, *Brave Black Regiment*, 88–91.

63. Quarles, *Negro in Civil War*, 21.

64. Sarah M. Palmer quoted in Jennifer L. Weber, "'If Ever War Was Holy': Quaker Soldiers and the Union Army," *North and South* (April 2002): 66.

65. Drake, *Quakers and Slavery*, 198.

66. James P. Jones quoted in Weber, "If Ever War Was Holy," 65.

67. Letter, Daniel Hooten to Miriam Green, July 11, 1861, Green Papers. Earlham College.

68. "Advice on War," *Minutes of Indiana Yearly Meeting (Orthodox)*: October 1, 1862. Wood Collection; and "Address," *Minutes of Western Yearly Meeting at Plainfield, IN*, September 19, 1861. Wood Collection.

69. McDaniel and Julye, *Fit for Freedom, Not for Friendship*, 146.

70. Chuck Fager, "Answers to the Sixth Query of Baltimore Yearly Meeting, 1865," in "Speaking Peace, Living Peace: American Quakers Face the Civil War," http://quakerhouse.org

71. Margaret H. Bacon, *In the Shadow of William Penn: Central Philadelphia Monthly Meeting* (Philadelphia: Friends General Conference, 2001), 12.

72. Rufus Jones, *The Later Periods of Quakerism* (London: Macmillan, 1921), 737–738.

73. *The Friend* (New York). Vol. 1, No. 6 (June 1866): 85

74. Brock, *Peace Testimony*, 179.

75. Thornburg, *Earlham*, 105.

76. Letter, Joseph Moore to John Hodgkin, Richmond, IN: June 3, 1862. Earlham College.

77. Letter, David Wills to AL, Gettysburg, PA: November 2, 1863 quoted in Carl Sandberg, *Abraham Lincoln: The War Years, 1861–64* (New York: Dell Publishing, 1975 paperback), 401.

78. *Washington (D.C.) Chronicle*: November 20, 1863.

79. Garry Wills, *Lincoln at Gettysburg. The Words That Remade America* (New York: Simon & Schuster, 1992), 33–34.

80. George Gitt, a 15-year-old boy, quoted in Philip B. Kunhardt, *Lincoln* (New York: Alfred A, Knopf, 1992), 312.

81. Trueblood, *Theologian of Anguish*, 132.

82. Sandburg, *War Years*, 402–403.

83. AL, "Gettysburg Address, November 19, 1863, *CW*, 7: 22.

84. Ward Hill Lamon, *Recollections of Abraham Lincoln, 1847–1865* (Washington, DC: Dorothy LamonTeillard, 1911), 171.

85. *Harper's Weekly*: November 25, 1863. For other newspaper accounts of the "Gettysburg Address" as well as of Lincoln's other speeches, see: Herbert Mitgang, editor, *Abraham Lincoln: A Press Portrait* (Athens, GA: University of Georgia, 1956).

86. *Chicago Times*: November 23, 1863.

87. *New York World*: November 27, 1863.

88. Letter, Edward Everett to AL, November 20, 1863 quoted in Goodwin, *Team of Rivals*, 586.

89. Historian James McPherson has called the *Gettysburg Address*, "The most eloquent expression of the new birth of freedom brought forth by reform liberalism." [See McPherson, *Drawn with the Sword: Reflections on the American Civil War* (New York: Oxford University Press, 1996), 185]. Garry Wills considers the speech an "authoritative expression of the American spirit—as authoritative as the Declaration of Independence itself." He believes that Lincoln told Americans what the Declaration actually meant by "correcting the Constitution" and its validation of human slavery "without overthrowing." In so doing, Lincoln sparked an "intellectual revolution" that placed the authority of the federal government above states' rights, changing America forever. [See Wills, *Lincoln at Gettysburg. The Words That Remade America* (New York: Simon & Schuster, 1992), 146–147]. Similarly, Douglas Wilson considers the *Gettysburg Address* an "American original" and "an alluring affirmation of the nation's ideals" that would "gradually become ingrained in the nation's consciousness." [See Wilson, *Lincoln's Sword: The Presidency and the Power of Words* (New York: Alfred A. Knopf, 2007), 235–236].

90. Burke Davis and Thomas L. Livermore, "Casualties in the American Civil War," www.civilwarhome.com/casualties, accessed on December 21, 2012. Although the most often quoted number of casualties is 620,000, some experts maintain that the toll reached 700,000. Regardless, the Civil War's casualty figures exceed U.S. losses in all other wars, from the Revolution

through Vietnam. The Union armies' manpower numbered between 2,500,000 and 2,750,000. Their estimated losses totaled 360,222: 110,070 in battle and 250,152 by disease. The Confederate strength, known less accurately because of missing records, was between 750,000 and 1,250,000 men. Their estimated losses totaled 258,000: 94,000 in battle and 164,000 by disease.

91. McPherson, *Battle Cry of Freedom*, 653–667. For casualty estimates, see: Davis and Livermore, "Casualties in Civil War." The most recent account of the Battle of Gettysburg is Allen C. Guelzo, *Gettysburg: The Last Invasion* (New York: Alfred Knopf, 2013).

92. Drew Gilpin Faust, *This Republic of Suffering: Death and the American Civil War* (New York: Vintage Books, 200), 189.

93. AL, "Speech at Springfield, Illinois, June 26, 1857," *CW*, 2: 403–409; See also: Wills, *Lincoln at Gettysburg*, 101.

94. AL, "Speech at Peoria, Illinois, October 16, 1854," *CW*, 2: 270–272, 274–276.

95. Wilson, *Lincoln's Sword*, 224.

96. Longwood Progressive Friends Meeting, "Memorial to the President": 6 mo.-5-7, 1862 in *Proceedings of the Pennsylvania Yearly Meeting of Progressive Friends Held at Longwood, Chester County* (New York: Oliver Johnson, 1862), 15–16.

97. Faust, *Republic of Suffering*, 210.

CHAPTER 4: REDEMPTION, 1864–1865

1. Whittier, *Life &Letters*, 3:21.
2. Brock, *Peace Testimony*, 180.
3. Coffin, *Reminiscences*, 349–350.
4. Bacon, *Valiant Friend*, 185.
5. Bacon, *Valiant Friend*, 185.
6. Kashatus, "Conflicts of Conscience," 33–34.
7. Bacon, *Mothers of Feminism*, 122, 124.
8. Chaplain of the 14th Wisconsin Volunteers quoted in Arthur G. Sharp, "Victims of Two Enemies: The Quakers in the Civil War," *Evangelical Friend* (Newberg, Oregon), Vol. 11, No. 3 (November 1978): 7.
9. Wright, *Conscientious Objectors in Civil War*, 126; Brock, *Peace Testimony*, 172; and Richard E. Wood, Evangelical Quaker Acculturation in the Upper Mississippi Valley, 1850–1875," *Quaker History*, Vol. 76, No. 2 (Fall 1987): 139.
10. Noah Brooks, *Washington in Lincoln's Time* (New York: Rinehart, 1896), 37; Stephen W. Sears, *Controversies and Commanders: Dispatches from the Army of the Potomac* (New York: Mariner Books, 2000), 80. Stanton had not been a political supporter of Lincoln before joining the cabinet. Nor did he have an easy relationship with the president. Stanton sometimes

refused to carry out Lincoln's requests for appointments, permits, or passes. Despite differences in personal temperament, Lincoln greatly respected Stanton's abilities and his tireless work to direct the military during the war. Stanton eventually became very devoted to Lincoln, and was known to obsess over the president's personal safety. [See Fletcher Pratt, *Stanton: Lincoln's Secretary of War* (New York: W.W. Norton, 1953), 225.]

11. Brock, *Peace Testimony*, 172.

12. Stanton was born on December 19, 1814, in Steubenville, Ohio. His father was a member of the Society of Friends, and his mother was a Methodist. They both despised slavery and instilled this belief in their son. At the age of 12 Stanton joined the Methodist Church. When his father died in 1827, Stanton was forced to leave school to help support his mother. He briefly worked at a general store before clerking at a Steubenville bookstore where he tutored himself. In 1831, Stanton applied to and was accepted as a student at Kenyon College, where he joined the Episcopal Church. Admitted to the bar in Ohio in 1836, Stanton practiced in Ohio, Pittsburgh, and in Washington, DC, where he had a large practice before the Supreme Court. He gained initial fame in 1858 when he was sent to California by the U.S. attorney general as a special federal agent for the settlement of land claims, where he succeeded in breaking up a conspiracy to defraud the U.S. government of vast tracts of land of considerable value. [See Frank A. Flower, *Edwin McMasters Stanton: The Autocrat of Rebellion, Emancipation, and Reconstruction* (New York: Western W. Wilson, 1905), 22–27, 73–79.]

13. Stanton quoted in Wright, *Conscientious Objectors in the Civil War*, 126.

14. "Report of Committee to Visit Secretary of War," *Meeting of Sufferings Minutes, Baltimore Yearly Meeting*: November 21, 1863. Wood Papers, Quaker Collection, Haverford College. The special committee consisted of members from the Baltimore, Indiana, New England, New York, Ohio, and Western Meetings for Suffering.

15. "Report of Committee to Attend Conference held in Baltimore," *Meeting of Sufferings Minutes, Baltimore Yearly Meeting*: December 22, 1863. Wood Papers, Quaker Collection, Haverford College.

16. Amendment to Enrollment Act of 1863 quoted in R. R. Russell, "Development of Conscientious Objector Recognition in the United States," *The George Washington Law Review* (Washington, DC), Vol. 20, No. 4 (March 1952): 418–420.

17. Brock, *Peace Testimony*, 169–171.

18. Letter, Lincoln to Gurney, September 4, 1864, *CW*, Vol. 7: 535–536. See also, Letter, Lincoln to Samuel Boyce, Washington, DC, March 19, 1862, *CW*, Vol. 5: 165; and Lincoln quoted in Letter, Joseph J. Lewis to Eli K. Price, West Chester, PA, October 11, 1889, *The Friend* (Philadelphia), Vol. 54 (1880): 101–102.

19. Letter, Eliza Gurney to AL, Earlham Lodge: September 8, 1864 in *Memoir and Correspondence of Eliza P. Gurney*, 321.

20. McPherson, *Ordeal by Fire*, 385–386. If the actual purpose of the draft was, as McPherson notes, to stimulate volunteering, it was a success. Nearly a million men enlisted or reenlisted during the two years the draft was in effect. Still, this argument is tempered by the strong possibility that voluntary enlistment would have been much greater had it not been for the existence of an outspoken peace movement composed of Democratic Copperheads as well as Quakers and other peace churches.

21. Donald, *Lincoln*, 501.

22. Coffin, *Reminiscences*, 12–13, 222–230, 107.

23. Coffin, *Reminiscences*, 110–111

24. Charles L. Blockson, *Hippocrene Guide to the Underground Railroad* (New York: Hippocrene Books, 1994), 229.

25. Coffin, *Reminiscences*, 147–151. Stowe's use of Coffin as a model for Simon Halliday in her novel *Uncle Tom's Cabin* is questionable. Although Coffin himself claims that many people believed he was the inspiration for the character, Stowe herself claims that Quaker stationmaster Thomas Garrett of Wilmington, Delaware, was the inspiration. Stowe also claims that Simon's wife, Rachel Halliday, was inspired by a Quaker woman no longer living. Since Levi Coffin's wife, Catharine, lived until 1881, it is doubtful that she inspired the character. [See Stowe, *The Key to Uncle Tom's Cabin* (Bedford, MA: Applewood Books, 2005), 115.]

26. Coffin, *Reminiscences*, 273.

27. Coffin, *Reminiscences*, 109–110.

28. Coffin quoted in Joseph E. Halliday, "Freedmen's Aid Societies in Cincinnati, 1862–1870," *Bulletin of the Cincinnati Historical Society*, Vol. 22 (1964): 175.

29. Coffin, *Reminiscences*, 658–659.

30. AL quoted in Coffin, *Reminiscences*, 666–667.

31. Coffin, *Reminiscences*, 712–713; and *Western Yearly Meeting Minutes*, 1867.

32. Coffin, *Reminiscences*, 711–712.

33. Coffin, *Reminiscences*, 712.

34. Lucretia Mott quoted in Philip S. Benjamin, *The Philadelphia Quakers in the Industrial Age, 1865–1920* (Ann Arbor: University of Michigan Press, 1971), 130.

35. Henrietta S. Jaquette, "Friends Association of Philadelphia for the Aid and Elevation of the Freedmen," *Bulletin of Friends Historical Association*, Vol. 46, No. 2, 69–70.

36. Thomas C. Kennedy, "The Last Days at Southland," *Southern Friend*, Vol. 8, No. 1 (Spring 1986): 3–19.

37. Jaquette, "Friends Association," 70.

38. Maragaret Hope Bacon, "The Heritage of Anthony Benezet: Philadelphia Quakers and Black Education," *For Emancipation and Education: Some*

Black and Quaker Efforts, 1680–1900, edited by Eliza Cope Harrison (Philadelphia: Awbury Arboretum Association, 1997), 29.

39. Barbour & Frost, *Quakers*, 198.

40. "Relief of Contrabands," *Quaker City Telegram* (Richmond, IN), November 12, 1864.

41. Elkanah and Irena Beard quoted in Selleck, *Gentle Invaders*, 50.

42. Barbour & Frost, *Quakers*, 198

43. Laura Haviland, *A Woman's Life-Work: Labors and Experiences* (Cincinnati: Walden & Stowe, 1881), 245–387.

44. McDaniel & Julye, *Fit for Freedom, Not for Friendship*, 150.

45. McDaniel & Julye, *Fit for Freedom, Not for Friendship*, 152–153.

46. Yardley Warner quoted in Susan T. Hatcher, "North Carolina Quakers: The Freedmen's Friends," *Southern Friend* (Spring 1981): 32.

47. Willie Lee Rose, *Rehearsal for Reconstruction: The Port Royal Experiment* (New York: Oxford University Press, 1976).

48. Monica M. Tetzlaff, "The Penn School, Penn Center and Friends," *Friends Journal*, Vol. 43, No. 3 (March 1997): 16–19.

49. Jaquette, "Friends Association," 76.

50. Bacon, *Quiet Rebels*, 119.

51. Bacon, *Mothers of Feminism*, 124.

52. Barbour & Frost, *Quakers*, 198.

53. Barbour & Frost, *Quakers*, 334–335.

54. Bacon, *Quakers*, 120.

55. Thomas C. Kennedy, "Southland College: The Society of Friends and Black Education in Arkansas," *Arkansas Historical Quarterly*, Vol. 42 (Summer 1983): 211.

56. Selleck, *Gentle Invaders*, 143–144.

57. John Hope Franklin & Evelyn Brooks Higginbotham. *From Slavery to Freedom: A History of African Americans* (New York: McGraw-Hill, 2011, ninth edition. Originally published, 1947), 252–255.

58. Franklin & Higginbotham, *From Slavery to Freedom*, 250.

59. Donald, *Lincoln*, 471–472.

60. Eric Foner, *Reconstruction: America's Unfinished Revolution, 1863–1877* (New York: Harper & Row, 1988), 61–62.

61. AL, "Second Inaugural Address," March 4, 1865, *CW*, Vol. 8: 333.

62. Ronald C. White, Jr., *Lincoln's Greatest Speech: The Second Inaugural* (New York: Simon & Schuster, 2002), 164–179.

63. Letter, John B. Dutton to Ann Dutton, Point of Rocks, Maryland, November 25, 1864 quoted in John E. Divine, *"To Talk Is Treason": Quakers of Waterford, VA, on Life, Love, Death and War in the Southern Confederacy* (Waterford, VA: Waterford Foundation, Inc., 1996), 88.

64. Letter, Lucretia Mott to Mary Robbins Post, "Roadside," Cheltenham, PA, March 14, 1865, *Letters of Lucretia Mott*, 355.

65. Donald, *Lincoln*, 423–426; Mark E. Neeley, Jr., *The Fate of Liberty: Abraham Lincoln and Civil Liberties* (New York: Oxford University, 1991. reprint 2007), 185–209; and Jennifer L. Weber. *Copperheads: The Rise and Fall of Lincoln's Opponents in the North* (New York: Oxford University Press, 2006). The reasons for Democratic Copperhead opposition to Lincoln were numerous but focused on Lincoln's declaration of martial law and suspension of *habeas corpus* in 1863, the negative impact of the war on banking and agriculture, and, for some, the *Emancipation Proclamation*. These reasons were identified in the Copperhead political pamphlet *Abraham Africanus I*, which satirically depicts Lincoln making a pact with the Devil to become the monarchical ruler of the United States. [See *Abraham Africanus I: His Secret Life, Revealed Under the Mesmeric Influence; Mysteries of the White House* (New York: J.F. Feeks, 1864).]

66. Dickinson quoted in James M. McPherson, *The Struggle for Equality: Abolitionists and the Negro in the Civil War and Reconstruction* (Princeton: Princeton University Press, 1964), 108.

67. James H. Young, "Anna Elizabeth Dickinson and the Civil War: For and Against Lincoln," *Mississippi Historical Review* (June 1944): 61.

68. Bacon, *Mothers of Feminism*, 122.

69. Dickinson's speech and its reception by the audience and Lincoln quoted in the *Cincinnati Gazette*, January 18 1864.

70. Dickinson's account is quoted in Boston's *Daily Courier*, April 28, 1864.

71. J. M. McKim quoted in "Anna Elizabeth Dickinson and the Civil War: For and Against Lincoln," *Mississippi Valley Historical Review*, Vol. 31 (June 1944): 72.

72. J. Matthew Galman, *America's Joan of Arc: The Life of Anna Elizabeth Dickinson* (New York: Oxford University Press, 2006), 3–4.

73. Goodwin, *Team of Rivals*, 624.

74. Samuel T. Pickard, *Life and Letters of John Greenleaf Whittier* (2 vols., London: Sampson Low, Marston & Co., 1895), Vol. 2: 486–487. Whittier had cast one of Massachusetts' electoral votes for Lincoln in both the presidential elections of 1860 and 1864. In the latter campaign, he was deeply concerned that a Fremont candidacy would divide the Republican Party, paving the way for a Democratic victory. [See Letter, Whittier to Theodore Tilton, Boston, MA, November 1864, Quaker Collection, Haverford College.]

75. Goodwin, *Team of Rivals*, 619, 629, 645.

76. F. B. Carpenter, "Personal Impression of Abraham Lincoln," Friends Intelligencer (Philadelphia), Vol. 22, No. 11 (May 20, 1865): 171.

77. Letter, Eliza Gurney to AL, Earlham Lodge, NJ, September 8, 1864, in Mott, *Memoir and Correspondence of Gurney*, 318–321.

78. Emmanuel Hertz, *Lincoln Talks* (New York: Viking, 1939), 580.

79. Letter, John Bright, member of Parliament, to Horace Greeley, Editor, *New York Tribune*: September 26, 1864.

80. See "The Presidential Election," Friends Review (November 5, 1864): 156–157; and Richard Wood, "Evangelical Quaker Acculturation in the Upper Mississippi River Valley, 1850–1875," *Quaker History*, Vol. 76, No. 2 (Fall 1987): 140.

81. Letter, Lucretia Mott to Martha Coffin Wright, "Roadside," PA, January 24, 1864 in Palmer, Selected Letters of Mott, 338.

82. Stephen W. Sears, *George B. McClellan: The Young Napoleon* (New York: Da Capo Press, 1988), 372–374.

83. McPherson, *Battle Cry of Freedom*, 805.

84. AL, "Response to a Serenade: February 1, 1865, *CW*, Vol. 8: 254.

85. The Senate passed the 13th amendment on April 8, 1864, by a vote of 38 to 6.

86. Goodwin, *Team of Rivals*, 687–689; and W. Sherman Jackson, "Representative James M. Ashley and the Midwestern Origins of Amendment Thirteen," *Lincoln Herald*, Vol. 80, No. 2 (1978): 83–95.

87. Walter Stahr, *Seward: Lincoln's Indispensable Man* (New York: Simon & Schuster, 2012), 418–419.

88. "Joint Resolution Submitting 13th Amendment to the States; signed by Abraham Lincoln and Congress." *The Abraham Lincoln Papers at the Library of Congress: Series 3. General Correspondence, 1837–1897.* Library of Congress, Washington, DC.

89. Eric L. McKitrick, *Andrew Johnson and Reconstruction* (Chicago: University of Chicago Press, 1960), 178; and Clara Mildred Thompson, *Reconstruction in Georgia: Economic, Social, Political, 1865–1872* (New York: Columbia University Press, 1915), 156. Lincoln was assassinated by John Wilkes Booth in April 1865. His successor vice-president Andrew Johnson strongly recommended that the ex-Confederate states ratify the amendment and also repeal their ordinances of secession. On December 18, 1865, Secretary of State William H. Seward proclaimed the amendment to have been adopted on December 6, 1865, when Georgia's ratification brought the total number of states to ratify to 27 of the then 36 states. Other Southern states continued to ratify the amendment during the early years of Reconstruction.

90. John Wilkes Booth quoted in James Swanson, *Manhunt: The 12-Day Chase for Lincoln's Killer* (New York: Harper Collins, 2006), 6.

91. For the most detailed accounts of the Lincoln assassination, see: Jim Bishop, *The Day Lincoln was Shot* (New York: Harper & Row, 1955); W. Emerson Reck, *A. Lincoln: His Last 24 Hours* (Columbia: University of South Carolina Press, 1994); and Charles A. Leale, *Lincoln's Last Hours* (Whitefish, MT: Kessinger Publishing, 2010).

92. Hoch, *Lincoln Trail in Pennsylvania*, 134–138.

93. Katherine Smedley, *Martha Schofield and the Religious Education of the South, 1839–1916* (Lewsiton, NY: Edwin Mellen Press, 1987), 69–70.

94. *Minutes of Philadelphia Monthly Meeting (Hicksite)*, April 19, 1865.

95. *Minutes of Green Street Monthly Meeting, 1854–1873*, April 25, 1865.

96. The monthly meeting minutes memorializing Lincoln are referenced in the records of *Philadelphia Yearly Meeting of Women Friends (Hicksite)*, May 19, 1865; and *Philadelphia Yearly Meeting (Orthodox)*, May 9, 1865.

97. Letter, Alice C. Chase to Carrie [Chase], Haverford, PA, April 19, 1865. Quaker Collection, Haverford College; and Philip C. Garrett, editor, *A History of Haverford College* (Philadelphia: Porter & Coates, 1892), 608.

98. Martha Schofield quoted in Smedley, *Schofield and Re-Education of the South*, 69–70.

99. Rachel W. Moore quoted in *Journal*, edited by George Truman (Philadelphia: T. Ellwood Zell, 1867), 229, 242–243.

100. Samuel M. Janney, *Memoirs of Samuel M. Janney* (Philadelphia: Friends Book Association, 1890, 4th edition), 235.

101. Rebecca K. Williams, *Journal*, April 23, 1865. Mary Elizabeth Pidgeon Family Papers, 1769–1979. Friends Historical Library, Swarthmore College.

102. Letter, J. M. Walker to Samuel Janney, Waterford, Virginia, April 25, 1865 in Samuel Janney Papers, Friends Historical Library, Swarthmore College.

CONCLUSION

1. Letter, AL to Albert G. Hodges, editor, *Frankfort (Ky) Commonwealth*, April 1864, *CW*, Vol. 7: 281–282.

2. AL, "Second Inaugural Address," March 4, 1865, *CW*, Vol. 8: 333.

3. Foner, *Fiery Trial*, 181.

4. Foner, *Fiery Trial*, 181–182.

5. Foner, *Fiery Trial*, 212–213, 223–224; and Goodwin, *Team of Rivals*, 459–460.

6. Pennsylvania Progressive Friends, "Memorial to the President" in *Proceedings*, 15–16.

7. Comstock, *Life and Letters of Comstock*, 180.

8. Gurney, *Memoir and Correspondence of Gurney*, 309–312.

9. Letter, AL to Eliza P. Gurney, October 26, 1862, *CW*, Vol. 5: 478.

10. Letter, AL to Eliza P. Gurney, September 4, 1864, *CW*, Vol. 7: 535–536.

11. Amendment to Enrollment Act of 1863 quoted in Russell, "Development of Conscientious Objector Recognition in the United States," 418–420.

12. Franklin & Higginbotham, *From Slavery to Freedom*, 252–255.

13. Herbert Hoover, the thirty-first president who served from 1929 to 1933, was a Quaker from West Branch, Iowa. Richard M. Nixon, the 37th president who served from 1969 to 1975, was a Friend from Yorba Linda, California.

14. Nellie Blessing-Eyster, "A Day among the Quakers," *Harper's New Monthly Magazine* (September 1870).

15. Nellie Blessing-Eyster, "Mr. Lincoln and the Crazy Quaker," *New Voice*, 1889.

16. Henry W. Wilbur, *Friends with Lincoln in the White House* (Philadelphia, 1912).

17. Carl Sandburg, *The War Years*, 1939.

18. Henry J. Cadbury, "Another Quaker Legend of Lincoln," *Friends Intelligencer*, Vol. 109, No. 6 (February 9, 1952): 75–76.

19. In 1909, Edwin Hadley, a descendant of Isaac and Sarah Harvey, delivered a Memorial Day speech at Springfield, Ohio, in which he stated that the Quaker couple "made a trip to Washington to confer with President Lincoln." Although he did not offer a specific date for the interview and admitted that "none of us ever knew the exact nature of the conference," Hadley stated his "firm belief" that the meeting was "the pivot on which turned the destinies of this nation." [See Edwin Hadley, "Memorial Day Speech," *Clinton Republican*: June 1, 1894]. Christine Hadley Snyder, another descendant, has completed painstaking research in the Springfield Friends Monthly Meeting Minutes to verify the Harvey's interview with Lincoln. While she admits that there is no request for a traveling minute to Washington in 1862, she did find evidence that the couple requested and received letters of introduction from the governors of Indiana and Illinois dated September 1861. [See e-mail, Christine Hadley Snyder to author, February 15, 2013; and Snyder, *Springfield Friends Meeting, 1809–2009* (Wilmington, OH: Springfield Monthly Meeting, 2009), 77–91]. Her discovery confirms this writer's findings in Roy Basler's Collected Works of Lincoln.

20. See "Statue honors Quaker heritage," *News Journal* [Clinton County, Ohio], September 22, 2009; and "Who Sends Thee? Statue Tells a Quaker Story," *Wilmington College News*, September 24, 2009, online at www2.wilmington.edu/prc/news/

21. Letter, AL to Eliza P. Gurney, Washington, DC, September 4, 1864, *CW*, Vol. 7: 535–536.

22. J. Bevan Braithwaite, "Obituary of Eliza P. Gurney," *Annual Monitor* (London, 1882), 12.

23. Richard F. Mott, editor, *Memoirs and Correspondence of Eliza P. Gurney* (Philadelphia, 1884), 322.

24. Augustus J. C. Hare, *The Gurneys of Earlham* (2 vols. London, 1895), Vol. 2: 328.

25. Amelia Mott Gummere, *The Quaker in the Forum* (1910), 316.

26. F. Lauriston Bullard, "Lincoln and the Quaker Woman," *Lincoln Herald*, Vol. 46, No. 2 (June 1944): 10; See also: Henry J. Cadbury, "The Letter in Lincoln's Pocket – Letter from the Past No. 47," *Friends Intelligencer*, Vol. 101, No. 7 (February 12, 1944): 102.

Selected Bibliography

MANUSCRIPTS

Newspapers and Periodicals

Broad Axe of Freedom (Richmond, IN)
Chicago Times
Cincinnati Gazette
Friend (New York)
Friend (Philadelphia)
Friends Intelligencer (Philadelphia)
Friends Journal (Philadelphia)
Harper's Weekly
National Anti-Slavery Standard (New York)
New York Herald
New York Times
New York World
North American & U.S. Gazette
Public Ledger (Philadelphia)
Quaker City Telegram (Richmond, IN)
Washington (D.C.) Chronicle

Religious Society of Friends: Yearly Meeting Minutes

Baltimore Yearly Meeting (Orthodox)
Indiana Yearly Meeting of Anti-Slavery Friends
Indiana Yearly Meeting (Orthodox)
London Yearly Meeting
New England Yearly Meeting (Orthodox)
New York Yearly Meeting (Hicksite)
New York Yearly Meeting (Orthodox)

Ohio Yearly Meeting
Philadelphia Yearly Meeting (Hicksite)
Philadelphia Yearly Meeting (Orthodox)
Western Yearly Meeting
Source: Manuscripts, Quaker Collection, Haverford College Library, Haverford, PA.

PRIMARY SOURCES

Arnold, Isaac N. *The Life of Abraham Lincoln*. Chicago: A.C. McClurg & Co., 1909. Originally published, 1880.
Bates, Edward. *The Diary of Edward Bates*, edited by Howard K. Beale. Washington, D.C.: United States Government Printing Office, 1933.
Bayne, Julia Taft. *Tad Lincoln's Father*. Lincoln: University of Nebraska, 2001. Originally published, 1931.
Carpenter, F. B. "Personal Impressions of Abraham Lincoln," *Friends Intelligencer*, Vol. 22, No. 11 (May 20, 1865): 171.
Coffin, Levi. *Reminiscences of Levi Coffin: The Reputed President of the Underground Railroad*. New York: Arno Press & *The New York Times*, 1968. Originally published, 1876.
Comstock, Elizabeth. *The Life and Letters of Elizabeth L. Comstock*, edited by C. Hare. London: Headley Brothers, 1895.
Douglass, Frederick. *The Life and Writings of Frederick Douglass*, 5 vols, edited by Philip S. Foner. New York: International Publishers, 1950–1973.
Edgerton, Walter. *A History of the Separation in Indiana Yearly Meeting*. Cincinnati, 1856.
Emilio, Luis F. *A Brave Black Regiment: History of the 54th Massachusetts Regiment*. Salem, NH: Ayer Company, 1990. Originally published, 1894.
Gurney, Eliza P. *Memoir and Correspondence of Eliza P. Gurney*, edited by Richard F. Mott. Philadelphia: J.B. Lippincott, 1884.
Hallowell, Norwood P. *Reminiscences.* Privately published manuscript, West Medford, MA, 1897.
Haviland, Laura. *A Woman's Life-Work: Labors and Experiences*. Cincinnati: Walden & Stowe, 1881.
Herndon, William. *Herndon's Lincoln: The True Story of a Great Life, 2 vols*. New York: Macmillan Company, 1917.
Janney, Samuel M. *Memoirs of Samuel M. Janney*. Philadelphia: Friends Book Association, 1890, 4th edition.
Keckley, Elizabeth. *Behind the Scenes, or, Thirty Years a Slave and Four Years in the White House*. New York: Oxford University Press, 1988. Originally published, 1868.
Lamon, Ward H. *Recollections of Abraham Lincoln: 1847–1865*, edited by Dorothy Lamon Teillard. Lincoln: University of Nebraska Press, 1994. Originally published, 1911.

Lincoln, Abraham. *The Collected Works of Abraham Lincoln*, 8 vols, edited by Roy P. Basler. New Brunswick, NJ: Rutgers University Press, 1953–1955.

McGowan, James A. *Station Master on the Underground Railroad: The Life and Letters of Thomas Garrett*. Jefferson, NC: McFarland, 2005.

Mitgang, Herbert, editor. *Abraham Lincoln: A Press Portrait*. Athens, GA: University of Georgia, 1956.

Moore, Rachel W. *Journal of Rachel Wilson Moore*, edited by George Truman. Philadelphia: T. Ellwood Zell, 1867.

Mott, Lucretia. *Selected Letters of Lucretia Coffin Mott*, edited by Beverly W. Palmer. Chicago: University of Illinois Press, 2002.

Nicolay, John G. *With Lincoln in the White House: Letters, Memorials & Other Writings of John G. Nicolay, 1860–1865*, edited by Michael Burlingame. Carbondale: Southern Illinois University Press, 2006.

Pennsylvania Yearly Meeting of Progressive Friends, *Proceedings, 1853–1862*. New York: Oliver Johnson, 1862.

Pringle, Cyrus. *The Record of a Quaker Conscience: Cyrus Pringle's Civil War Diary, 1863*. New York: Macmillan Company, 1918.

Seward, Frederick W., editor. *Seward at Washington, as Senator and Secretary of State: A Memoir of His Life, with Selections from His Letters, 1861–1872*. New York: Derby and Miller, 1891.

Thayer, William R. *The Life and Letters of John Hay*. Boston: Houghton Mifflin, 1915.

Welles, Gideon. *Diary of Gideon Wells, Secretary of the Navy Under Lincoln and Johnson*, 3 vols. Boston: Houghton Mifflin, 1911. Reprinted, 1960.

Whittier, John G. *Life and Letters of John G. Whittier*, 3 vols., edited by Samuel T. Pickard. London: Sampson Low, Marston & Company, 1895.

SECONDARY SOURCES

Adams, Ephriam D. *Great Britain and the American Civil War*, 2 vols. New York: Russell & Russell, 1924.

Ausubel, Herman. *John Bright: Victorian Reformer*. New York: Wiley, 1966.

Bacon, Margaret H. *The Quiet Rebels: The Story of Quakers in America*. New York: Basic Books, 1969.

Bacon, Margaret H. *Valiant Friend: The Life of Lucretia Mott*. New York: Walker & Co., 1980, paper.

Baker, Jean H. *James Buchanan*. New York: Times Books, 2004.

Baker, Jean H. *Mary Todd Lincoln: A Biography*. New York: W.W. Norton, 1989.

Barbour, Hugh. *The Quakers in Puritan England.* New Haven: Yale University, 1964.
Barbour, Hugh and J. William Frost. *The Quakers.* Westport, CT: Greenwood Press, 1988.
Bassuk, Daniel. *Abraham Lincoln and the Quakers.* Wallingford, PA: Pendle Hill Publications, 1987.
Bennett, Lerone, Jr. *Forced into Glory: Abraham Lincoln's White Dream.* Chicago: Johnson Publishing Company, 2000.
Braithwaite, William C. *The Beginnings of Quakerism.* Cambridge, England: Cambridge University Press, 1961, 2nd edition.
Brock, Peter. *The Quaker Peace Testimony, 1660 to 1914.* York, England: William Sessions, Ltd., 1990.
Bullard, F. Lauriston. "Lincoln and the Quaker Woman," *Lincoln Herald,* Vol. 46, No. 2 (June 1944): 9–12.
Burlingame, Michael. *The Inner World of Abraham Lincoln.* Urbana: University of Illinois Press, 1994.
Cadbury, Henry J. "1863 Bright: Letter from the Past—No. 202," *Friends Journal,* Vol. 9, No. 14 (July 15, 1963): 311–312.
Cadbury, Henry J. "Another Quaker Legend of Lincoln," *Friends Intelligencer,* Vol. 109, No. 6 (February 9, 1952): 75–76.
Cadbury, Henry J. "The Hunt for Lincoln's Quaker Ancestors," *Friends Journal* (February 1, 1966), 12–14.
Cadbury, Henry J. "The Letter in Lincoln's Pocket—Letter from the Past No. 47," *Friends Intelligencer,* Vol. 101, No. 7 (February 12, 1944): 102.
Cadbury, Henry J. "Negro Membership in the Society of Friends," *Journal of Negro History,* Vol. 21 (1936): 151–213.
Carter, Max L. "Elizabeth Kirkbride Gurney's Correspondence with Abraham Lincoln: The Quaker Dilemma," *Pennsylvania Magazine of History and Biography,* Vol. 133, No. 4 (October 2009): 389–396.
Carwardine, Richard. *Lincoln: A Life of Purpose and Power.* New York: Alfred A. Knopf, 2006.
Cash, Bill. *John Bright: Statesman, Orator, Agitator.* London: I.B. Tauris, 2012.
Cuthbert, Norma B., editor. *Lincoln and the Baltimore Plot, 1861.* San Marino, CA: Huntington Library, 1949.
Dennett, Tyler. *Lincoln and the Civil War in the Diaries and Letters of John Hay.* New York: Dodd, Mead & Company, 1939.
Doherty, Robert W. *The Hicksite Separation: A Sociological Analysis of Religious Schism in Early Nineteenth Century America.* New Brunswick, NJ: Rutgers University, 1967.
Donald, David Herbert. *Lincoln.* New York: Simon & Schuster, 1996, paperback.
Drake, Thomas E. *Quakers and Slavery in America.* Gloucester, MA: Peter Smith, 1950.

Faulkner, Carol. *Lucretia Mott's Heresy: Abolition and Women's Rights in Nineteenth Century America*. Philadelphia: University of Pennsylvania, 2011.
Faust, Drew Gilpin. *This Republic of Suffering: Death and the American Civil War*. New York: Vintage Books, 2008.
Fleischner, Jennifer. *Mrs. Lincoln and Mrs. Keckley: The Remarkable Story of the Friendship between a First Lady and a Former Slave*. New York: Broadway Books, 2003.
Foner, Eric. *The Fiery Trial: Abraham Lincoln and American Slavery*. New York: W.W. Norton, 2010.
Foner, Eric. *Free Soil, Free Labor, Free Men: The Ideology of the Republican Party before the Civil War*. New York: Oxford University Press, 1995, revised edition.
Foner, Eric. *Reconstruction: America's Unfinished Revolution. 1863–1877*. New York: Harper & Row, 1988.
Franklin, John Hope. *The Emancipation Proclamation*. New York: Doubleday, 1965, paperback edition.
Franklin, John Hope and Evelyn Brooks Higginbotham. *From Slavery to Freedom: A History of African Americans*. New York: McGraw-Hill, 2011, 9th edition. Originally published, 1947.
Galman, J. Matthew. *America's Joan of Arc: The Life of Anna Elizabeth Dickinson*. New York: Oxford University Press, 2006.
Garrett, Philip C., editor. *A History of Haverford College*. Philadelphia: Porter & Coates, 1892.
Geary, James W. *We Need Men: The Union Draft in the Civil War*. DeKalb, IL: Northern Illinois University Press, 1991.
Goodwin, Doris Kearns. *Team of Rivals: The Political Genius of Abraham Lincoln*. New York: Simon & Schuster, 2005.
Guelzo, Allen C. *Abraham Lincoln: Redeemer President*. Grand Rapids, MI: Wm. B. Eerdmans Publishing Company, 1999.
Guelzo, Allen C. *Gettysburg: The Last Invasion*. New York: Alfred Knopf, 2013.
Guelzo, Allen C. *Lincoln's Emancipation Proclamation: The End of Slavery in America*. New York: Simon & Schuster, 2004.
Hamm, Thomas D. *The Transformation of American Quakerism: Orthodox Friends, 1800–1907*. Bloomington: Indiana University, 1988.
Hare, Augustus J.C. *The Gurneys of Earlham*, 2 vols. London: George Allen, 1895.
Hatcher, Susan T. "North Carolina Quakers: The Freedmen's Friends," *Southern Friend* (Spring 1981): 32–38.
Heidler, David S. and Jeanne T. Heidler, *Henry Clay: The Essential American*. New York: Random House, 2010.
Hirst, Margaret E. *The Quakers in Peace and War*. London: Swarthmore Press, 1923.

Hoch, Bradley R. *The Lincoln Trail in Pennsylvania: A History and Guide.* University Park, PA: Penn State Press, 2001.

Holzer, Harold, editor. *Dear Mr. Lincoln: Letters to the President.* Reading, MA: Addison-Wesley, 1993.

Holzer, Harold. *Lincoln at Cooper Union: The Speech That Made Abraham Lincoln President.* New York: Simon & Schuster, 2006.

Holzer, Harold. *Lincoln President-Elect: Abraham Lincoln and the Great Secession Winter 1860–1861.* New York: Simon & Schuster, 2008.

Ingle, H. Larry. *Quakers in Conflict: The Hicksite Separation.* Knoxville: University of Tennessee Press, 1986.

James, Sydney V. *A People among Peoples: Quaker Benevolence in Eighteenth-Century America.* Cambridge, MA: Harvard University Press, 1963.

Jaquette, Henrietta S. "Friends' Association of Philadelphia for the Aid and Elevation of the Freedmen," *The Bulletin of the Friends Historical Association*, Vol. 46, No. 2 (Autumn 1957): 68–73.

Jones, Rufus M. *The Later Periods of Quakerism.* London: Macmillan & Co., 1921.

Jordan, Ryan P. *Slavery and the Meetinghouse: The Quakers and the Abolitionist Dilemma, 1820–1865.* Bloomington: Indiana University Press, 2007.

Kashatus, William C. "Conflict of Conscience: The Richmond Quakers Face the Civil War, 1860–1865," *Indiana Military History Journal* (Indianapolis), Vol. 5, No. 3 (October 1980): 27–35.

Kashatus, William C. *Just Over the Line: Chester County and the Underground Railroad.* West Chester, PA: Chester County Historical Society, 2002.

Keiser, David S. "Quaker Ancestors for Lincoln," *Lincoln Herald* 63 (1961): 134–137.

Kunhardt, Philip B., Jr., Philip B. Kunhardt III, and Peter W. Kunhardt, *Lincoln: An Illustrated Biography.* New York: Alfred A. Knopf, 1992.

Leech, Margaret. *Reveille in Washington, 1860–1865.* New York: Harper & Brothers, 1941.

Mangus, Michael S. " 'A Cruel and Malicious War': The Society of Friends in Civil War Loudoun County, Virginia," *Quaker History*, Vol. 88, No. 1 (Spring 1999), 40–52.

Mansfield, Stephen. *Lincoln's Battle With God: A President's Struggle with Faith and What It Meant for America.* Dallas, TX: Thomas Nelson, 2012.

Marietta, Jack D. *The Reformation of American Quakerism, 1748–1783.* Philadelphia: University of Pennsylvania Press, 1984.

McDaniel, Donna and Vanessa Julye. *Fit for Freedom, Not for Friendship: Quakers, African Americans, and the Myth of Racial Justice.* Philadelphia: Quaker Press, 2000.

McPherson, James M. *Battle Cry of Freedom: The Civil War Era.* New York: Oxford University Press, 1988.

McPherson, James M. *Drawn with the Sword: Reflections on the American Civil War.* New York: Oxford University Press, 1996.

McPherson, James M. *The Negro's Civil War. How American Blacks Felt and Acted During the War for the Union.* New York: Ballantine Books, 1991.

McPherson, James M. *Ordeal by Fire: The Civil War and Reconstruction.* New York: McGraw-Hill, 2001, 3rd edition.

Mekeel, Arthur J. *The Quakers and the American Revolution.* York, England: William Sessions, 1996. Originally published, 1979.

Miers, Early Schenk. *Lincoln Day by Day: A Chronology, 1809–1865.* Dayton, OH: Morningside, 1991.

Miller, William L. *Lincoln's Virtues: An Ethical Biography.* New York: Vintage, 2003.

Moore, John M., editor. *Friends in the Delaware Valley: Philadelphia Yearly Meeting, 1681–1981.* Haverford, PA: Friends Historical Association, 1981.

Moskos, Charles C. and John Whiteclay Chambers, editors. *The New Conscientious Objection: From Sacred to Secular Resistance.* New York: Oxford University Press, 1993.

Neely, Mark E., Jr. *The Fate of Liberty: Abraham Lincoln and Civil Liberties.* New York: Oxford University Press, 1992.

Neely, Mark E., Jr. and R. Gerald McMurty. *The Insanity File: The Case of Mary Lincoln.* Carbondale: Southern Illinois University Press, 1986.

Nelson, Jacquelyn S. *Indiana Quakers Confront the Civil War.* Indianapolis: Indiana Historical Society, 1991.

Neuburger, Otto E. "Quaker Documents in the Lincoln Collection," *Friends Intelligencer*, Vol. 105, No. 33 (August 14, 1948): 467–469.

Nicolay, Helen. *Lincoln's Secretary: A Biography of John G. Nicolay.* New York: Longman, Green, 1971.

Noll, Mark A. *The Ambiguous Religion of Abraham Lincoln.* Grand Rapids, MI: William B. Eerdmans, 1992.

Oakes, James. *The Radical and the Republican: Frederick Douglass, Abraham Lincoln, and the Triumph of Antislavery Politics.* New York: W.W. Norton & Co., 2007.

Oates, Stephen. *With Malice Toward None: A Life of Abraham Lincoln.* New York: Harper & Row, 1977.

Packard, Jerrold M. *The Lincolns in the White House: Four Years That Shattered a Family.* New York: St. Martin's Press, 2005.

Periano, Kevin. *Lincoln in the World. The Making of a Statesman and the Dawn of American Power.* New York: Crown Publishers, 2013.

Pratt, Fletcher. *Stanton: Lincoln's Secretary of War.* New York: W.W. Norton, 1953.

Quarles, Benjamin. *The Negro in the Civil War*. New York: Da Capo Press, 1989. Originally published, 1953.
Randall, J.G. *Lincoln the President: Last Full Measure*. New York: Dodd, Mead and Co., 1955.
Randall, Ruth Painter. *Lincoln's Sons*. Boston: Little, Brown & Co., 1955.
Randall, Ruth Painter. *Mary Lincoln: Biography of a Marriage*. Boston: Little, Brown & Co., 1953.
Reed, Pat B. *Westtown: In Word & Deed, 1799–1999*. Westtown, PA: Westtown School, 1998.
Ridley, Jasper. *Lord Palmerston*. New York: Dutton, 1970.
Russell, R.R. "Development of Conscientious Objector Recognition in the United States," *George Washington Law Review* (Washington, D.C.), Vol. 20, No. 4 (March 1952): 418–420
Sandberg, Carl. Lincoln: *The War Years*, 3 vols. New York: Harcourt, Brace & Co., 1939.
Selleck, Linda. *Gentle Invaders: Quaker Women Educators and Racial Issues During the Civil War and Reconstruction*. Richmond, IN: Friends United Press, 1995.
Shenk, Joshua Wolf. *Lincoln's Melancholy: How Depression Challenged a President and Fueled His Greatness*. Boston: Houghton Mifflin, 2005.
Simon, John Y. "Abraham Lincoln and Ann Rutledge." *Journal of the Abraham Lincoln Association* 11 (1990): 13–34.
Smedley, Katherine. *Martha Schofield and the Religious Education of the South, 1839–1916*. Lewiston, NY: Edwin Mellen Press, 1987.
Smith, Thomas H. "Ohio Quakers and the Mississippi Freedmen: 'A Field to Labor,'" *Ohio History*, Vol. 78, No. 3 (Summer 1969): 160–167.
Soderlund, Jean R. *Quakers and Slavery. A Divided Spirit*. Princeton: Princeton University Press, 1985.
Stahr, Walter. *Seward: Lincoln's Indispensable Man*. New York: Simon & Schuster, 2012.
Stashower, Daniel. *The Hour of Peril: The Secret Plot to Murder Lincoln Before the Civil War*. New York: Macmillan, 2013.
Stephenson, Nathanial W. *Abraham Lincoln and the Union*. New Haven: Yale University Press, 1918.
Stephenson, Nathanial W. *An Autobiography of Lincoln*. New York: Blue Ribbon Books, 1926.
Striner, Richard. *Father Abraham: Lincoln's Relentless Struggle to End Slavery*. New York: Oxford University, 2006.
Suppinger, Joseph E. "The Intimate Lincoln," *Lincoln Herald*, Vol. 85, No. 3 (Fall 1983): 161.
Thornburg, Opal. *Earlham: The Story of the College, 1847–1962*. Richmond, IN: Earlham College, 1963.
Tripp, C.A. *The Intimate World of Abraham Lincoln*. New York: The Free Press, 2005.

Trueblood, D. Elton. *Abraham Lincoln: Theologian of American Anguish.* New York: Harper& Row, 1973.
Turner, Justin G. and Linda L. Turner. *Mary Todd Lincoln: Her Life and Letters.* New York: Alfred A. Knopf, 1972.
Wahl, Albert J. "The Congregational or Progressive Friends in the Pre-Civil War Reform Movement." PhD dissertation, Temple University, Philadelphia, Pennsylvania, 1951.
Ward, Geoffrey C., Ric Burns, and Ken Burns. *The Civil War: An Illustrated History.* New York: Alfred A. Knopf, 1990.
Waring, Eileen. "Four Friends Drop in on Lincoln," *Friends Journal*, Vol. 11, No. 10 (May 15, 1965): 253–255.
Warren, Gordon H. *Fountain of Discontent: The Trent Affair and Freedom of the Seas.* Boston: Northeastern University Press, 1981
Weber, Jennifer L. *Copperheads: The Rise and Fall of Lincoln's Opponents in the North.* New York: Oxford University Press, 2006.
Weeks, Stephen. *Southern Quakers and Slavery.* Baltimore: Johns Hopkins Press, 1896.
White, Ronald. *Lincoln's Greatest Speech.* New York: Simon & Schuster, 2002.
Wilbur, Henry W. *Friends with Lincoln in the White House.* Philadelphia, 1912.
Williams, T. Harry. *Lincoln and the Radicals.* Madison: University of Wisconsin Press, 1960.
Wills, Garry. *Lincoln at Gettysburg. The Words That Remade America.* New York: Simon & Schuster, 1992.
Wilson, Douglas L. *Honor's Voice: The Transformation of Abraham Lincoln.* New York: Vintage, 1999.
Wilson, Douglas L. *Lincoln's Sword: The Presidency and the Power of Words.* New York: Alfred A. Knopf, 2007.
Wolf, William J. *The Almost Chosen People: A Study of the Religion of Abraham Lincoln.* Garden City, NY: Doubleday & Co., 1959.
Worrall, Arthur J. *New England Quakerism, 1656–1830.* PhD dissertation, Indiana University, 1969.
Wright, Edward N. *Conscientious Objectors in the Civil War.* PhD dissertation, University of Pennsylvania, 1930.
Zeitz, Joshua. *Lincoln's Boys: John Hay, John Nicolay, and the War for Lincoln's Image.* New York: Viking, 2014.

Index

abolitionism, 4–5, 64, 88; and Quakers, 4–5, 12–14, 16–19, 52–53, 70, 72–73, 101–3, 104–5
Agnew, Eliza, 47, 53, 120
American Republican (West Chester, PA), 52
Andrew, Gov. John A., 75
Antietam, 63, 122
Arnold, Isaac, 44
Ashley, James, 113

Baker, Edward, 93
Baltimore Conference, 99–100
Baltimore Yearly Meeting, 16, 18, 35, 89, 99
Barnard, William, 47–49, 53, 120
Bates, Judge Edward, 40, 58
Battle of Wilderness, 101
Beard, Elkanah, 105
Beard, Irena, 105
Blair, Montgomery, 58–59
Blessing-Eyster, Nellie, 123
Booth, John Wilkes, 114
border states, 12, 25, 29–31, 61, 72
Bright, John: champions abolitionism in Parliament, 32–33, 64; relations with U.S. Congress, 34–35; relationship with Lincoln, 33–35, 83–84, 112; and Trent Affair, 32–34
Brinton, Joseph, 72
Broad Axe of Freedom (Richmond, IN), 82
Brock, Peter, 27, 89
Brown, William Wells, 60
Browning, Orville, 22, 43
Buchanan, James, 22
Bundy, Thomas, 26
Burleigh, Charles, 52
Burnside, Gen. Ambrose E., 68–69

Cadbury, Henry J., 123
Cameron, Simon, 40
Camp William Penn, 98
Canada, 34
Carey, James, 1, 65, 99–100
Carpenter, F. B., 111
Chase, Salmon, 12, 40, 53, 58, 122
Chicago Times, 92
Chicago Tribune, 64
Child, Maria, 64
Cincinnati, OH, 21, 86, 102–3
Clark, Alida, 106–7
Clark, Calvin, 106–7
Clay, Henry, 17
Cobden, Richard, 35
Coffin, Catharine, 98, 102–3
Coffin, Elijah, 17
Coffin, Levi, 17, 86–87, 98; background of, 102–4; and inspiration for *Uncle Tom's Cabin*, 102; and relief of freedmen, 103–4; and *Reminiscences*, 98, 103; underground railroad activities, 102–3
colonization, 12, 18, 56–58, 59–61, 120
Comstock, Elizabeth, 69–70, 121

Confederate Army: at Antietam, 63; casualties, 93; at Fort Wagner, 87–88; and Peninsula campaign, 53
Confederate States of America: and "cotton diplomacy," 31, 37; prisoners of war, 75–76; and slavery, 9; Reconstruction, 107–8; relations with Britain, 31–32, 37, 64
Confiscation Acts (1861), 29–31, 55; (1862), 55–58, 74
conscientious objection, 77–78, 79–80, 82–90, 98–101
Conscription Acts (1863), 5, 76; (1864), 5, 100; statistics, 76, 101
Cornelius, James M., 49–50
Cromwell, Oliver, 78–79
Curtin, Governor Andrew, 19, 90, 123
Cuyler, Theodore, 10

Dakin, Peter, 82–83
Davis, Edward M., 28, 87–88
Davis, Jefferson, 44, 63–64
Declaration of Independence, 9–11, 21, 73, 93, 94–96, 115
Delany, Martin R., 60
Democrat Party: "Copperheads" (Peace Democrats), 77–78, 114; criticism of Lincoln, 21, 25, 78, 109; and Fourteenth Amendment, 113–14; and presidential election of 1860, 10; and presidential election of 1864, 111–13
Dickinson, Anna Elizabeth, 109–10
doctrine of necessity, 7, 46, 54, 67–68, 94
Douglas, Stephen, 21
Douglass, Frederick, 60–61, 74–75
Dow, Neal, 88
Dutton, John B., 108

Earlham College, 27, 89
Edgerton, Walter, 17
Ellsworth, Elmer, 93
emancipation, 30–31, 53–54, 55–59, 64, 71–75, 94–95
Emancipation Proclamation: and enlistment of black soldiers, 74–75; preliminary draft, 56–57, 58–59, 62, 63–64, 120–21, 124; Quaker reaction to, 72–73, 85, 110; significance to the war, 71–72, 74, 113
Enrollment Act (1863). *See* Conscription acts
Evans, Thomas, 84–85
Everett, Edward, 90–91, 93

Fenton, Sallie, 65
Fisher, George, 30
Ford's Theater (Washington, D.C.), 86, 114
Fort Sumter (Charleston, SC), 25, 26
Fort Wagner (Charleston, SC), 87–88
freedmen: Quaker aid to, 103–7
Freedmen's Bureau, 104, 105, 107, 117, 122
Fremont, Gen. John C., 28, 29, 87, 110
French–Indian War, 79–80
Friend, The (Philadelphia, PA), 72
Friends Association for Aid to Freedmen, 104
Friends Freedmen's Association, 104, 106
Friends Intelligencer (Philadelphia, PA), 77
Fugitive Slave Law (1850), 50–51, 120

Garnet, Henry H., 60
Garrett, Thomas, 47, 51, 53, 120
Garrison, William Lloyd, 52, 88–89, 97
Germantown Anti-Slavery Protest, 12–13
Germantown (PA) Monthly Meeting, 62
Gettysburg, PA, 84, 90–96; battle of, 93–94
Gettysburg Address, 91–93, 94
Gibbons, Abbey Hopper, 98
Gladstone, William, 35, 64
Grant, Gen. Ulysses, 53
Greeley, Horace, 61–62, 64, 112
Green Street Monthly Meeting, 24, 115
Grellet, Rachel, 69–70, 121
Guelzo, Allen, 6–7
Gummere, Margaret, 26
Gurley, Rev. Phineas, 45–46

Gurney, Eliza, 1–4, 65, 70; correspondence with Lincoln, 3–4, 66–67, 85–86, 101, 111, 124–25; interview with Lincoln, 1–4, 65, 121
Gurney, Joseph J., 16, 65, 124

Halleck, Gen. Henry W., 55
Hallowell, Edward, 87–88
Hallowell, Norwood, P., 26, 87–88
Hallowell, Richard, 87–88
Hambleton, Alice, 47, 53, 120
Hamm, Thomas, 17, 28
Hancock, Cornelia, 106
Harper's Weekly, 92
Harrisburg, PA, 19
Harvey, Isaac, 122–24, 125
Harvey, John, 27
Harvey, Sarah, 122–24, 125
Haverford College, 26, 116
Haviland, Laura, 98, 105
Hay, John, 86
Herndon, William, 6
Hicks, Elias, 16, 64
Hicksite Separation, 15–16
Hollingsworth, Robert, 83
Holzer, Harold, 6–7
Hooker, Gen. Joseph, 93
Hopkins, James, 72
Hopper, Maria, 98
Howland, Emily, 106
Hunter, Gen. David, 53

Independence Hall, 9–10, 115
Indiana Yearly Meeting, 16–18, 20, 25–26, 27–28, 88
Indiana Yearly Meeting of Anti-Slavery Friends, 17–18, 105
Inner Light doctrine, 3, 12, 16, 78
Iowa Yearly Meeting, 20

Janney, Samuel, 83, 117
Johnson, Gov. Andrew, 76
Johnson, Oliver, 47–48, 51, 53, 120
Johnston, Gen. Joseph E., 53
Jones, James Parnell, 88

Kansas–Nebraska Act, 11
Keckley, Mary, 42

Kelley, William D., 110
Kennett Monthly Meeting (Hicksite), 50
King, Levinus, 27

Lamborn, Thomas, 72–73
Lamon, Ward, 49
Lay, Benjamin, 13
Lee, Gen. Robert E., 63, 68–69, 91, 93–94, 114
Lincoln, Abraham: *Annual Message to Congress* (1862), 67, 73; assassination of, 86, 114, 124–25; British criticism of, 32; on colonization, 12, 57–58, 59–61, 120; as congressman, 11; correspondence with Eliza Gurney, 1–4, 66–67, 85–86, 101, 111, 124–25; and depression, 43–45; and doctrine of necessity, 7, 46, 50, 54, 62, 67–68; and emancipation, 30–31, 53–54, 55–59, 71–75, 94–95; *First Inaugural Address*, 23–25; at Gettysburg, 90–96; *Gettysburg Address*, 91–93, 94; *House Divided Speech*, 47–48; humor of, 22, 44, 57; inauguration, 22–24; interviews with Quakers, 1–2, 35–36, 47–49, 65–70, 72–73, 84–85, 121; *Meditation on the Divine Will*, 62, 67–68, 121; mythologized by Quakers, 122–25; plan for gradual compensated emancipation, 30–31, 53–54; presidential campaign of 1860, 6, 19; presidential campaign of 1864, 111–13; Quaker ancestry, 6, 49–50; and Reconstruction, 107–9, 110; relationship with cabinet, 29, 40, 44, 57–59, 71; relationship with Congress, 55–56, 67, 73, 74–76, 103–4, 107, 109; relationship with McClellan, 39–40, 111–13; relationship with Quakers, 119–22; religious beliefs, 6–7, 45–46, 49, 62, 66–67, 89–90, 119; reverence for *Declaration of Independence*, 9–11, 21; *Second Inaugural Address*, 67–68,

108–9; on slavery, 8, 11–12, 21–22, 23, 48, 57–59, 73–74; and war powers, 25, 56, 58, 113, 119
Lincoln, Edward "Eddie," 41
Lincoln, Mary Todd, 42–43, 70, 84
Lincoln, Robert, 22, 40–41, 125
Lincoln, Thomas "Tad," 40–42
Lincoln, Willie, 40–42, 46, 54; death of, 42–43, 84
London Yearly Meeting, 35, 79
Longstreth, Lydia, 62
Longwood (PA) Progressive Friends Meeting, 47–54; *Exposition of Sentiments*, 51–52
Loudoun County, VA, 27, 83

Macomber, Lindley, 82–83
Mason, James, 32, 34
McClellan, Gen. George B.: and 1864 presidential campaign, 111–13; background, 39–40; compared to other Union generals, 39–40, 69; and "Quaker Gun" affair, 53; and relationship with Lincoln, 40, 53, 55; and reluctance to attack, 53, 63; replaced by Halleck, 55
Meade, Gen. George, 90–91, 93–94
Medill, Joseph, 64
Meditation on the Divine Will, 62, 67–68, 121
Mendenhall, Isaac, 51
Mendenhall, Dinah, 47, 51, 53, 120
Mexican War, 81
Michigan Freedmen's Aid Commission, 105
Mitchell, James, 56, 60
Moore, Joseph, 89
Moore, Rachel Wilson, 64, 117
Mott, Hannah B., 1, 65
Mott, Lucretia: and abolitionist activities, 52, 64–65, 98; freedmen's relief, 104; views on Lincoln's policies, 24, 28–29, 72, 108–9, 113

Nelson, Thomas A. R., 64
New England Yearly Meeting, 25, 36, 72, 80
Newport, Elizabeth, 24

Newport, IN, 21, 102
Newton, Isaac, 68, 70, 83, 84, 85
New York Times, 29, 60
New York Tribune, 61, 64, 112
New York World, 92
New York Yearly Meeting, 16, 72, 80, 106
Nicolay, John, 42, 66
North Carolina Yearly Meeting, 18, 80

Ohio Yearly Meeting, 16, 18, 105, 106
Osborn, Charles, 17
Otis, James D., 72

Parliament: pro-war sentiment, 32–34; and Quaker Peace Testimony, 78–79
Peace Testimony: and Baltimore Conference, 99–100; and French–Indian War, 79–80; origins of, 13–14, 78–79; and Quaker dilemma, 5–6, 70, 81, 89; and young Quaker males, 27, 28, 82
Penn School, 106
Pennsylvania Abolition Society, 105
Pennsylvania Anti-Slavery Society, 18
Pennsylvania legislature, 19, 79–80
Pennsylvania Yearly Meeting of Progressive Friends. *See* Longwood Progressive Friends Meeting
Philadelphia, PA, 9–10, 12–14, 21, 115–16
Philadelphia Meeting for Sufferings, 25, 80, 84
Philadelphia Yearly Meeting, 13–14, 16, 25, 50, 80
Pickett, Gen. George E., 94
Pinkerton, Allan, 10
Pinkerton National Detective Agency, 10
Port Royal Relief Committee, 105–6
Prairie Grove (Iowa) Monthly Meeting, 65
Pratt, Joseph, 26
Primitive Friends, 72–73
Pringle, Cyrus, 82–83

Quaker City Telegram (Richmond, IN), 81–82

Index

Quakers: and abolitionism, 4–5, 12–14, 16–19, 52–53, 70, 72–73, 101–3; British, 16, 31–36, 112; and colonization, 18; and conscientious objection, 82–90, 98–101; and conscription, 76–78; and emancipation, 5–6, 47–49, 65–70, 72–73; and enlistment in Union Army, 27–28, 87–89; Gurneyite, 16–18, 27, 72; Hicksites, 15–16, 77, 89, 104–5, 115–16; and humanitarian reform, 50, 52–53, 80–81, 97–98, 103–7, 122; and interviews with Lincoln, 1–2, 35–36, 47–49, 65–70, 72–73, 84–85; Orthodox, 15–16, 17–18, 89, 105, 116; and Peace Testimony, 5–6, 77–80, 89, 99–100; Primitive, 72–73; Progressive (Congregational), 47–53, 95; and relationship with Lincoln, 8, 62–63, 119–22; and relief of freedmen, 103–7; and reverence for Lincoln, 29, 115–18; schisms, 15–19; and slavery, 4, 15, 18, 20–21, 62–63, 72–73; theology, 3–6, 12, 15–16, 17–18, 78–79, 96; and Underground Railroad, 5, 18, 98, 102–3; voting patterns, 20; Wilburite, 16–18, 72

Reconstruction, 107–8, 110, 117, 122
Religious Society of Friends. *See* Quakers
Republican Party: 1860 platform, 20–21, 55; conservatives, 10, 109; moderates, 10; radicals, 10, 12, 29, 64, 72–73, 109
Richmond, IN, 17, 27, 81–82, 98
Richmond Sanitary Commission, 98
Rubery, Alfred, 83–84
Russell, Caleb, 65
Russell, John, 37, 64

Schofield, Martha, 24, 98, 116–17
Schofield, Mary, 62–63
Scott, Gen. Winfield, 23
secession, 9–10, 24, 31, 64

Seward, William: as cabinet member, 12, 40; and *Emancipation Proclamation*, 54, 56–57, 59; and passage of Fourteenth Amendment, 113–14; Trent Affair, 32, 34
Sharpless, Henry H. G., 29
Shaw, Col. Robert Gould, 75–76
slavery: Lincoln's views on, 8, 11–12, 21–22, 48, 57–59, 73–74, 77; population of, 30–31; Quaker views on, 4, 15, 18, 20–21, 62–63, 72–73
Slidell, John, 32, 34
Smiley, Sarah, 107
Stanton, Edwin: as cabinet member, 40; death of infant son, 54; and Lincoln's death, 114; and Lincoln's humor, 44; and organization of black troops, 75; and Quaker resistors, 83, 84, 99–101; support for *Emancipation Proclamation*, 59
Stevens, Thaddeus, 64
Stoddard, William, 70
Storey, Wilbur F., 92
Sumner, Sen. Charles, 34, 75
Swift, Henry D., 81

Taney, Chief Justice Roger B., 23
Temple, Henry John (Lord Palmerston), 32–34, 64
Thomas, E. M., 60
Tobey, Samuel Boyd, 36–37
Trent Affair, 32–34
Trueblood, D. Elton: *Abraham Lincoln: Theologian of American Anguish*, 7; on doctrine of necessity, 46; on Lincoln's inspiration for emancipation, 63
Truth, Sojourner, 52
Tubman, Harriet, 51

Underground Railroad: and Fugitive Slave Law, 18, 50; Quaker involvement in, 12, 18, 21, 50, 86–87, 98, 102–3
Union Army: at Antietam, 63; Battle of Wilderness, 101; casualties, 93, 101; and black enlistments, 71–72, 74–76; and conscription statistics,

76, 101; enlistments, 27–28; 54th Massachusetts, 75–76, 87–88; at First Bull Run, 39; at Fort Wagner, 87–88; at Fredericksburg, 68–69; at Gettysburg, 84, 93–94; Peninsula campaign, 53; persecution of Quakers, 81–83; U.S. Colored Troops, 98

U.S. Colored Troops, 98. *See also* Union Army

U.S. Congress: and conscientious objection, 100–101, 121–22; and conscription, 76; and emancipation, 29–31; and Fourteenth Amendment, 113–14; relations with Britain, 34; relations with Lincoln, 55–56, 67, 73, 74–76, 103–4, 107, 109; relief of freedmen, 103–4, 107; Wade–Davis bill, 108

Wade, Benjamin F., 64
Walton, Margaretta, 24–25
Ward, Samuel Ringgold, 60
Warner, Yardley, 105
Washington Mission for Freedmen, 105
Wells, Gideon, 40, 54, 56, 59
Western Freedmen's Aid Society, 103–4
Western Yearly Meeting, 20, 25, 27–28, 36, 88, 105, 106

Westtown Friends Boarding School, 26
Whig Party, 17, 20
Whitaker, Alfred, 26
Whitall, John M., 1–2, 65–66
White, Col. E. V., 83
White, Ronald C., 67
Whittier, John Greenleaf, 19, 97, 111
Wilbur, Henry w., 123
Wilbur, John, 16, 18
Wilbur, Julia, 106
Wilburite–Gurneyite controversy, 16–18
Williams, Rebecca, 117
Williams, William, 83
Wilmington College, 124
Wilmot Proviso, 11
Wistar, Isaac J., 26
Wood, Edward, 26
Wooten, Daniel, 27, 88

Yearly meetings: Anti-Slavery Friends, 17–18; Baltimore, 16, 18, 35, 89, 99; Indiana, 16–18, 25–26, 27–28, 88, 105; Iowa, 20; London, 35, 79; New England, 25, 36, 72; New York, 16, 18, 72, 106; North Carolina, 18; Ohio, 16, 18, 105, 106; Philadelphia, 13–14, 16, 18, 25, 50; Western, 20, 25, 27–28, 36, 88, 105, 106

About the Author

William C. Kashatus, PhD, is a historian, educator, and writer. A product of and former teacher in Philadelphia's Quaker schools, his published works include ABC-CLIO's *Harriet Tubman: A Biography* as well as *Just Over the Line: Chester County and the Underground Railroad*; *A Virtuous Education: William Penn's Vision for Philadelphia's Schools*; and *Conflict of Conviction: A Reappraisal of Quaker Involvement in the American Revolution*. After studying under D. Elton Trueblood at Earlham College, Kashatus received his master's degree in history from Brown University and his doctorate from the University of Pennsylvania.